Challenger SECOND EDITION 8

ADULT READING SERIES

Corea Murphy

New Readers Press

Acknowledgments:

"Houdini: His Legend and His Magic" adapted from *Houdini: His Legend and His Magic* by Doug Henning with Charles Reynolds. Copyright © 1977, 1978 by Doug Henning. Warner Books, Inc.

Entry for "Houdini, Harry" from *Funk & Wagnall's New Standard Dictionary* (Thomas Y. Crowell). Copyright 1920 by Harper & Row, Publishers, Inc. Reprinted by permission of Harper & Row, Publishers, Inc.

"Names That Have Made the Dictionary" excerpted from pp. 42, 43, 94, 104, 177, 180, 205, and 248 of *Thereby Hangs a Tale: Stories of Curious Word Origins* by Charles Earle Funk. Copyright 1950 by Harper & Row, Publishers, Inc. Renewed © 1978 by Beulah M. Funk. Reprinted by permission of HarperCollins Publishers, Inc.

"Mirror, Mirror, on the Wall . . ." adapted from pp. 8, 9, 14, 22, 27, 47, 50, 58, and 187 of *The Decorated Body* by Robert Brain. Copyright © 1979 by Robert Brain. Reprinted by permission of HarperCollins Publishers, Inc.

"Keeping up with the Joneses" excerpted from "Keeping Up With the Joneses" (pp. 141–142) in *Heavens to Betsy and Other Curious Sayings* by Charles Earle Funk. Copyright © 1955 by Charles Earle Funk. Reprinted by permission of Harper & Row, Publishers, Inc.

Adapted from "While the Auto Waits" by O. Henry from *Collected Stories of O. Henry.* Edited by Paul J. Horowitz. Copyright ©1977 by Crown Publishers, Inc. Used by permission of Crown Publishers, Inc.

"A Fable for Tomorrow" from *Silent Spring* by Rachel Carson. Copyright © 1962 by Rachel L. Carson, renewed 1990 by Roger Christie. Reprinted by permission of Houghton Mifflin Harcourt Publishing Company. All rights reserved.

Rachel Carson biographical data from *Heroes of Conservation* by C.B. Squire. Copyright ©1974 by Fleet Press Corporation, New York. Used by permission.

"The Good Earth: Two Points of View" from *Encounters with the Archdruid* by John McPhee. Copyright © 1971 by John McPhee. Originally appeared in *The New Yorker.* Reprinted by permission of Farrar, Straus and Giroux, Inc.

Adaptation of "Antaeus" by Borden Deal. Copyright © 1961 by Southern Methodist University Press. Used by permission of Ashley D. Matin, Brett Deal and Shane Townsend.

"The Forecast" from *Reflections on a Gift of Watermelon Pickle* by Dan Jaffe. Used by permission of Dan Jaffe.

"Life Without Furnace, Pipe, or Water" abridged from *Home Sweet Home in the 19th Century* by Buehr, Walter. Copyright © 1965 by Harper & Row, Publishers, Inc. Reprinted by permission of HarperCollins Publishers.

"Heir to Tradition" from *How to Think About Ourselves* by Bonaro W. Overstreet. Copyright 1948 by Harper & Brothers, renewed © 1976 by Bonaro W. Overstreet. Reprinted by permission of W.W. Norton & Company.

"The Negro Speaks of Rivers," from *The Collected Poems of Langston Hughes* by Langston Hughes, edited by Arnold Rampersad with David Roessel, Associate Editor, copyright © 1994 by The Estate of Langston Hughes. Used by permission of Alfred A. Knopf, a division of Random House, Inc.

Images courtesy of:

p. 15, p. 31, p. 39, p. 42, p. 52, p. 54, mermaid, dragon: p. 64, p. 74, p. 94, p. 95, p. 111, p. 112, p. 114, p. 121, p. 129, p. 138, p. 146, p. 147, p.148, p. 179, p. 181, flag: p. 186, p. 191: © 2008 Jupiterimages Corporation; p. 17, cosmetics: p. 44, p. 55, p. 87, p. 110, p. 158, p. 208: istockphoto.com; p. 7, p. 8, p. 10, p. 16, p. 56, p. 58, unicorn, kraken, griffin: p. 64, p. 65, p. 75, p. 77, p. 78, p. 85, p. 161, p. 162, President Obama: p. 186, p. 188, p. 190, p. 204: Public Domain (Wikimedia Commons); p. 97, p. 103: NASA; p. 163: Library of Congress Prints & Photographs Division

Challenger 8, 2nd Edition
ISBN 978-1-56420-575-9

Proceeds from the sale of New Readers Press materials support professional development, training, and technical assistance programs of ProLiteracy that benefit local literacy programs in the U.S. and around the globe.

Developmental Editor: Terrie Lipke
Contributing Writers: Terry Ledyard, Nina Shope, S. Dean Wooton
Creative Director: Andrea Woodbury
Production Specialist: Maryellen Casey
Art and Design Supervisor: James P. Wallace
Cover Design: Carolyn Wallace

Table of Contents

UNIT 1
Appearances

The theme of this unit—*appearances*—is a very interesting and complex concept. One meaning of *appearance* deals with the way people look—the images they project. These images deliver messages, telling other people something about themselves. Another meaning of *appearance* suggests deception or giving a false impression. Used in this sense, *appearance* implies an illusion, a contrast between what something seems to be and what it really is.

The reading for Lesson 1 deals with appearance as deception or illusion. In this selection, "Houdini: His Legend and His Magic," you will read about one of the most famous magicians of all times—Harry Houdini.

The reading for Lesson 2, "Mirror, Mirror on the Wall . . . ," examines the notion of personal appearance. In this selection, you will learn how, throughout the ages, people have used cosmetics and other forms of body art to deliver messages about themselves.

The reading for Lesson 3 is entitled "Celebrity vs. Reality." In this selection, the author discusses America's obsession with celebrity and how that obsession is fueled. The reading also explains how the line between celebrity life and real life can often become blurred.

Most of us have heard the expression, "Keeping up with the Joneses," the title of the reading for Lesson 4. This reading, taken from a book that was written at the end of the last century, explores how people go about trying to appear wealthy and powerful. As you study the ideas in this reading, it will be helpful to consider whether or not the author's ideas about the time and money people spend creating the appearance of wealth and power still hold true today.

The reading for Lesson 5 is a short story by the American author O. Henry. In this story, titled "While the Auto Waits," you will see what happens when two characters decide that deception is more interesting than reality.

Words for Study

Houdini	dismember	publicity	sustain
extrication	memoirs	exhibition	ruptured
feat	Americanization	shackles	neutrality
chloroform	concentrate	portable	disentangle

LESSON 1
Houdini: His Legend and His Magic

by Doug Henning with Charles Reynolds

In the year 1920, Harry Houdini, then at the peak of his career, was justly proud that his name had become an accepted part of the English language. That year's edition of *Funk and Wagnall's New Standard Dictionary* carried the following entry:

> Hou di-ni, Harry (4/6 1874–) American mystericist, wizard and expert in extrication and self release. hou di-nize, vb. To release or extricate oneself from (confinement, bonds, or the like), as by wriggling out.

The verb *to houdinize* has hardly found its way into standard usage, but the name of Houdini has become part of the vocabulary not only of American culture, but of cultures throughout the world. If we say a person is a *Houdini*, what we mean is immediately understood. That Houdini escaped from handcuffs, packing boxes, and straitjackets; that he made an

elephant disappear on the stage of the world's largest theater; that he could swallow needles and thread and bring the needles up threaded; that at one point in his career he performed the astonishing feat of walking through a brick wall—these are all parts of the legend. And today, to be a Houdini is to be able to do the seemingly impossible.

Houdini's origins have, until very recently, been shrouded in mystery. One reason for this mystery is that both Houdini and members of his family gave false information to the public. In hundreds of interviews with the press, for example, Houdini always gave his date of birth as April 6, 1874, and his birthplace as Appleton, Wisconsin. Yet careful research has revealed that Houdini's true date and place of birth were March 24, 1874, in Budapest, Hungary.

Houdini's real name was Ehrich Weiss, and he is said to have been the son of a Hungarian rabbi. When he was still an infant, his family moved to the United States and settled in Milwaukee, Wisconsin. Houdini comments on those years in Milwaukee as a time when "such hardships and hunger became our lot; the less said on the subject the better."

It was during the years in Milwaukee that Ehrich Weiss was first exposed to magic. Most professional magicians become fascinated with magic by seeing and being astonished by another magician, and Houdini was no exception. It is likely that this happened when Rabbi Weiss took his son to a stage performance of a traveling magician named Dr. Lynn.

Dr. Lynn's magic act featured an illusion in which he pretended to give chloroform to a man and then, after tying him in place inside a cabinet, proceeded to dismember the man with a huge butcher knife, cutting off his legs and arms and finally his head. The pieces were then thrown into the cabinet and the curtain was pulled. Moments later, the victim appeared from the cabinet restored to one living piece, and seemingly none the worse for the ordeal. Many years later Houdini purchased this illusion (reportedly for $75) from Dr. Lynn's son and presented it without the chloroform during the last two years of his show.

In 1888, Rabbi Weiss moved his family to New York City. Ehrich had run away from home on his twelfth birthday in an attempt to find work and help support the family, but he joined them at their new house on East 69th Street and found employment as a cutter in a necktie factory. It was during this period that Ehrich became seriously interested in the art of magic. One of the books he was reading at the time was *The Memoirs of Robert-Houdin,* the biography of the great French magician who is generally considered to be "the father of modern magic."

Ehrich told a friend of his desire to be as great as Robert-Houdin, and his friend suggested that if he added the letter *i* to Houdin's name, it would mean "like Houdin," and he could call himself Houdini. This, with the Americanization of his nickname, Ehrie, into Harry, produced the name that was, forever after, to mean *magic*— Harry Houdini.

In 1891, Harry Houdini left his job at the necktie factory and made the plunge into a career as a professional magician. He barely managed, and by 1893, he was doing as many as twenty shows a day at a salary of twelve dollars per week. The following year he met Wilhelmina Beatrice Rahner, an eighteen-year-old girl from Brooklyn. It was love at first sight, and within two weeks they were married. The marriage marked the beginning of "the Houdinis," with Bess, as his wife was called, being an attractive addition to his magic act.

Five years of hardship and struggle followed. For very little money, Harry and Bess gave thousands of shows in front of the toughest and most demanding kinds of audiences. Houdini used these years of struggle to polish and perfect the escape act that only a few years later would make him a headliner at fabulous salaries in the most important theaters in the world.

Just how Houdini began to concentrate on escapes is not known. One theory is that, again, he was influenced by reading a rare book he had come upon in which the author revealed how a person could escape from rope ties, metal collars, and knotted and sealed bags. When, at the turn of the century, he finally began to get the recognition he had struggled so hard for, Houdini came to be known as "the handcuff king." The idea of escaping from handcuffs was not a new one, but Houdini's brilliant idea of allowing people to bring real cuffs to restrain him made him famous for his handcuff escapes.

Then, too, Houdini was a master at handling the press and gaining publicity for himself. There was scarcely a town where Houdini played that he was not on the front pages of the local newspaper. Here, for example, is an excerpt from an article which appeared in a Virginia newspaper in April 1900.

> Houdini, in an exhibition given in the City Hall yesterday before Chief Howard, Captain Angle, and many other of the police force, puzzled these officers and some thirty or forty other gentlemen who were present. Houdini seems to have fairly won his title, the King of Handcuffs. He stripped himself of all clothing so it could not be charged that he had keys or springs concealed about his person, and with his mouth sealed with plaster, and bound with a handkerchief, he removed four pairs of irons that had been placed upon him by Captain Angle.

> Dr. C.W.P. Brock attended to thoroughly closing the "King's" mouth, and then Captain Angle placed the shackles upon the performer. Irons were put not only upon Houdini's wrists, but also upon his feet, and then his hands were shackled to his legs. Houdini did not remove the irons in the presence of spectators, but got behind a chair over which a rug was thrown. However, he was almost entirely within the sight of those in the room, and many even saw the performer as he worked upon his shackles. In 2 minutes he stepped from behind the chair holding the four pairs of irons in his hands. It was simply a wonderful exhibition and every one in the room admitted that the King of Handcuffs was one too many for them . . .

Houdini used the "naked test" jailbreak as a top publicity stunt for many years to come. At times he added such newsworthy pranks as opening all the other cells in the jail and moving the prisoners to different cells or opening the cell in which his clothes were locked and appearing in front of his audience not only free but fully dressed.

One of Houdini's most widely reported challenge escapes was from a prison van during his tour of Russia in 1903. The portable steel cells, lined with zinc and mounted on a wagon body, were pulled by a team of horses used to transport prisoners. To this day, it is not known how Houdini managed to escape the van. One theory is that Bess had the necessary tools hidden in her mouth and passed them to the naked Houdini as she gave him a farewell kiss.

In addition to the standard jail escape, Houdini devised special escapes that were offered to him as challenges by merchants and local organizations in each city he played. He escaped from paper bags (without tearing the paper), zinc-lined piano boxes, padded cells, U.S. mail pouches, coffins, straitjackets of many different designs, a large football made by a local sporting goods manufacturer, a roll-top desk, various burglar-proof safes, wet packs used to subdue the violently insane, a plate glass box, a diving suit, and various types of steel boilers.

Tragically, the challenges that brought him worldwide fame and fortune also brought him death. In October 1926, Houdini was playing in Montreal. He was backstage in his dressing room preparing for the show when there was a knock at the door. Two college students had come to see the great Houdini and especially to find out for themselves if one of the well-publicized stories about the illusionist was true. It was said that Houdini had such control over all of his muscles that he could sustain punches to his stomach without injury. When asked about this by the boys, Houdini agreed that he was able to do this. Suddenly, before Houdini had time to brace himself, one of the students punched him hard in the stomach. Houdini recovered from the force of the blow, and the students left.

It is very odd that Houdini, who always made one hundred percent sure of the success of each of his feats, would let two strange men into his dressing room and then let one of them punch him. But this is what happened on that fateful day of October 21, 1926. Houdini dismissed the incident. But, unknown to him, the unexpected blow had ruptured his appendix. Through sheer willpower he continued to perform in ever-increasing pain, but after a performance a few days later he collapsed.

On Halloween of 1926, the most famous magician who had ever lived passed quietly away.

1 Understanding the Reading. Put the letter of the best answer on the line.

1. This reading is an excerpt from a(n) _____.
   a. autobiography   **b.** biography   **c.** essay   **d.** short story

2. Houdini's motive in running away from home when he was twelve was _____.
   a. to become a magician
   b. to escape family pressures
   c. to help his family
   d. to seek adventure

3. Henning's reason for writing about Dr. Lynn is _____.
   a. to cite evidence of the good relationship Houdini enjoyed with his father
   b. to describe an early influence on Houdini's chosen career
   c. to reveal the tricks used by an illusionist
   d. to show how audiences responded to illusionists

4. We can guess that Houdini's first meeting with the woman who was to become his wife was _____.
    a. business-like   b. romantic   c. stormy   d. uneventful

5. Which of the following did *not* contribute to Houdini's fame as "the Handcuff King"? _____
    a. He greatly admired Robert-Houdin, the fabulous French magician.
    b. He dared people to present him with seemingly impossible challenges.
    c. He knew how to use publicity in order to broadcast his talent.
    d. He worked hard to perfect his talent as an illusionist.

6. In which sentence does Henning present information as if he is *not* certain that it is true? _____
    a. "...his friend suggested that if he added the letter *i* to Houdin's name, it would mean *like Houdin* ..."
    b. "Houdini purchased this illusion (reportedly for $75) ..."
    c. "To this day, it is not known how Houdini managed to escape the van."
    d. "It was said that Houdini had such control over all of his muscles that he could sustain punches ... without injury"

7. In the newspaper excerpt, which of the following is *not* a statement of opinion? _____
    a. "...he was almost entirely within the sight of those in the room ..."
    b. "Houdini ... puzzled these officers and some thirty or forty other gentlemen who were present."
    c. "Houdini seems to have fairly won his title, the King of Handcuffs."
    d. "It was simply a wonderful exhibition and every one in the room admitted ..."

8. Probably the greatest stumbling block to Henning in researching the facts about Houdini's life was _____.
    a. accounts reported in the newspapers
    b. finding the books that inspired Houdini
    c. his lack of knowledge about magic
    d. the false information provided by Houdini's family

9. Based on this reading, Henning's main intent is _____.
    a. to add his own knowledge to the Houdini legend
    b. to explore the mysterious circumstances regarding Houdini's death
    c. to expose the truth about the real Houdini
    d. to present information about Houdini's life

10. Henning's attitude toward Houdini seems to be one of _____.
    a. admiration   b. disbelief   c. neutrality   d. scorn

2 What Do You Think? Answer the following questions in good sentence form.

1. If you had been a member of the audience during one of Houdini's performances, would you hope that he could escape his latest challenge or would you hope that someone had finally outsmarted him? Include at least one reason to help to explain your answer.

_____

_____

_____

2. If Houdini were performing today, do you think he would enjoy the same degree of fame and fortune that he enjoyed in his own lifetime? Be sure to include reasons to support your opinion.

_____

_____

_____

_____

3 Synonyms. *Synonyms* are words that have similar meanings. From the choices listed, choose the best synonym for the word in bold-faced type, and write it on the line to the right. The first one has been done to get you started.

1. **exhibition:**	commotion	discovery	display	drama	_display_
2. **shackle:**	ambush	confine	entangle	punish	
3. **rupture:**	burst	decay	enlarge	separate	
4. **publicize:**	advertise	expose	narrate	pronounce	
5. **fascinated:**	appreciative	attentive	mindful	spellbound	
6. **astonishing:**	amazing	attractive	pleasant	mysterious	
7. **worldwide:**	earthy	foreign	national	universal	
8. **legend:**	biography	memoirs	myth	rumor	myth
9. **feat:**	achievement	exception	extrication	illusion	
10. **extricate:**	discharge	disentangle	disjoin	dismember	
11. **subdue:**	overload	overpower	overturn	overwork	
12. **shrouded:**	deathly	disorderly	hidden	treacherous	
13. **plunge:**	dive	glide	orbit	whirl	
14. **sustain:**	dismiss	overwhelm	support	welcome	dismiss

4 Names That Have Made the Dictionary. Houdini is not the only person whose name has become a household word. Complete the sentences with the names listed below. Do you know the word that is derived from each name? In some cases, the word is exactly the same as the person's name. You may need to use a dictionary or the Internet to look up the name or word. The first one has been done for you.

✓Braille	Fahrenheit	Lynch	Poinsett
Derick	Jacuzzi	Nicot	Sandwich

1. Blinded in 1812, the Frenchman Louis __**Braille**__ later devised a system of printing for the blind which bears his name.

2. Joel R. _____, having served as a special minister to Mexico during the middle 1800s, returned to the United States with these large, flaming flowers, which have become a favorite decoration during the Christmas season.

3. In the 1950s, the _____ brothers created and marketed the first portable water therapy pump. In 1968, the brothers invented the first self-contained whirlpool bath.

4. Gabriel David _____, in the early years of the 18th century, constructed the first mercury thermometer, which made recording temperatures much easier.

5. Colonel Charles _____ of Virginia, a county court justice, may have given us this word. During the Revolutionary War he was unable to safely transport people accused of felonies to the court in Williamsburg, so he set up a court, tried the cases, and imposed punishment himself.

6. The fourth Earl of _____, an Englishman of the 18th century, had such a passion for gambling that during one 24-hour session, he refused to stop for any meals and instead ordered his servant to bring him slices of bread with roast beef nested between them.

7. This hoisting device was named after Godfrey _____, a famous 17th-century hangman at an English prison, who invented a gallows that used this device.

8. Jean _____, the French ambassador to Portugal in 1560, was curious about some seeds that had been brought from America. He sent some of the seeds on to France where they were planted, producing the first tobacco raised in Europe. His name was given to the poisonous substance found in tobacco.

5 Challenges. Perhaps these challenges are not so dramatic as Houdini's, but you might enjoy trying them out on your friends anyway. First, you must put the steps of each challenge in a sensible order. The first challenge has been started for you.

1. _____ Add that only *one* glass can be moved.

   _____ Then challenge your friend to rearrange the glasses so that each full glass is next to an empty glass.

   _____ When your friend gives up, pick up the middle glass, drink the water, and put the glass back in its place.

   _____ Pour water into the three middle glasses.

   __1__ Set five glasses side by side on a table.

2. _____ After your friend gives up, cut through one of the loops of the bow, and you've successfully met the challenge.

   _____ Challenge your friend to cut the string without letting the cup fall to the floor.

   _____ Mention that the cup is not to be touched either.

   _____ Now hand your friend a pair of scissors.

   _____ Hang a china cup from a doorknob by looping a piece of string through the handle of the cup and tying the string around the doorknob in a bow.

3. _____ Be sure to use the word *figures* and not *numbers*.

   _____ However, when you write them for your puzzled friend, write:

$$\begin{array}{r} 17 \\ 1 \\ 1 \\ \underline{1} \\ 20 \end{array}$$

_____ State that you can write five odd figures that will add up to twenty.

_____ The figures you will use are 1, 1, 1, 1, and 7.

_____ Your friend will be puzzled because, as everybody knows, an odd number of odd numbers always adds up to an odd number.

Words for Study

fascination	economies	identification	mutilate
primitive	techniques	Melanesia	petroleum
civilized	symbolic	patriotic	executive
anthropologist	initiation	missionaries	perception

LESSON 2
Mirror, Mirror, on the Wall . . .

by Robert Brain

Throughout recorded history, men and women have had a fascination for changing their appearance by using cosmetics and other forms of body art. *Cosmetics*, as defined by the United States Federal Food, Drug and Cosmetic Act, is a word which can be equally applied to African, Asian, and Western body art: "articles intended to be rubbed, poured, sprinkled or sprayed on, introduced into, or otherwise applied to the human body or any part thereof for cleansing, beautifying, promoting attractiveness, or altering the appearance."

In this reading, the author describes the role cosmetics have played in different cultures. The author also presents some interesting thoughts for us to consider in his discussion of the concepts *primitive* and *civilized*.

* * *

I am attempting a description of the decoration of the human body in various cultures, whether by painting, tattooing, or otherwise changing its surface. As an anthropologist, one of my main aims is to lessen the traditional gap between the primitive and the civilized, and a comparison of body art is as good a means as any other.

I must apologize at once for using such terms as *primitive* and *civilized*. I use *primitive* to refer to people who live in small groups, who can neither read nor write, and who have very simple economies. The word *civilized* means "having a highly-developed society or culture." I also use *Western* to refer to those societies which in general pursue a European or American way of life. And I shall be describing Western practices of body decoration as measurements by which we can understand *exotic*—that is *different*—techniques. I believe that fashionable Western techniques of make-up, plastic surgery, and hair-styling differ very little from those of primitive body art, except that primitive body decoration has more religious and social functions. In Western societies, paint and pattern do not celebrate the physical and social body, but rather are used to conform to fashion.

'The Head of a Chief of New Zealand, the face curiously tataowd, or mark'd, according to their manner.'

Non-Western body art is a symbolic statement in which the decoration sends messages about groups or individuals. The native Australians paint their bodies as part of their religion. For religious ceremonies, people use the patterns and colors that have been passed down from generation to generation. In everyday life, however, they make themselves attractive by painting themselves with any pattern and any color. A whole family may spend long hours improving each other's appearance, painting detailed designs on different parts of the body. Parents paint their children and display them proudly to other members of the group.

Before coming into much contact with Europeans, many North American Indians also delighted in transforming the natural body into a work of art. One northwestern group, the Haida, painted their faces daily for cosmetic purposes. For dances and special ceremonies, designs and colors were more carefully applied. Both the men and women of the Haida tribe wore earrings. If they were of high rank, royal crests were tattooed on their legs and arms.

The Thompson Indians, who lived between the Rocky Mountains and the Thompson River, were masters at cosmetic decoration. As a rule, individuals painted themselves. Water or sheets of mica were used as looking glasses. Most young people painted their faces for cosmetic reasons, experimenting with designs and colors, even changing their face and body patterns several times a day.

Each Thompson Indian acquired a guardian spirit during initiation ceremonies and took on the qualities connected with that guardian spirit. During the winter dances, the singers and dancers painted themselves with designs representing the individual's guardian spirit, the spirit having indicated to him the designs to paint. Warriors painted their bodies before going to war. Each warrior had an individual pattern, but in all the paintings, the main idea was to bring good luck to the warrior and ill luck to the enemy.

As the Indians of North and South America increased their contact with Europeans, most stopped painting themselves. The Indians looked on the pale-faced Europeans with scorn, but unable to explain the importance and value of their body art, they abandoned it. Today, body painting has all but disappeared as a living art among the North American Indians, and in South America it is still popular only among the more remote tribes.

Another cosmetic practice that has enjoyed widespread use is tattooing. Like painting, tattooing has been used for many different reasons: decoration, identification, magic, an ordeal to prove courage, initiation ceremonies, a way to prevent old age and illness, relationships with guardian spirits, and a property mark on slaves.

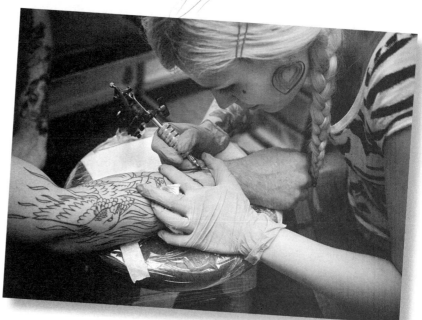

The great chiefs of New Zealand had their faces and their bodies covered with tattooed designs of delicate beauty, and all free men were permitted to do the same. Personal, individual designs were made on men's faces, which made them easily noticed in war and attractive to women. A face tattoo was also a kind of personal signature, and they believed that their personalities were reflected in these face patterns. When the chiefs signed deeds of land sales to Europeans, instead of a signature or a cross, they drew their face patterns, without the aid of mirrors and with great ease.

In many parts of the world, but particularly in Africa and in Melanesia, a group of islands in the South Pacific, young girls are tattooed in recognition of their important roles as future wives and mothers in the community. Tattooing was also used on other important occasions. In 19th-century Hawaii, for instance, the tips of the tongues of women were tattooed as a sign of mourning the death of a chief or some other tragic event.

Tattooing died out in Europe in the Middle Ages because the Christian church disapproved of it. But it flourished again after contact with the Far East and the South Seas in the 19th-century. England's Duke of York (later King George V), his brother the Duke of Clarence, and Tsar Nicholas of Russia were all tattooed by the same Japanese artist. For a time tattooing had an immense popularity in England. When Edward VII was crowned in 1901, many people, including Lady Randolph Churchill, had tattoos done with the royal arms or a patriotic motto.

Through the centuries, people in civilized cultures have tended to think that their cultures are superior to primitive cultures and that their practices are "natural" while those of others are "unnatural." Early travelers and missionaries who journeyed to the islands of the South Pacific and the remote regions of Africa expressed these views. Blind to their own powdered wigs and tight laces, these travelers and missionaries considered the decorated bodies of the people they met on their journeys as signs of savage and uncivilized behavior.

Our language helps to maintain this unnatural division between primitive and civilized societies. *We* have make-up, cosmetics, scents, creams, and dyes; *they* have twigs and swabs, animal fats and dyes. *We* have plastic surgery; *they* mutilate themselves. An anthropologist studying a South American Indian during a special ceremony describes the patterns of colored clay applied with pork fat and the ground charcoal dabbed around the eyes. It is highly unlikely that he would describe his wife's make-up in the same terms; yet she is most likely also wearing a red dye mixed with wax on her lips; blue, green or white pigments mixed with petroleum jelly on her eyelids, and soot and pig's fat on her brows and lashes.

To further explore the similarities between primitive and civilized societies, let us compare a New Guinea trader with an American business executive. The main goal of both these men is the same: to appear attractive so they can make the best deal. The old trader knows that he will not make a deal without artificial aids. He would not dream of setting out without his cosmetic kit. He attempts to make himself attractive to his business friends through the use of spells and cosmetics. He rubs himself with fragrant leaves and coconut oil, arranges his hair and draws designs on his face. Youthfulness and attractiveness are magically applied to his body in the form of scents, dyes, and paints.

Like the South Pacific trader, the American executive realizes that in our culture also, an ugly, old face cannot be a successful one. He must consider his clothes, his figure, and his wrinkles. The American businessman is beginning to use cosmetics for the same reasons as women do—to promote good health, or the appearance of good health, by artificial means. He turns to the hair surgeon, the cosmetic surgeon, and the make-up specialist with the idea of looking younger and rested. He uses beauty products to make him feel bold, rugged, and commanding. For both the New Guinea trader and the American businessman, cosmetics are magical aids to success in business.

It is the belief in the power of cosmetics that makes them effective, since both the New Guinea trader and American businessman believe that they are young and attractive. This feeling, in turn, injects self-confidence into their behavior.

Cosmetics help an individual's appearance, and as Tolstoy, a Russian writer, remarked, "Nothing has so marked an influence on the direction of a man's mind as his appearance, and not his appearance itself, so much as his conviction that it is attractive or unattractive." This is how we should understand the satisfaction of a man smeared with soot and ocher in the New Guinea mountains or of a woman smeared with soot and ocher in a Miami bar.

Attention to the body is an attempt to put on a new skin, a cultural as opposed to a natural skin. It is a basic need which is practiced among all the peoples of the world. The matter goes even deeper. Body painting, tattooing, even hair styles are concerned with the questions all human beings ask: "Who am I? Who are we?" As long as there is an attempt to find an answer, people will continue to make up. A sane perception of self is closely linked with a sane perception of the body. As we paint our eyes, trim our body hair, put on our ties, belts, and ribbons, we are creating a self-portrait. Through decorating our bodies we are telling other people that we are special kinds of individuals.

1 Understanding the Reading. Put the letter of the best answer on the line.

1. The author of this article, Robert Brain, is an anthropologist. From your reading of this article, what do you think an anthropologist is? _____
    a. a tour guide
    b. a person who studies different cultures
    c. a fashion designer
    d. a make-up artist

2. When Brain states: ". . . one of my main aims is to lessen the traditional gap between the primitive and the civilized . . ." he means that one of his main aims is to _____.
    a. teach primitive people to act the same way civilized people do
    b. point out the differences between primitive and civilized cultures
    c. show that primitive people have been around longer than civilized people
    d. show that primitive and civilized peoples are more alike than many of us believe

3. The fact that North American Indians, South American Indians, and native Australians painted their bodies suggests that body painting _____.
    a. is limited to warm climates
    b. was more common in the Northern Hemisphere
    c. was once popular in many parts of the world
    d. was unknown to people living in Africa

4. Peoples lessened their use of body painting as they _____.
    a. increased their contact with Western societies   c. became more interested in tattooing
    b. ran out of materials needed for body painting   d. stopped fighting with other tribes

5. Which of the following practiced tattooing? _____
    a. Hawaiian women   b. New Zealand chiefs   c. girls in Melanesia   d. all of these people

6. Brain suggests that cosmetics used by both primitive and civilized people _____.
    a. are made from similar materials   c. are difficult to remove
    b. can cause infection   d. often have unpleasant fragrances

7. One argument put forth by Brain is that _____.
    a. primitive people are often more civilized than so-called advanced people
    b. both primitive and civilized people use cosmetics for the same reason, to make them look attractive
    c. primitive people are less vain than civilized people
    d. the use of cosmetics is a relatively new practice

8. Brain suggests that _____.
    a. anthropologists who study primitive people are prejudiced
    b. the use of cosmetics is an example of mankind's foolishness
    c. as long as people are concerned with their sense of identity, they will use cosmetics
    d. the past culture of the North American Indians was more advanced than that of the present South Pacific groups

2 More about *We* and *They*.

1. Brain talks about *we* and *they* in terms of civilized and primitive cultures. Sometimes people in our own culture also talk about *we* and *they*. Briefly describe what *we* (the people in italicized type) might say about *they* in the following situations. The first one has been done to get you started.

Situation 1: Waiting to use the bathroom

A. A *teenage boy* waits outside the bathroom for his twin sister to finish getting ready for a date.

 Girls waste so much time putting on make-up and looking at themselves in the mirror. We have better things to do with our time.

B. *His twin sister* waits outside the bathroom for him to finish getting ready in the morning.

 Boys take forever getting ready to leave. We have better things to do in the morning.

Situation 2: Waiting for the phone

A. A *mother* waits for her son to finish talking on the phone.

_____

_____

B. *Her son* waits for his mother to finish talking on the phone.

_____

_____

Situation 3: Being disturbed by loud noises

A. *Nick Thompson* is awakened very early on a Saturday morning by his neighbor's loud hammering.

_____

_____

B. *His neighbor* is kept awake very late on Saturday night by the loud music coming from Nick's home.

_____

_____

2. Describe a *we* and *they* situation from your own experience.

_____

_____

_____

3. What conclusions can you draw about *we* and *they* thinking?

_____

_____

_____

_____

3 Antonyms. *Antonyms* are words that are opposite in meaning. From the choices listed, choose the best antonym for the word in bold-faced type, and write it on the line to the right.

1. gradually:	eventually	finally	justly	suddenly	_____
2. beautify:	deprive	disfigure	overpower	shackle	_____
3. primitive:	advanced	American	brand-new	natural	_____
4. portable:	complex	fixed	heavy	inexpensive	_____
5. attentive:	careless	hateful	indignant	uncivilized	_____
6. thrive:	dwindle	endure	maintain	sustain	_____
7. rugged:	frail	generous	humble	unskilled	_____
8. thrift:	budget	economy	prosperity	wastefulness	_____
9. poised:	disgraceful	heartless	jittery	unsuspecting	_____
10. stunning:	abnormal	homemade	plain	uninformed	_____
11. seemingly:	apparently	certainly	reportedly	usually	_____
12. relieve:	confine	inflict	linger	sacrifice	_____
13. fascinated:	annoyed	ignorant	indifferent	unconvinced	_____
14. gloss:	dullness	heartiness	stubbornness	thickness	_____

4 The Suffix -logy. The suffix *-logy* indicates the science, theory or study of; for example, *anthropology* is the study of the origin and of the physical, social, and cultural development of man. Use a dictionary to help you match the following *-logies* with the correct description.

| archaeology | biology | etymology | meteorology | psychology | theology |
| astrology | ecology | geology | pathology | sociology | zoology |

zoo _____ **1.** the biological science of animals

meteorology _____ **2.** the science dealing with occurrences in the atmosphere, especially weather and weather conditions

biology _____ **3.** the science of life and life processes, including the study of structure, functioning, growth, origin, evolution, and distribution of living organisms

psychology _____ **4.** the science of mental processes and behavior

ecology _____ **5.** the science of relationships between organisms and their environment

archeology _____ **6.** the scientific study of man's life and past culture

pathology _____ **7.** the scientific study of the nature of disease, its causes, processes, development, and consequences

geology _____ **8.** the scientific study of the origin, history, and structure of the earth

sociology _____ **9.** the study of human social behavior; especially, the study of institutions and the development of human society

Theology _____ **10.** the study of the nature of God and religious truth

etymology _____ **11.** the study of the origin and historical development of words

astrology _____ **12.** the study of the positions and aspects of heavenly bodies with a view to predicting their influence on the course of human affairs

5 More about Melanesia. Use the map to answer the questions that follow.

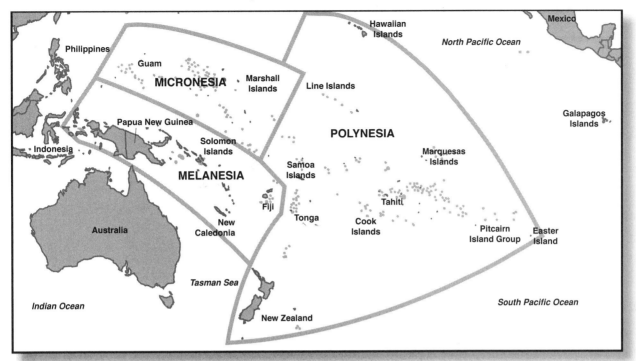

The Three Main Pacific Island Groups The Pacific Islands can be divided into three main groups: (1) Melanesia, meaning *black islands;* (2) Micronesia, meaning *small islands;* and (3) Polynesia, meaning *many islands.* This grouping is based on the race and customs of the native peoples and on the islands' geography.

1. *Melanesia* means _____.
   - **a.** black islands
   - **b.** many islands
   - **c.** Pacific islands
   - **d.** small islands

2. Which of the following island groups is not part of Melanesia? _____.
   - **a.** Solomon Islands
   - **b.** New Caledonia
   - **c.** Fiji Islands
   - **d.** Samoa Islands

3. To travel from New Caledonia to Indonesia, you would go _____.
   - **a.** northeast
   - **b.** northwest
   - **c.** southeast
   - **d.** southwest

4. Which of the following is closest to Mexico? _____
   - **a.** Marshall Islands
   - **b.** Marquesas Islands
   - **c.** Galapagos Islands
   - **d.** Line Islands

5. Which of the following statements is false? _____.
   - **a.** Polynesia covers more territory than Melanesia.
   - **b.** Melanesia is located in the Pacific Ocean.
   - **c.** Tonga is west of Melanesia.
   - **d.** New Zealand is not part of Melanesia.

Words for Study

Hollywood	obsession	googled	episodes
tabloid	appetites	ultra	footage
National Enquirer	airwaves	contestant	syndrome
skyrocketed	spin-off	Bachelor	advent

LESSON 3
Celebrity vs. Reality

Americans have had a love affair with celebrities ever since the first actors and actresses stepped onto the silver screen in the early 1900s. The excitement of seeing those movie stars in their glamorous outfits set our hearts racing and left us breathless. Right away, photos of celebrities began gracing the pages of newspapers and magazines. Regular people living ordinary lives were able to gaze at the sparkling gowns and trendy hairstyles of the actresses, see the stylish suits worn by the actors, and feel like they were a part of that glamorous life. Movie stars' lives looked like fairy tales full of exciting adventures. Many people dreamed of living the Hollywood life.

But what do these images have to do with reality? In 1926, a weekly magazine took the celebrity-watching world by storm. The tabloid magazine was printed on cheap newsprint and offered current photos of the most sought after celebrities—actors, actresses, entertainers, sports stars, and more. Yes, it offered the most up-to-date news and gossip about these celebrities to give people the latest on their favorite stars. But not only did it offer the good—it offered the bad and the ugly, too! The tabloid gave the public all the dirt on celebrity crime, scandals, and heartbreak. The magazine? It was to become what is today *National Enquirer*. At its height,

National Enquirer had a weekly circulation rate of over six million copies. In the 1980s, its slogan was, "Inquiring minds want to know." Today, *National Enquirer* reaches just over one million, thirty thousand people each week. And the tabloid has plenty of competition.

We've all seen them on the racks at the grocery store checkout lines. At times, there are half a dozen weekly tabloids, as well as other entertainment magazines aimed at giving readers the latest celebrity and entertainment news, gossip, and photos.

Not much is left private by supermarket tabloid and entertainment magazines. The reality is that celebrities are real people. Underneath all of the glamour and makeup and beautiful gowns, they are just like the rest of us. They eat. They sleep. They play on the beach with their kids. They get in fights with their husbands and wives. They get in trouble with the law. The only difference is that they do all of it in front of a camera. And the pictures wind up in the tabloids and magazines sold across America. The public is hungry for all the celebrity news it can get.

One such entertainment magazine is *People* magazine, which reaches 3.6 million readers each week. *US Weekly* boasts an average weekly circulation of 1.9 million readers. Another weekly celebrity magazine is *In Touch Weekly*. This tabloid has more than 1.2 million readers each week.

How did gossip become such a big business? A drastic change in celebrity-watching took place after World War II. People began watching their favorite stars right in their own living rooms. That's when TV usage skyrocketed in the U.S. Before the war, TV sets were very expensive. The average person could not afford to have one. But in 1947, one company made a TV set that sold for under $200. That finally made TV affordable for millions of Americans. People could see all of their favorite celebrities in action—without going to the movies. Plus, a whole new crop of stars was born. These were TV stars—people who acted on TV series, entertained in variety shows, or were part of other programming. Fans could watch their favorite stars day after day and week after week. TV had become another way people could continue their romance with the stars.

By 1954, 55.7 percent of households had a TV set. By the early 1960s, 90 percent of households had one. Today, 98 percent of homes have a TV—and most of those homes have more than one!

How many TV sets do you have in your home? Two? Three? Five? What kinds of shows do you like to watch? Are you interested in what celebrities are doing, where they are going, and what they are wearing? Or do you enjoy hearing about celebrities who have gotten in trouble with the law? Partied too hardy, or whose marriages are on the rocks? Have the latest teen idols inspired your son or daughter to want to look like them or want to dress like them? It seems that in America, our interest in celebrities has become an obsession.

In 1981, a new type of TV show helped to feed our appetites for celebrity gossip. That year,

Entertainment Tonight (ET) hit TV airwaves to rave reviews. The daily TV entertainment news show calls itself "the most watched entertainment newsmagazine in the world." Today, *ET* continues to air in the U.S., Canada, and around the globe, making it the longest-running TV newsmagazine in history. The show offers, in its own words, "all the Hollywood news you crave and desire." *ET* dives headfirst into celebrity successes and scandals. The show's spin-off, *The Insider,* also airs weeknights. *ET* and *The Insider* aren't the only shows that dish the dirt on celebrities. There's *Access Hollywood, EXTRA, TMZ, E! News,* and more. But *ET* still remains one of the top 10 highest rated shows. It seems that viewers can't get enough of the good or the bad about their favorite stars.

Since the development of cable and satellite TV stations in the 1970s, people have had even more channels to watch to keep up with what their favorite celebrities are doing. And with the computer revolution of the 1990s and the introduction of the Internet, now celebrity news is just a mouse click away. Search engines offer easy access on their startup pages to the latest entertainment news. MSN Entertainment, AOL, Yahoo News, and online newspapers all offer entertainment pages. Some even have hot links for instant access to the latest celebrity doings. Among popular stars, it's a competition to see who is most googled!

Anyone can become a celebrity with the current trend in TV programming—the reality show. In recent years, the reality show has become ultra-popular. Reality shows take regular people—people who would normally be TV viewers—and make them TV stars. Reality shows include programs such as *The Real World* or *Survivor. The Real World,* which takes a group of seven young men and women and puts them together in a house to see what happens, claims to be the first reality show. Each week, it follows the housemates as they fight, bond, love, and grow. *Survivor,* which is still going strong after 10 seasons, pits a group of people against each other in an uninhabited location in the hopes that one contestant will outlast all of the others. There are many other types of reality shows—some are job-based shows that offer a prize at the end and center around a certain career. Others are dating shows such as *The Bachelor* or *The Bachelorette,* in which viewers watch as contestants vie for the affections of a prized partner over several episodes.

How real are reality shows? People who watch reality shows week after week see what looks like reality—but really it is not. Many reality shows are edited to make viewers think what is going on is real life. There is talk that some episodes are scripted or that contestants are prompted to do or say certain things that will create conflict or excitement. Much of what is shown on reality TV is only a small part of what is really happening. The footage is carefully edited so that viewers see only the most interesting interactions. That's what keeps the audience coming back for more.

1 Understanding the Reading. The reading gives ways in which the American public has kept the love of celebrity news, gossip, and photos alive over time. Look at the events listed below, and explain how each event has contributed to our obsession with celebrities.

1. Going to the movies became popular in the early 1900s.

    _____

    _____

2. In 1926, *National Enquirer* is founded.

    _____

    _____

3. The TV set began selling for under $200 in 1947.

    _____

    _____

4. The TV newsmagazine, *Entertainment Tonight,* first airs in 1981.

    _____

    _____

5. The Internet exploded into American life in the 1990s.

    _____

    _____

6. Reality shows become a reality.

    _____

2 Reality Check. Read the following section about reality shows. It gives information about a disturbing syndrome that doctors are seeing now that reality TV programming is so widespread. Answer the questions below using complete sentences.

In recent years, doctors are seeing a new type of mental disorder relating to reality shows. Experts are calling it Truman syndrome after a 1998 movie. In the movie "The Truman Show," actor Jim Carrey stars as a man whose life is normal until he finds out that none of it is real. He is actually living his life on a TV set. His friends are actors. And every moment of his life is being shown on TV.

In real life, Truman syndrome affects a person's belief system about the world at large. Nothing seems real to them. Some patients even bring up "The Truman Show" when discussing their symptoms with their doctors. In 2006, doctors who researched reality TV disorders presented their findings at medical schools across the nation. By the end of 2008, about 75 people had been diagnosed with Truman syndrome.

Some experts say the syndrome shows just how strong the effect of pop culture is on mental disorders. But one of the researchers says he does not believe that reality shows can make healthy people sick. He believes that people who would become ill anyway are just becoming ill more quickly or in a different way.

1. Do you watch reality TV shows? If yes, which ones? What do you like about them? If you don't watch them, why not?

_____

_____

_____

_____

2. Have you or someone you know seen the movie, "The Truman Show?" If yes, describe what you or they remember about it.

_____

_____

_____

_____

3. Do you think a person can develop a mental illness from watching too much reality TV? Why or why not?

_____

_____

4. Do you think that watching too much reality TV can affect how a person thinks about real life? Why or why not? What effect do you think it might have?

_____

_____

_____

_____

3 Synonyms and Antonyms. If the pair of words is similar in meaning, write *synonyms* on the line to the left. If the pair is opposite in meaning, write antonyms. The first one has been done to get you started.

antonyms	**1.** beautify—disfigure
	2. executive—laborer
	3. advent—introduction
antonyms	**4.** fantasy—reality
antonyms	**5.** obsession—indifference
	6. extricate—shackle
syn	**7.** engrave—carve
antonyms	**8.** neutral—prejudiced
synonyms	**9.** imaginary—fictional
syn	**10.** phase—aspect
ant	**11.** publicize—conceal
synonyms	**12.** reliable—trustworthy
ant	**13.** retain—discard
ant	**14.** inquire—respond
synonyms	**15.** contestant—competitor
syn	**16.** worldwide—universal

4 The Suffix -ist. The suffix *-ist* indicates a person who does, makes, produces, operates, plays, or is connected with a particular thing. Match each person below with the response he or she might make after having read the article about celebrity.

activist	archaeologist	etymologist	meteorologist
alarmist	conformist	hypnotist	nonconformist
anthropologist	dramatist	journalist	novelist

Hypnotist 1. "Some people think TV shows do the same thing I do every day—put people in trances."

Novelist 2. "Creating a cast of characters who live in modern America but have never seen a magazine, movie, or TV show would make a very interesting plot for my next book."

dramatist 3. "With all the channels on cable and satellite TV these days, not as many people go to the theater."

Journalist 4. "Maybe I can get an interview with a reality show contestant and submit a story to my magazine publisher."

Activist 5. "I'm so disturbed by the trash that's on TV these days that I'm going to organize a campaign and get everyone to write our Congresswoman immediately."

Anthropologist 6. "I want to read some more studies of cultures that don't have TV or movies before I draw any conclusions about how they affect people."

Etymologist 7. "*Celebreality* is a word that combines the words *celebrity* and *reality*. It was created to describe the TV shows that put current or has-been celebrities in a reality-show format."

Archaeologist 8. "If I were living hundreds of years from now, I wonder what my reaction would be upon digging up a battered TV set among the ruins of some civilization."

Alarmist 9. "If I'm right, we are all just actors in one big show that the world is watching!"

Conformist 10. "If all my friends watched the latest cable TV shows and I didn't, I'd really feel left out."

nonconform 11. "Just because most people watch TV doesn't mean everyone should. I don't even own a TV!"

meteorologist 12. "TV offers round-the-clock weather forecasts for everyplace in the world. It's easy to find what the weather will be where you live."

5 Working with Headings. There are many different types of TV shows that people enjoy watching. Put the correct heading with each group of words that describe things you see on a TV show. Study the example before you begin.

Cooking Show	Game Show	News Broadcast	Sitcom
Crime Drama	Nature Show	Newsmagazine	Sporting Event

1. __Cooking Show__
   restaurant chefs
   healthy recipes
   food competitions
   quick meals

2. __Sitcom__
   taped laughter
   funny characters
   day-to-day life
   weekly show

3. __Newsmagazine__
   celebrity gossip
   interviews with newsmakers
   movie previews
   Hollywood romances

4. __News broadcast__
   political figures
   national and international events
   breaking news
   live news conferences

5. __Crime drama__
   police officers
   criminals
   evidence
   FBI agents

6. __Sporting Event__
   domed stadiums
   All-Stars
   athletic equipment
   championship trophies

7. __Nature Show__
   dangerous animals
   wilderness encounters
   jungle explorers
   natural disasters

8. __Game show__
   trivia questions
   money and prizes
   word puzzles
   host or hostess

Extra Credit. If you watch TV often, these categories might remind you of shows you have seen. Can you name a TV show or a network that fits each category?

1. _____
2. __Friends__
3. __Bravo__
4. __CNN__

5. __Dexter__
6. __Olympics__
7. __Discovery__
8. __Jeopardy__

Words for Study

leisure	dishonorable	status	offensive
captives	manual	proportion	ingrained
ambition	instinct	contraption	elimination
significant	necessities	obviously	accumulate

L E S S O N   4
Keeping up with the Joneses

by Thorstein Veblen

The American social philosopher Thorstein Veblen (1857–1929) wrote a book entitled *The Theory of the Leisure Class* in which he described what he thought people throughout the ages have worked at harder than anything else—"keeping up with the Joneses." As you read this excerpt from his highly respected work, consider whether or not what he had to say still holds true today.

* * *

In order to gain and to hold the respect of men, it is not enough merely to possess wealth or power. The wealth or power must be displayed, for the respect which we get from others is awarded only on evidence.

Throughout history, man's evidence of wealth has been based on owning things. There is every reason to believe that one of the earliest forms of ownership in history was the ownership of women by the able-bodied men of primitive communities. The original reason for the capture of women seems to have been their usefulness as trophies. This practice, in turn, gave birth to a form of ownership-marriage, resulting in households ruled by males.

This was followed by an extension of slavery to other captives, besides women, and by an extension of ownership-marriage to other women than those seized from the enemy. From the ownership of people, the concept of ownership extended itself to include the products of their industry. Thus, there arose the ownership of things as well as of persons.

It has often been thought that when people have struggled over goods—be they people, products, or property—they have done so because they had to in order to stay alive. This is not so. The motive that lies at the root of ownership is ambition—ambition to be as good or better than the next person.

Of course, in a community where nearly all goods are private property, it is necessary to earn a livelihood. Most of us live in such communities, and we are aware of the importance of earning a living. On the other hand, we must admit that the *basic* needs of food, shelter, and clothing do not really play a significant role in earning this living. When all is said and done, owning things still has the nature of a trophy.

These trophies—our possessions—provide the foundation on which we seek and gain respect from others. In order to stand well in the eyes of the community, it is necessary to come up to a certain commonly accepted standard of wealth. This standard is never very clearly defined; nevertheless it exerts its influence on us. Those members of the community who fall short of this undefined standard are considered failures.

To a great extent, the ambition to be as good as or better than everybody else determines what we decide to own. Just consider how often our purchases are based on "what everybody else has" or "what nobody else has yet." Besides this, the very means of livelihood we choose is also, to a great extent, based on this ambition to gain respect from others through ownership. Thus, "How much does it pay?" is often a far more important question when considering a new job than "What is the nature of the work?"

For those who do not have to labor in order to show their superior wealth, the concept of working for a living is a dishonorable one. From the days of the Greek philosophers right down to the present, a degree of leisure and freedom from hard work has been recognized as absolutely necessary in order to live a worthy or beautiful life. In some cultures, the sense of shamefulness of manual labor is so strong that it even overrides the instinct to survive. For instance, there are stories of certain Polynesian chiefs who preferred to starve to death rather than carry their food to their mouths with their own hands. There is also the story of a certain king of France whose servant happened to be absent one day. One of the duties of this servant was to move the king's throne when the heat from the roaring fireplace became too hot. Because the king refused to move his own throne, he suffered his royal person to be toasted beyond recovery.

For those who must labor in order to show wealth, the ways in which they gain and maintain respect take other forms. The desire here—and this applies to most of us since most of us have to work for a living—is not so much to be better, but to keep up with the accepted standards of what is considered decent ownership. Decency, in terms of our ambition to be respected, can be defined as owning goods which make us feel as if we enjoy a "higher" standard of living.

Quite often, these goods, which are usually wasteful, become more necessary to our sense of well-being than the basic necessities of life. For example, a family might delay repairing a faulty furnace in order to buy unnecessary furniture. This suggests that our concept of a high standard of living is based not on what we have, but on an ideal of ownership that is just beyond our reach. And, generally speaking, our ideals are set by the group of people who display just a bit more wealth than we do. Thus, the ambition to own more becomes a never-ending activity.

Perhaps no method of putting ownership on display provides such a fine example of showy and wasteful spending as dress. The clothes that we wear have always given an indication of our social status to all observers at first glance. And probably at no other point is our sense of shabbiness so keenly felt if we fall short of the standard set by society as in the matter of dress.

We not only buy clothes to impress others; we strive to buy as expensive clothes as we can. Inexpensive clothes are regarded as "cheap and nasty" without our even being conscious of the fact that we have passed this judgment. We tend to find things beautiful somewhat in proportion to their cost.

The function of dress as evidence of an ability to pay does not end with simply showing that the wearer consumes goods that have nothing whatsoever to do with physical comfort. Dress can also show that the wearer is not under the necessity of earning a livelihood or that, if a livelihood is involved, the wearer does not have to do manual labor.

The dress of women goes much farther than that of men in demonstrating status. In China, for example, it was once the custom to bind the feet of girls from the wealthier families. Because the feet could not grow properly, the girls grew to become women who could barely walk, thus indicating that they did not have to work. The Western version of this custom is the high heel which makes any manual work extremely difficult, and thus shows observers that the wearer is free from this type of labor. In the last century, the corset was commonly worn by fashionable women in spite of the fact that it did nothing to improve their appearance. A corset, for the benefit of modern readers who might have never heard of such a contraption, is an extremely tight-fitting undergarment. What this painful undergarment did offer, however, was an announcement to the world that its wearer did not have to work; for corsets were so uncomfortable that they made women unfit for work.

Dress must not only be obviously expensive and inconvenient to wear; it must at the same time be up-to-date. It is not known exactly how the custom of changing fashions originally started. What is obvious, however, is that if clothing is permitted to be popular for only a brief time, the wasteful buying of clothes will be greatly increased.

The same wastefulness that is apparent in fashionable clothing can be easily observed in other areas of buying as well. What is to be remembered is that this wastefulness has a strong effect on our beliefs about what is honest, beautiful, or useful.

In the matter of beauty and usefulness, beauty is usually the key factor, *but* beauty is often defined as expensiveness. Sometimes, beauty and expensiveness go hand in hand, as is the case with gold. Yet the usefulness of gold is due less to its beauty than to the fact that it is expensive. To use a not-so-beautiful example, the shine on a successful businessman's expensive shoes is no more beautiful than the shine on a beggar's threadbare sleeve. Yet the first is considered beautiful while the latter is considered highly offensive.

It is a well-known fact that shoppers are guided more by the finish and workmanship of the goods than by any signs of lasting usefulness. Goods, in order to sell, must have the marks of decent expensiveness in addition to usefulness. This, of course, makes each item more costly and leads us to believe that cheaper goods are automatically poorer in quality.

So completely has the habit of approving the expensive and disapproving the inexpensive been ingrained into our thinking that we automatically insist upon at least some measure of wasteful expensiveness in the goods we buy. Thus, it has come about that there are today no goods supplied anywhere which do not contain some unnecessary frill or feature in greater or lesser degree. Any consumer who wishes to insist on the elimination of all wealth symbols from his purchases would be unable to supply his most insignificant wants in the modern marketplace.

1 Understanding the Reading. Put the letter of the best answer on the line.

1. According to Thorstein Veblen, our possessions have value for us when _____.
   a. they are displayed
   b. they are useful
   c. we have had to work hard for them
   d. we have not had to work hard for them

2. Veblen presents his discussion of women as trophies in primitive communities as _____.
   a. biased opinion b. false assumption c. proven fact d. reasonable theory

3. According to Veblen, _____ is at the heart of our desire for possessions.
   a. advertising b. ambition c. comfort d. survival

4. Veblen defines ambition as the desire _____.
   a. to avoid manual labor
   b. to succeed in one's chosen career
   c. to enjoy at least an acceptable social status
   d. to use one's abilities to the fullest

5. According to Veblen, the standard of wealth a person must reach to gain the respect of others is _____.
   a. comical b. fair c. unimportant d. vague

6. Which example is *not* used by Veblen to demonstrate how people have scorned labor throughout the ages? _____
   a. a French king b. Chinese women c. businessmen d. the Greeks

7. According to Veblen, our sense of what is beautiful is determined by _____.
   a. commercials b. cost c. education d. income

8. Veblen maintains that most of our purchases contain at least one _____ feature.
   a. shabby b. tasteful c. thoughtless d. unnecessary

9. If Veblen's ideas are correct, the consumer who wishes to avoid all status symbols in his purchases would probably _____.
   a. have a hard time finding anything to buy
   b. have no impact on the buying habits of others
   c. buy well-made clothes
   d. have more time for important pursuits

10. The tone of this excerpt from *The Theory of the Leisure Class* is _____.
    a. amusing b. critical c. neutral d. questioning

2 What Do You Think? Answer the following questions in good sentence form. Be sure to include reasons or examples in your answers.

1. If Thorstein Veblen were alive today, what do you think his reaction would be upon entering a modern department store or supermarket?

   _____

   _____

   _____

   _____

2. Do you think Veblen is correct—that our main ambition is displaying our possessions in order to prove that we're as good as or better than everyone else? Explain.

   _____

   _____

   _____

   _____

   _____

3. Imagine inviting Mr. Veblen into your home and giving him permission to throw out three of your possessions that he considered examples of wasteful spending. List three items he might throw out. After each item, write an objection you might offer in which you explain why the item is really necessary to your well-being.

Item	Objection
1. _____	_____
	_____
2. _____	_____
	_____
3. _____	_____
	_____

3 Word Relationships. On the line, write the letter of the answer that best completes each statement.

1. Houdini is to illusionist as ___b___.
   a. Capricorn is to equator
   b. Edison is to inventor
   c. Jacuzzi is to anthropologist
   d. Veblen is to immigrant

2. Meteorology is to weather as ___c___.
   a. etymology is to dictionary
   b. pathology is to corpse
   c. psychology is to behavior
   d. zoology is to microscope

3. Hawaii is to Polynesia as ___c___.
   a. Fiji is to Micronesia
   b. Guam is to Melanesia
   c. Tahiti is to Polynesia
   d. Tonga is to Indonesia

4. Petroleum is to fuel as ___a___.
   a. chloroform is to hospital
   b. commercial is to talk show
   c. derrick is to construction
   d. straitjacket is to contraption

5. Contestant is to game show as ___d___.
   a. game show is to reality
   b. murder is to crime drama
   c. channel is to television
   d. actor is to sitcom

6. Ambassador is to government as ___c___.
   a. captive is to imprisonment
   b. ecologist is to environment
   c. missionary is to church
   d. Haida is to Indian tribe

7. Midway is to island as ___b___.
   a. Mecca is to city
   b. Norse is to country
   c. Polynesia is to continent
   d. Vietnam is to colony

8. Google is to search engine as ___c___.
   a. laptop is to Internet
   b. footage is to film
   c. AOL is to computer
   d. *People* is to magazine

9. Accumulate is to distribute as ___/___.
   a. attach is to engage
   b. civilize is to tame
   c. disentangle is to snare
   d. mutilate is to eliminate

10. Budapest is to Hungary as ___c___.
    a. Honolulu is to Hawaii
    b. Tehran is to Iran
    c. Montreal is to Canada
    d. Oslo is to Sweden

4 The Suffix *-ism*. The suffix *-ism* indicates a practice, characteristic behavior, system, theory, or condition of being. Match the *isms* listed below with the situations they best describe. Refer to a dictionary for any words you are not sure of. The first one has been done to get you started.

capitalism	favoritism	idealism	patriotism
cynicism	heroism	individualism	skepticism
✓escapism	hypnotism	materialism	terrorism

escapism   1. In order to avoid doing chores he disliked, Godfrey often convinced himself that he was exhausted and lay down to take a nap.

Cynicism   2. Believing that people are basically selfish, Gail distrusted anyone who enjoyed doing favors for others without expecting a reward in return.

individualism   3. Charles never went along with the crowd; instead he did exactly what he wanted to do—when he wanted to do it.

heroism   4. When Chris saw the man fall into the path of the oncoming subway train, he jumped onto the tracks and rescued him.

Terrorism   5. Wanting desperately to return to his homeland, the man hijacked a plane and held the passengers hostage for two days.

materialism   6. Jack spent every penny he had trying to "keep up with the Joneses" and never had a cent left to give to charity.

favoritism   7. Because Aunt Martha liked Sally better than her other nieces, she gave her expensive birthday presents and sent the others only cards.

capitalism   8. Ehrich never regretted immigrating to the United States where, through hard work over the years, he had built his company from a one-person operation to one that employed 500 people.

Hypnotism   9. Tired of his addiction to nicotine, Scott asked his psychiatrist to put him into a trance to help him kick the cigarette habit.

Skepticism   10. When Joyce announced that she was going to turn over a new leaf and stop spending every cent she earned, her sister said, "Oh, really? Well, we'll just have to see."

Idealism   11. Harry truly believed that people never committed acts of evil on purpose and envisioned a world in which love would conquer all.

Patriotism   12. Every Fourth of July, Jack Jefferson hung the American flag from his porch before leaving to march in the parade.

5 Spelling Check. In each of the sentences below, one underlined word may be misspelled. Write that word, spelled correctly, on the line. If all the words in the sentence are correct, write *correct* on the line.

_____ 1. The respected <u>etymologist</u>, Charles Earle Funk, <u>received</u> a letter one day in which the <u>origen</u> of the <u>expression</u> "keeping up with the Joneses" was explained.

following 2. The letter was from Arthur R. "Pop" Momand, and the <u>folowing</u> <u>sentences</u> are an <u>abridged</u> <u>version</u> of his letter.

_____ 3. Here is how it happened: At the age of 23, I was making $125 a week (good money in those days, with no income tax). I <u>married</u> and moved to Long Island, joined a <u>country</u> club, rode <u>horseback</u> <u>daily</u>, and had a maid.

_____ 4. Well, it was not long until the <u>butcher</u>, the baker, <u>ect.</u>, were <u>knocking</u> gently but firmly on the old front door. In the end we pulled up <u>stakes</u>, headed for New York and moved into a cheap apartment.

humorous 5. Our Long Island <u>experience</u> was a rude <u>awakening</u>, but I saw the <u>humorus</u> side of it. We had been living far beyond our means. I also noted that most of our <u>friends</u> were doing the same.

_____ 6. I decided it would make good comic-strip <u>material</u>, so I drew six strips. At first I <u>thought</u> of calling it "Keeping up with the <u>Smiths</u>," but <u>finally</u> decided on "Keeping up with the Joneses."

_____ 7. "Keeping up with the Joneses" was <u>launched</u>—and little did I <u>realize</u> it was to run for <u>twenty-eight</u> years and take us across the Atlantic <u>fourty-two</u> times.

Bulletin 8. The feature was released in February of 1913 and appeared first in the *New York Globe, Chicago Daily News, Boston Globe, <u>Philadelphia Bullitin</u>* and ten <u>minor</u> papers.

cartoon 9. The strip gained in <u>popularity</u> each year; it appeared in two-reel <u>comedies</u>, was put on as a <u>musical</u> comedy, and published in a <u>carton</u> book.

portraits 10. After <u>twenty-eight</u> years on the old <u>treadmill</u>, I tired of it. Today I paint <u>portrats</u>, <u>landscapes</u>—and, yes, I hate to admit it, we are still trying to "keep up with the Joneses."

Words for Study

hovered	humility	luxuries	impels
trivial	humanity	monotony	Pierre
distinguished	modestly	accurate	parallel
recipient	marionettes	drone	Arabian

LESSON 5
While the Auto Waits

by O. Henry

Promptly at the beginning of twilight, there came again to that quiet corner of that quiet small park the girl in gray. She sat upon a bench and read a book, for there was yet half an hour left in which one could still read outside.

To repeat: Her dress was gray and quite plain. A large-meshed veil masked her hat and also her face which shone through it with a calm and unconscious beauty. She had come there at the same hour on the previous day and on the day before that, and there was someone in the park who knew it.

The young man who knew it hovered near, offering small prayers to that great lady, Luck. His prayers were rewarded; for, in turning a page, her book slipped from her fingers and bounded from the bench a full yard away.

The young man pounced upon it with eagerness and returned it to its owner with the kind of style that seems to flourish in parks and public places—a mixture of manly politeness and hope and watchful respect for a policeman who might happen by.

In a pleasant voice, he risked a trivial remark about the weather—a topic which is responsible for so much of the world's unhappiness—and stood poised for a moment, awaiting his fate.

The girl looked him over leisurely; at his ordinary, neat clothes and his features, which were not particularly distinguished.

"You may sit down, if you like," she said in a deep, rich voice. "Really, I would like you to sit down. The light is too bad for reading, and I would prefer to talk."

The recipient of Lady Luck's attention slid upon the seat by her side with ready obedience.

"Do you know," he said, speaking the formula with which park gentlemen begin their conversations, "that you are the most stunning girl I have seen in a long time? I had my eye on you yesterday. Didn't know somebody was bowled over by your beauty, did you, sweet thing?"

"Whoever you are," said the girl in icy tones, "you must remember that I am a lady. I will excuse the remark you have just made because the mistake was, doubtless, not an unnatural one—in your circle. I asked you to sit down; if the invitation leads to your rudeness, consider it withdrawn."

"I earnestly beg your pardon," pleaded the young man. His expression of satisfaction had changed to one of regret and humility. "It was my fault, you know—I mean there are girls in parks, you know—that is, of course, you don't know, but—"

"Drop the subject, please. Of course I know. Now, tell me about these people passing and crowding along these paths. Where are they going? Why do they hurry so? Do you think they're happy?"

The young man had promptly discarded his flirting role. His cue was now for a waiting part; he could not guess the new role he would be expected to play.

"It is interesting to watch them," he replied, studying her mood. "It is the wonderful drama of life. Some are going to supper and some to—er—other places, I guess. One wonders what their histories are."

"I don't," said the girl. "I'm not so curious. I come here to sit because here only can I be near the great, common, throbbing heart of humanity. Can you guess why I spoke to you, Mr.—?"

"Parkenstacker," said the young man. He now looked eager and hopeful.

"No," said the girl, holding up a slender finger and smiling slightly. "You would recognize it immediately. It is simply impossible to keep one's name out of print. Or even one's portrait. This veil and this hat of my maid furnish me with a disguise. You should have seen the chauffeur stare at it when he thought I wasn't looking. I spoke to you, Mr. Stackenpot—"

"Parkenstacker," corrected the young man modestly.

"—Mr. Parkenstacker, because I wanted to talk, for once, with a natural man—a man unspoiled by that hateful gloss of wealth and imagined superiority. Oh! you do not know how weary I am of it—money, money, money! And of the men who surround me, dancing like little marionettes all cut by the same pattern. I am sick of pleasure, of jewels, of travel, of society, of luxuries of all kinds."

"I always had an idea," the man said hesitatingly, "that money must be a pretty good thing."

"Perhaps. But when you have so many millions that—!" She concluded the sentence with a gesture of despair. "It is the monotony of it," she continued, "that bores me. Drives, dinners, theaters, dances. Sometimes the very tinkle of the ice in my champagne glass nearly drives me mad."

Mr. Parkenstacker looked innocently interested. "I have always liked," he said, "to read and hear about the ways of wealthy folks. I suppose I'm a bit of a snob. But I like to have my information accurate. Now, I had formed the opinion that champagne is cooled in the bottle and not by placing ice in the glass."

The girl gave a musical laugh of genuine amusement.

"You should know," she laughed, as if she were speaking to a slow-witted child, "that we of the non-useful class depend for our amusement upon breaking with custom. Just now, it is a fad to put ice in champagne."

"I see," admitted the young man humbly. "These special amusements of the inner circle do not become known to the common public."

"Sometimes," continued the girl, "I have thought that if I ever should love a man, it would be one of lowly station. One who is a worker and not a drone. But, doubtless, the claims of class and wealth will prove stronger than my desire. Just now I am chased by two. One is a Grand Duke from Germany. I think he has, or has had, a wife somewhere who has been driven mad by his cruelty. The other is an English Lord, so cold and heartless that I even prefer the cruelty of the Duke. What is it that impels me to tell you these things, Mr. Packenstaker?"

"Parkenstacker," breathed the young man. "Indeed, you cannot know how much I appreciate your telling me these things."

The girl looked at him with a calm, cool regard that suited the difference in their stations in life.

"What is your line of business, Mr. Parkenstacker?" she asked,

"A very humble one. But I hope to rise in the world. Were you really in earnest when you said that you could love a man of lowly position?"

"Indeed I was. No calling could be too humble were the man what I would wish him to be."

"I work," declared Mr. Parkenstacker, "in a restaurant."

The girl shrank slightly.

"Not as a waiter?" she said, a little pleadingly. "Labor is noble, but—"

"I am not a waiter. I am cashier in"—on the street they faced that bounded the opposite side of the park was the brilliant electric sign RESTAURANT—"I am cashier in the restaurant you see there."

The girl consulted a tiny watch set in a bracelet of rich design upon her left wrist and rose hurriedly. She thrust her book into a glittering bag for which, however, the book was too large.

"Why are you not at work?" she asked.

"I am on the night shift," said the young man. "It is yet an hour before I start. May I not hope to see you again?"

"I do not know. Perhaps—but the whim may not seize me again. I must go quickly now. There is a dinner and a box seat at the theater—and, oh! the same old round. Perhaps you noticed an automobile at the upper corner of the park as you came. One with a white body."

"And red running gear?" asked the young man, knitting his brows thoughtfully.

"Yes. I always come in that. Pierre waits for me there. He supposes me to be shopping in the department stores across the square. Imagine the chains binding the life in which we must deceive even our chauffeurs. Good night."

"But it is dark now," said Mr. Parkenstacker, "and the park is full of dangerous men. May I not walk—?"

"If you have the slightest regard for my wishes," said the girl firmly, "you will remain at this bench for ten minutes after I have left. Again, good night."

Swift and stately she moved away through the dusk. The young man watched her graceful form as she reached the pavement at the park's edge and turned up along it toward the corner where the automobile stood. Then he began to dodge and skim among the park trees and shrubbery in a course parallel to her route, keeping her well in sight.

When she reached the corner, she turned her head to glance at the automobile, and then passed it, continuing on across the street. Sheltered behind a cab, the young man followed her movements closely with his eyes. Passing down the sidewalk of the street opposite the park, she entered the restaurant with the blazing sign. The place was one of those glaring establishments where one may dine cheaply. The girl went to the back of the restaurant but soon reappeared without her hat and veil.

The cashier's desk was at the front. A red-haired girl on the stool climbed down, glancing angrily at the clock as she did so. The girl in gray mounted in her place.

The young man thrust his hands into his pockets and walked slowly back along the sidewalk. At the corner his foot struck a small, paperback volume

lying there, sending it sliding to the edge of the grass. By its quaint cover, he recognized it as the book the girl had been reading. He picked it up carelessly and saw that its title was "New Arabian Nights." He dropped it again upon the grass, and stood there, undecided, for a minute. Then he stepped into the automobile, stretched out among the cushions, and said four words to his chauffeur:

"To the club, Henri."

1 Understanding the Story. Write the letter of the best answer on the line.

1. The girl most likely wore a veil _____.
   a. for religious reasons
   b. to disguise herself
   c. to protect her complexion
   d. to shade her eyes

2. Mr. Parkenstacker's prayer was probably a plea that _____.
   a. he'd be granted an opportunity to meet the girl
   b. a police officer wouldn't interrupt his romantic pursuit
   c. the chauffeur wouldn't come to get him
   d. it wouldn't start to rain

3. The girl excuses Mr. Parkenstacker's bold compliment because she believes _____.
   a. all men are coarse and common
   b. all men begin conversations with young ladies in this way
   c. he is ignorant due to his social position
   d. he is mistaken about her social position

4. Mr. Parkenstacker ceases to flirt with the girl because _____.

    a. he decides to play "hard to get"

    b. his attention is drawn to the people passing by

    c. his interest in her is fading

    d. his strategy isn't working

5. According to the girl, the most tiresome feature of wealth is _____.

    a. marriage   **b.** romance   **c.** servants   **d.** the life style

6. Mr. Parkenstacker's probable motive for declaring that he works in a restaurant is _____.

    a. to make fun of the girl's employment

    b. to stall for more time

    c. to win the affection of the girl

    d. to offer sympathy for the girl's working conditions

7. When Mr. Parkenstacker tells the girl that he is a cashier, she _____.

    a. calls him a liar   **c.** feels ashamed that she has deceived him

    b. realizes that it's time to go to work   **d.** decides not to see him again

8. Which of the following excerpts from "While the Auto Waits" has the least bearing on the plot? _____

    a. "... the weather—a topic which is responsible for so much of the world's unhappiness ..."

    b. "It is the wonderful drama of life."

    c. "Just now, it is a fad to put ice in champagne."

    d. "To the club, Henri."

9. A synonym for *quaint* as in "By its quaint cover, he recognized it as the book the girl had been reading" is _____.

    a. costly   **b.** inexpensive   **c.** old-fashioned   **d.** ragged

10. We can guess that New Arabian Nights is a collection of _____.

    a. essays about wealth   **c.** romantic adventures

    b. murder mysteries   **d.** science fiction stories

2 What Do You Think? *A pretense* is a false appearance or action that is intended to deceive someone else. In "While the Auto Waits," for example, the girl's pretense is that of a wealthy lady of high society. Answer these questions about pretenses in good sentence form.

1. What is Mr. Parkenstacker's pretense, and why do you think he chooses to act in this way?

   _____

   _____

   _____

   _____

2. What might have happened in the story if Mr. Parkenstacker had not adopted a pretense in his conversation with the girl?

   _____

   _____

   _____

   _____

3. What might have happened in the story if the girl had not acted in such a pretentious manner with Mr. Parkenstacker?

   _____

   _____

   _____

   _____

3 Which Word Does Not Fit? Choose the word in each row which does *not* fit with the other words, and write it on the line.

1.	argue	bicker	dispute	question	wrangle	_____
2.	glaring	insignificant	petty	puny	trivial	_____
3.	magazine	book	printing	tabloid	newspaper	_____
4.	restaurant	appetite	taste	hunger	flavor	_____
5.	evident	idealistic	obvious	straightforward	unmistakable	_____
6.	Dover	Milwaukee	Montreal	Oakland	Pittsburgh	_____
7.	admiration	approval	fascination	regard	respect	_____
8.	humble	lowly	meek	modest	self-seeking	_____
9.	ultra	super	valuable	very	especially	_____
10.	pretentious	showy	splashy	swank	stately	_____
11.	flicker	flutter	hover	soar	waver	_____
12.	doubting	skeptical	uncertain	unconvinced	unsuspecting	_____
13.	tragedy	cheerless	glum	depressed	miserable	_____
14.	impel	incite	motivate	spur	suggest	_____
15.	boredom	dullness	monotony	routine	stillness	_____
16.	Adolph	Ehrich	Henri	Pierre	Wilhelmina	_____

4 More about O. Henry. For each sentence, fill in the three best words from the set at the left to complete the sentence correctly.

cleverly
continually
gradually
modestly
scholarly

1. For several generations now, O. Henry (1862–1910), the author of "While the Auto Waits," has been admired by the reading public for his _____ written stories despite the fact that _____ critics have _____ refused to recognize him as a major American author.

determinedly
eventually
hesitatingly
obviously
originally

2. Named William Sydney Porter at birth, O. Henry _____ came from North Carolina but _____ moved to Texas where he _____ pursued the two lines of his artistic interest—drawing and writing.

humility
majority
necessity
prosperity
quantity

3. The _____ of earning a living led him finally to take a position as teller at the First National Bank in Austin where he spent the _____ of his working hours drawing, writing, and—in a desperate effort to improve the _____ of a newspaper he was running on the side—embezzling.

attractive
impressive
objective
offensive
subjective

4. To this day, admirers of O. Henry try to come up with _____ evidence that proves their idol could never have committed such a(n) _____ crime, but the judge at the trial must have declared such evidence highly _____, for he sentenced O. Henry to jail.

bearable
reasonable
unbearable
unmistakable
valuable

5. Although he found prison life _____, the three years he spent in the Ohio Penitentiary were nonetheless _____ in that it was as Prisoner Number 30664 that he developed the _____ style that would earn him success as a writer.

abbreviation
assumption
confirmation
opposition
variation

6. No _____ of this idea exists, but one _____ is that O. Henry, William Sydney Porter's pen name, is a(n) _____ for the name of a French pharmacist which he had come upon in a reference book while working in the prison pharmacy.

expectation
indication
limitation
objection
quotation

7. One _____ that as a self-educated writer O. Henry felt a sense of _____ from his lack of formal schooling is a(n) _____ from a biography of his life: "I'd give my eyes for a formal education."

boundless
changeless
cheerless
countless
defenseless

8. In 1901 O. Henry stepped forth from the _____ walls of the Ohio Penitentiary and into the bustling twentieth century. After living briefly with his daughter Margaret in Pittsburgh, he moved to New York City where his writing energy seemed _____, for he managed to produce _____ stories for different magazines in a remarkably short period of time.

accompaniment
bewilderment
bombardment
enrichment
fulfillment

9. Managing money continued to be a source of _____ for O. Henry, whose _____ of a dream as a successful author was darkened by the _____ of the creditors who were forever hounding him to pay his many debts.

attraction
observation
proportion
relations
separation

10. Many students of O. Henry's stories share the _____ that his plots, whether they deal with business, marriage, or social _____, describe escapes from reality—escapes with which he was sympathetic, for O. Henry suffered from a painful sense of _____ from the world in which he lived.

5 Pretenses in the Park. Match the people listed below with the statements they might make if, like the characters in "While the Auto Waits," their park bench conversations were completely pretentious. The first one has been done to get you started.

alarmist	immigrant	Scrooge
braggart	manipulator	skeptic
escapist	quibbler	✓wallflower

_____ **wallflower** _____   **1.** "Being popular is such a nuisance, isn't it? You're always right in the middle of all the excitement!"

_____   **2.** "Don't you think people should confront their problems rather than running from them the minute the least little thing goes wrong?"

_____   **3.** "This country is getting too crowded. I think people should live in the country in which they were born."

_____   **4.** "I can't stand these doubting Thomases who can never accept anything—and I mean anything—at face value."

_____   **5.** "I have better things to do with my time than have a nervous breakdown every time the six o'clock news brings the latest world crisis into my living room."

_____   **6.** "If people would be a lot more interested in giving and a lot less interested in receiving, this world would be a much better place."

_____   **7.** "Some people—the minute they meet someone—try to figure out how to use them. But not me—I think people should be respected."

_____   **8.** "When you ask me what I think is my most valuable trait, the first thing that comes to my mind is my modesty."

_____   **9.** "You know, if you waste your time quarreling over every little dispute that arises during the course of the day, before you know it your life is nothing but one long argument."

Review: Lessons 1–5

1 Definitions. Match the words listed below with the correct definitions.

assumption	fiction	modesty	prosperity
economy	illusion	neutrality	status
excerpt	leisure	organism	technique
feat	luxury	penalty	trivia

_____ **1.** any living individual; any plant or animal

_____ **2.** anything that adds physical comfort; the enjoyment of riches

_____ **3.** freedom from time-consuming duties, or activities; rest

_____ **4.** insignificant matters

_____ **5.** social standing; the legal condition of a person or thing

_____ **6.** the condition of having good fortune or financial success

_____ **7.** the systematic procedure by which any task is accomplished

_____ **8.** the state or policy of not actively taking sides in a matter under dispute

_____ **9.** a passage or scene selected from a speech, book, film, play, or the like

_____ **10.** a statement accepted or supposed true without proof or demonstration

_____ **11.** any act or deed of skill, courage, imagination, or strength; an achievement

_____ **12.** the state or quality of showing a reasonable regard for one's own talents, ability, and value

_____ **13.** the careful or thrifty use or management of resources, such as of income, materials, or labor

_____ **14.** an incorrect perception of reality; the state or condition of being deceived by such perceptions or beliefs

_____ **15.** an event, statement, or occurrence that has been invented or pretended rather than having actually taken place

_____ **16.** a punishment established by law or authority for a crime or offense; the disadvantage or painful consequences resulting from such an action

2 Word Review. Fill in the blanks with the set of words that makes the best sense in each sentence.

1. Many people in the audience squirmed uncomfortably in their seats as the _____ recited _____ examples of how the typical American household abuses our natural resources.
   - **a.** archaeologist—obvious
   - **b.** ecologist—glaring
   - **c.** etymologist—impressive
   - **d.** geologist—distinguished

2. The _____ was _____ calm considering that his boss had just informed him he was fired and told him to clear out of the building.
   - **a.** executive—remarkably
   - **b.** immigrant—continually
   - **c.** manufacturer—occasionally
   - **d.** applicant—amazingly

3. Even though he was known to be _____ to public criticism, Beatrice wrote a letter to the mayor in which she sharply accused him of political _____.
   - **a.** immune—favoritism
   - **b.** hardened—heroism
   - **c.** attached—idealism
   - **d.** addicted—cynicism

4. _____ is the capital of _____.
   - **a.** Charleston—South Carolina
   - **b.** Milwaukee—Wisconsin
   - **c.** Montreal—Canada
   - **d.** Pierre—South Dakota

5. David was such a(n) _____ that he thought conversations about the latest fad were _____.
   - **a.** conformist—unfashionable
   - **b.** illusionist—unsuccessful
   - **c.** materialist—unsettling
   - **d.** nonconformist—unbearable

6. Usually, a(n) _____ has read many books or articles about _____.
   - **a.** ambassador—patriotism
   - **b.** minister—theology
   - **c.** dramatist—marionettes
   - **d.** designer—tattoos

7. Not sure that he was using a word _____, Arthur checked the _____ in his abridged dictionary.
   - **a.** accurately—entry
   - **b.** effectively—aspect
   - **c.** precisely—quotation
   - **d.** reasonably—verb

8. "The _____ maintain(s) that we don't have a chance of winning this election," stated the candidate. "_____, we will continue our campaign efforts."
   - **a.** critics—Whereupon
   - **b.** cynics—Thereafter
   - **c.** experts—Furthermore
   - **d.** opposition—Nonetheless

9. _____ is the study of _____.
   - **a.** Anthropology—ancient ruins
   - **b.** Biology—organisms
   - **c.** Geology—environmental waste
   - **d.** Sociology—primitive cultures

10. A Greek dramatist once defined the _____ human being as a person who would always be in the right by _____.

    a. ideal—instinct   **c.** motivated—leisure

    b. modest—luxury   **d.** rugged—escapism

3 Synonyms and Antonyms. Choose a synonym to fill in the first blank in each sentence. Choose an antonym to fill in the second blank. The first one has been done to get you started.

Synonyms

cheerless –

confined –

elimination –

frill

imaginary –

meekly

modest –

✓plentiful –

significant –

skepticism –

unbiased

upright –

Antonyms

actual

addition

boastfully

boundless

conviction

dishonorable

lighthearted

necessity

pretentious

✓scarce

subjective

uneventful

1. Ample and ___*plentiful*___ are antonyms for ___*scarce*___.

2. Doubt and ___*skepticism*___ are antonyms for _____.

3. Fictional and ___*imaginary*___ are antonyms for ___*actual*___.

4. Glum and ___*cheerless*___ are antonyms for _____.

5. Humbly and _____ are antonyms for _____.

6. Removal and ___*elimination*___ are antonyms for ___*necessity*___.

7. Limited and ___*confined*___ are antonyms for _____.

8. Luxury and ___*upright*___ are antonyms for _____.

9. Meek and _____ are antonyms for _____.

10. Moral and _____ are antonyms for ___*pretentious*___.

11. Noteworthy and ___*significant*___ are antonyms for _____.

12. Objective and ___*unbiased*___ are antonyms for ___*subjective*___.

4 A Poem about Appearances. Read this well-known poem, and then answer the questions that follow.

The Blind Men and the Elephant
by John Godfrey Saxe

It was six men of Indostan
To learning much inclined,
Who went to see the Elephant
(Though all of them were blind),
That each by observation
Might satisfy his mind.

The First approached the Elephant,
And happening to fall
Against his broad and sturdy side,
At once began to bawl:
"God bless me! but the Elephant
Is very like a wall!"

The Second, feeling of the tusk
Cried, "Ho! what have we here
So very round and smooth and sharp?
To me 'tis very clear
This wonder of an Elephant
Is very like a spear!"

The Third approached the animal
And happening to take
The squirming trunk within his hands
Thus boldly up he spake:
"I see," quoth he, "the Elephant
Is very like a snake!"

The Fourth reached out an eager hand,
And felt about the knee:
"What most this wondrous beast is like
Is very plain," quoth he;
"Tis clear enough the Elephant
Is very like a tree!"

The Fifth, who chanced to touch the ear,
Said: "E'en the blindest man
Can tell what this resembles most;
Deny the fact who can
This marvel of an Elephant
Is very like a fan!"

The Sixth no sooner had begun
About the beast to grope
Than, seizing on the swinging tail
That fell within his scope,
"I see" quoth he, "the Elephant
Is very like a rope!"

And so these men of Indostan
Disputed loud and long
Each in his own opinion
Exceeding stiff and strong.
Though each was partly in the right,
They all were in the wrong!

1. What illusion does each of the blind men have about his ability to know what an elephant is like?

_____

_____

_____

2. What is the reason that the blind men "disputed loud and long"?

_____

_____

_____

3. Would the blind men agree with the last two lines of the poem? Why or why not?

_____

_____

_____

4. What message about reality is offered to us in this poem?

_____

_____

_____

_____

_____

_____

5 Faraway Places. The places below have all been mentioned in the readings in this unit. With the help of a dictionary or the Internet, match these faraway places with the correct descriptions.

Australia	Fiji	Hawaii	New Guinea	Tasmania
Budapest	Guam	Hollywood	Tahiti	Vietnam

_____ 1. A U.S. air and naval base is located on this Pacific island which is also a territory belonging to the United States.

_____Vietnam_____ 2. A tropical country in Southeast Asia, it was here that the longest conflict (1957–1975) in which the United States has ever taken part occurred.

_____Budapest_____ 3. Although much of this city was destroyed during World War II, it is a thriving eastern European capital today.

_____Hawaii_____ 4. Captain Cook named these the Sandwich Islands in 1778. Near the middle of the Pacific Ocean, this is the only state in the United States that does not lie on the mainland of North America.

_____Fiji_____ 5. Comprised of about 250 scattered islands, this South Pacific country gained its independence from England in 1970. Its capital, Suva, is located on the largest island.

_____Hollywood_____ 6. A district near Los Angeles, California, this is known as the historical center of movies and movie stars.

_____Australia_____ 7. South of the equator, this faraway place is the sixth largest country and the smallest continent in the world.

_____Tahiti_____ 8. Surrounded by a broken coral reef, this is the largest island of the Society Islands and is famous for its beauty.

_____New Guinea_____ 9. Located north of Australia, this is the second largest island in the world.

_____Tasmania_____ 10. This small island state of the Australian Commonwealth is a favorite vacation spot for Australians.

UNIT 2
Explorers

Unit 2 takes us on an exciting and amazing journey—to places most of us could only dream about going. Follow these groundbreaking explorers as they make history by traveling the earth, the sea, and the universe.

This first reading, *Marco Polo*, follows a mid-13th-century explorer as he heads out to explore the far corners of the world. Marco Polo's tales of his travels may be even more fantastic than his actual experiences.

Lesson 7, *The Journals of Lewis and Clark*, presents excerpts from journals the pair kept as they were traveling across the wild western territory of the U.S. in 1805. The excerpts tell of an encounter Lewis and Clark—along with their interpreter and their Shoshone guide—have with the Shoshone Indians.

Lesson 8 offers passages adapted from the book *South*, written by British explorer Sir Ernest Shackleton. The passages offer a gripping, first-hand account of Shackleton's 1914 expedition in which he attempts to become the first explorer to cross the Antarctic by land.

There is still so much to know about life in the world's great oceans. The reading for Lesson 9, *Exploring the Deep*, follows the 1930s undersea adventures of explorers William Beebe and Otis Barton. These two men dared to explore the bottom of the sea—deeper than anyone had ever gone before.

Lesson 10 presents *A Brief History of Space Exploration*, starting from the time of ancient sky watchers right up to the most current celestial discoveries. The article tells where we've been, where we are, and where we may be going—in the universe.

Words for Study

unicorns	bandit	Gryphon	exaggerated
Sepulcher	'tis	dictated	currency
VIP	comrades	manuscript	document
inscribed	astray	controversial	navigated
reverence	perished	resolve	medieval

LESSON 6
Marco Polo

The world, and what people knew about it, was vastly different 800 years ago from what it is today. In fact we probably know more about outer space than most people of that era knew about countries on the other side of the planet. Remember, this was a time when people didn't know if the world was flat or round. They thought monsters lived in the deep oceans and unicorns raced through the forests of distant lands. So imagine what it must have been like for a 17-year-old boy setting out on a trip that would last years and take him to the far corners of the world. That was the prospect that awaited Marco Polo in 1271.

In reality, Marco knew more about what this trip held in store for him than most people of his time. He lived in Venice, Italy, a great trading nation of the period. Venetian merchants traveled to the most remote parts of the known world. His father, Niccolo Polo, and his uncle, Maffeo Polo, were merchants. They had traveled all over the Middle East to trade the goods of Europe for the spices, ivory, silk, perfumes, and other goods of the East. And in 1266, after a journey that lasted 6 years, they had actually visited Cathay—the country we now know as China. There, they met the great Mongol ruler of China, Kublai Khan.

The Khan was impressed with the Polo brothers. When they prepared to go home to Europe, he invited them to return again to his court. He wanted them to bring scholars back who could teach him about western religion and science. He also wanted them to ask the Pope to send him sacred oil from the Holy Sepulcher in Jerusalem. To aid the brothers on their travels, the Khan gave them what amounted to a VIP passport. It was a tablet of gold, 12 inches long by three inches wide. On it were inscribed these words: "By the strength of the eternal Heaven, holy be the Khan's name. Let him that pays him not reverence be killed." This passport was of great value. The Mongols governed much of Asia, and their rule extended as far west as Russia and Poland. The Great Khan and his Mongol armies were, moreover, feared by everyone. Having this tablet ensured the Polos of whatever assistance they needed on their journey. They were given horses, food, lodging, and armed protection as they traveled through countries on their way home.

The brothers reached Venice in 1269. Soon they set about planning a return to Cathay, a trip that began late in the year 1271. They took the young Marco with them. Most of their journey was by land. They crossed Armenia, Persia, Afghanistan, and passed along the northern parts of Tibet. They crossed the Pamirs, some of the highest mountains in the world, and then they crossed the unforgiving Gobi Desert.

Although the Mongols were both powerful and feared, the world was still a dangerous place. Bandits, pirates, and war were a constant menace, as were sickness and brutal travel conditions. Marco Polo described the Lop Nor, a desert in northwest China, as "so great that 'tis said it would take a year and more to ride from one end of it to the other. And here, where its breadth is least, it takes a month to cross it. 'Tis all composed of hills and valleys of sand, and not a thing to eat is to be found on it." Travelers made the journey on foot, horseback, and camel. Their awkward wagons and carts were slow and bogged down in mud and sand.

Dangers—both real and imagined—were everywhere. Speaking again of the Lop Nor, Polo wrote that "there is a marvelous thing related to this Desert, which is that when travelers are on the move by night, and one of them chances to lag behind or to fall asleep or the like, when he tries to gain his company again he will hear spirits talking, and will suppose them to be his comrades. Sometimes the spirits will call him by name; and thus shall a traveler ofttimes be led astray so that he never finds his party. And in this way many have perished."

The Polos persisted and finally arrived at the court of Kublai Khan. It had taken them three and a half years to travel 5,600 miles. The Great Khan greeted them warmly. In time, Marco became a great favorite of the Khan and served him in different roles. He was sent on missions representing the Khan to provinces of China as well as to Myanmar and India.

Marco Polo described many of the wonders of Kublai Khan's China. He told about the Khan's great, moveable palace. Its walls were covered with gold and silver. Six thousand people could dine in it at once. Most amazingly, it was made of cane held together by silk cords. The entire palace could be taken apart and moved when the Khan moved.

Polo, who traveled far and wide in the service of the Khan, tells of seeing, or at least hearing about, strange and legendary beasts. On islands south of Myanmar, he says there were "wild elephants in the country, and numerous unicorns, which are very nearly as big. They have hair like that of a buffalo, feet like those of an elephant, and a horn in the middle of the forehead, which is black and very thick." He may have been describing an animal he saw in Indonesia, perhaps a rhinoceros.

On Madagascar, Marco Polo says there lived a huge bird like an eagle. He calls it the Gryphon, but he says the islanders call it the Ruc. It is a bird of "enormous size," he says. "Its wings covered an extent of 30 paces . . . And it is so strong that it will seize an elephant in its talons and carry him high into the air, and drop him so that he is smashed to pieces."

What seemed to amaze Marco Polo more than any of these beasts, though, was paper money, black stones that burned, and the Khan's system of communication. Polo could not quite grasp how paper could be used as a substitute for gold or silver, yet it was used throughout China, and people could buy anything they wished with it.

Polo also described a black rock that was found in China that was burned to produce heat. The stone exists "in beds in the mountains, which they dig out and burn like firewood. . . . It is true that they have plenty of wood also, but they do not burn it, because those stones burn better and cost less." Although coal was known in Europe at this time, Marco Polo evidently did not know about it. His description of coal is one of the earliest recorded.

Kublai Khan's system of communication was perhaps the best in the entire ancient world. It impressed Polo as well as modern historians. It resembled our postal system with three grades of delivery service. The ordinary messages were carried by runners who handed off their messages every three miles. What might be called first-class mail was carried on horseback. The horses were changed every 25 miles. Still faster service, used for the Khan's messages, were also carried by horse. These riders traveled at a gallop, however, and the horses were changed frequently. The riders could cover 300 miles in a day.

The Polos remained in China for seventeen years. Toward the end of this time, they became restless and began asking the Khan for permission to leave. The Polos missed home. They also worried about what might happen when the aging Kublai Khan died. They had amassed great treasure and feared that it would be hard to get it out of the country without the Khan's support. At first he refused their request: their services were too valuable. Finally, in 1291, the Khan asked the Polos to escort a Mongol princess to Iran where she would be married.

The Polos began their journey by ship. They traveled along the south coast of China and Southeast Asia. Marco Polo left few details about this leg of his travels, but it was one of great hardship and loss. Many crew members and passengers died, and the Polos were robbed of much of their wealth. After leaving the princess in Iran, however, the Polos finally reached Venice again, much to the surprise of their family who thought they must have died many years before.

Upon his return, Marco Polo tried to settle back into a normal life, but adventure followed him. Three years after returning, he was in command of a Venetian warship that was captured during a war with Genoa, Venice's rival. Polo spent the next year in prison. To pass the time, he dictated the story of his travels to a fellow prisoner who happened to be a writer. The book became known as *The Travels of Marco Polo*.

When the war was over, Polo published the book. It became popular throughout Europe. Over the next fifty years, hundreds of manuscript copies were sold in several languages. The book was also controversial, and remains so to this day. It is a good story of great adventure and tells of marvelous things that Polo saw during his travels. But some of these stories seem so fantastic that many people wonder if his tales were made up. Some even question whether Marco Polo visited China at all. They point out that Polo's book fails to mention things that it would have been impossible to overlook. For example, Polo doesn't mention drinking tea or using chopsticks. Moreover, Polo's name never comes up in the Chinese records of the period. Still, many of his descriptions and stories of events are historically accurate. *The Travels of Marco Polo* is an important resource for Chinese historians because it gives more details about some historical events than their own written histories do.

Scholars continue to study the facts of Marco Polo's travels in order to resolve the mystery, but the debate is not completely settled. What seems most likely, though, is that Polo, with the help of his prison-mate, the writer, simply exaggerated some of the events of his journey.

He may also have reported some tales of things he heard about but did not see. The doubters stung Marco who insisted to his last breath that the stories were true. When he died in 1324, Polo's last words were said to have been "I have only told the half of what I saw!"

1 Understanding the Reading. Put the letter of the best answer on the line.

1. Marco Polo grew up in _____.
   a. Venice   b. China   c. Mongolia   d. Russia

2. Niccolo and Maffeo Polo went to Cathay, which is another name for _____.
   a. Lop Nor   b. China   c. Jerusalem   d. Madagascar

3. Kublai Khan wanted Niccolo and Maffeo Polo to bring him _____.
   a. wild elephants from Myanmar
   b. a VIP passport
   c. spices and silk from Europe
   d. sacred oil from the Holy Sepulcher

4. The Mongols were a powerful and dangerous people who _____.
   a. tried to prevent Europeans from traveling to Asia
   b. made travel to Asia dangerous
   c. ruled China and much of the rest of Asia
   d. lived deep in the Lop Nor

5. It took Marco Polo and his father and uncle about _____ to reach Kublai Khan's court.
   a. three and a half years   b. 17 years   c. a year   d. a month

6. Marco Polo described a huge bird that was like an eagle that could lift an elephant in its talons. He called it the _____.
   a. unicorn   b. rhinoceros   c. gryphon   d. buffalo

7. One reason the Polos wanted to leave the Khan's court and go home was because _____.
   a. they wanted to tell the people of Europe about Cathay
   b. the Ruc was hunting and killing people
   c. Venice was at war with Genoa and they wanted to help their city
   d. they wanted to leave the country before Kublai Khan died

8. While the Polos were traveling home, _____.
   a. Marco Polo wrote his book about his travels
   b. they were robbed of much of their wealth
   c. they had to cross the Gobi Desert
   d. Marco Polo was captured by a warship from Genoa

9. Marco Polo's book was controversial because _____.
   a. people didn't believe the fantastic stories he told
   b. people knew Marco Polo had not written the book himself
   c. he does not tell what happened on his voyage home
   d. they knew Marco Polo had worked for Kublai Khan

10. When Marco Polo was dying, he _____.
    a. admitted that many of his stories were exaggerated
    b. said that he had never worked for Kublai Khan
    c. said "I have only told the half of what I saw!"
    d. claimed that "I have always been honest with people"

2 What Do You Think? Read the question. Then write your answer in good sentence form.

1. Did Marco Polo really see a gryphon?

   _____

   _____

2. Marco Polo says it would take a year to travel the Lop Nor from end to end. Is this believable? Why do you think so?

   _____

   _____

3. Why was Marco Polo so impressed with the Khan's communication system? Do you think he was justified in having this opinion? Explain.

   _____

   _____

4. Did Polo really visit China? Explain.

   _____

   _____

3 Ancient China. Use context clues and some intelligent guessing to complete these statements about ancient China.

bamboo	evidence	knowledge	press	technology
books	explorer	language	revolution	type
commerce	explosive	legend	rockets	warfare
currency	invention	magnets	society	wealthy

1. There is a Chinese _____ that tells of the invention of paper in AD 105.

2. Historic _____ shows paper was invented two hundred years earlier.

3. The first paper was made of _____.

4. The Chinese were also the first to use moveable _____ for printing.

5. Chinese _____ didn't benefit much from the printing press.

6. The Chinese _____ has 5,000 characters compared to 26 characters in the English alphabet. Finding the correct character from among 5,000 made setting type very slow.

7. Three hundred years later, Johann Gutenberg independently invented the printing _____ in Europe.

8. Europe benefited much more than China from this new printing _____.

9. This new system allowed _____ to be printed quickly and cheaply.

10. The printing press started a(n) _____ in Europe as books became cheap. Suddenly, many people had access to books and knowledge. Society changed rapidly.

11. In the past, only the _____ could afford books.

12. Cheap, easily available books led to the spread of _____.

13. The compass is another ancient Chinese _____.

14. Chinese scientists in the third century knew how to make _____. They used magnets to manufacture compasses.

15. The Chinese _____ Zheng He was the first sailor known to use a compass for navigation.

16. Gunpowder was first invented by the Chinese, who used this _____ for fireworks.

17. They put gunpowder into tubes of bamboo to make the first _____.

18. Gunpowder was later introduced into Europe, where it was used as a weapon that completely changed _____.

19. Paper money was probably first used as legal _____ in about the year 1,000 by the Chinese.

20. The use of paper money instead of heavy coins helped improve trade and _____.

4 Early Explorers. Use the words on the left to complete sentences about some other ancient explorers.

discovered
extraordinary
explorers
vague
document

1. When most people think of great _____, names like Marco Polo and Christopher Columbus usually come to mind. But there were many other early explorers who traveled great distances and _____ amazing lands. We hear little about these early travelers largely because they left few records behind to _____ their journeys. Like Marco Polo's book, the records are _____, leaving historians to wonder exactly where these explorers did go, and whether they actually made the _____ journeys at all.

ancient
colonized
continent
scholars
traders

2. The Phoenicians were great _____ in the ancient world. Their home was in the eastern Mediterranean, but they _____ other areas, establishing _____ cities such as Carthage. Sometime in the fifth century BC, **Hanno,** one of Carthage's leaders, set out with 60 ships and about 30,000 men and women to found colonies on the north coast of Africa. Afterwards, he sailed down the west coast of that _____. Hanno sailed far down the coast. Some _____ say he sailed around the entire continent and reached Arabia.

flimsy
similar
treacherous
sailed
navigated

3. People have been exploring and discovering new places since the beginning of time. **St. Brendan** of Ireland, who lived from about AD 486 to 578, is one of the earliest whose trips were recorded. He _____ the _____ waters of the Atlantic Ocean in small, _____ vessels made of ox hide. The skins were stretched over wooden frames. _____ boats are still _____ in Ireland today.

fantastic
traditional
validity
underlie
legends

4. St. Brendan did not leave written records of his voyage, but _____ Irish tales tell of _____ events during a seven-year voyage. He may have reached Iceland, Greenland, and even North America. Many historians doubt the _____ of these tales, claiming they are simple _____. Others think some truth may _____ these ancient stories.

5. **Zheng He** was a(n) _____, or sailor, who lived between 1371 and 1435. His _____ came from Arabia but he was brought to the Chinese court to serve the emperor. Zhen He made seven _____ altogether between 1405 and 1433. His purpose was to _____ the power and glory of China. Some of his voyages _____ to the Cape of Good Hope at the very tip of Africa.

ancestors
exhibit
mariner
voyages
extended

6. According to what is known about Zheng He's voyages, everything was on a huge _____. His _____ numbered as many as 317 ships with crews and passengers numbering 28,000. His _____ ships were huge; some _____ measured 400 feet in length. _____ this to Columbus's first fleet of three ships, the longest of which measured just 85 feet.

scale
compare
treasure
fleets
vessels

7. Although many early explorers left little to document their _____, one _____ is **Ibn Battutah** of Morocco. Battutah is known as the greatest traveler of the ancient world. He _____ his first journey in 1325 when he was 21 years old. Over the _____ 29 years, he journeyed 75,000 miles, which is three times the distance Marco Polo traveled. He was the only _____ traveler to visit every country governed by a Muslim ruler.

commenced
following
medieval
travels
exception

8. When Battutah returned from his last journey in 1354, the sultan of Morocco asked him to _____ his adventures. The _____, which took three months to complete, was recorded by a young scholar. The _____ book, the *Rihla*, gives a _____ account of Battutah's travels as well as unmatched _____ into the Muslim world of that period.

resulting
narrative
recount
insight
complete

5 Animals of Myth. The world occupied by ancient peoples was vast and mysterious. People knew little about distant places, but sometimes travelers told stories of beasts they had seen or maybe only heard about in far away lands. The stories were told over and over. Each time the stories changed a little and the animals grew into new and strange creatures. Read about some of these mythic animals below. Then read the questions, and write your answers in complete sentences.

Unicorn Unicorns were almost always pure white. They had a horse's body and a single long, horn. These were powerful beasts, but peaceful.

Kraken Kraken were huge sea monsters. Some were described as more than a mile long with many arms. Kraken were dangerous creatures of the deep ocean.

Gryphon The gryphon lived high up in the mountains. It had the body and legs of a lion, the tail of a snake, and the wings of an eagle. Gryphons were fierce and powerful.

Mermaid A mermaid is half woman and half fish. They are beautiful and have lovely voices that may lure men to their deaths.

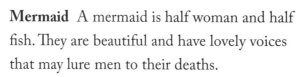

Dragon Dragons live deep in caves or in swamps. They sleep during the day and hunt at night. Many have wings and they breathe fire. They are feared wherever they hunt.

1. Which animal would a sailor fear the most? Why do you think so?

   _____

   _____

2. Why might sailors fear a mermaid?

   _____

   _____

3. Would you rather meet a unicorn or a dragon? Why?

   _____

   _____

4. Where would you most expect to see a gryphon?

   _____

   _____

Words for Study

Meriwether	Minnetaree	prone	reluctant	emphasized
Charbonneau	expedition	ammunition	suspicion	disposition
Sacagawea	Cameahwait	prey	fickle	merchandise
Shoshone	imperfect	ermine	rejoined	compensate

LESSON 7
The Journals of Lewis and Clark

In 1803, President Thomas Jefferson sent Meriwether Lewis and William Clark to explore the western half of the U.S. At the time, very little was known about that part of the country. Lewis and Clark were supposed to map the area, report on the wildlife and plant life they found, and make peaceful contact with the Native American tribes they encountered.

The pair hired an interpreter, Charbonneau, along with his pregnant Native American wife, Sacagawea, to accompany them. Sacagawea belonged to the Shoshone tribe but, as a young woman, had been captured by the Minnetaree Indians.

Lewis and Clark kept journals describing the expedition. The adapted entries below relate to Lewis's encounter with the Shoshone Indians. At the time, Lewis and Clark were searching for a route across the Rocky Mountains to the Pacific Ocean. The pair had briefly split up in order to explore the area, and Sacagawea and Charbonneau were traveling with Clark.

* * *

[Lewis, August 13, 1805]

We had not traveled far when we were lucky enough to meet three female savages. I laid my gun down and advanced towards them. They appeared much alarmed but saw that we were too near for them to escape. I gave the women gifts and painted their cheeks with red paint, which is a symbol of peace for the Shoshone. I informed them by signs that I wished them to lead us to their camp. They readily obeyed.

We had marched about two miles when we met a party of 60 warriors mounted on excellent horses. I advanced towards them with the flag, leaving my gun behind. The chief and two other warriors spoke to the three women, who showed the presents we had given them. The men then advanced and embraced me very warmly. After smoking a few pipes with them, I informed the chief that the object of our visit was a friendly one and that after we reached his camp I would try to fully explain who we were, where we came from, and where we were going. The chief, Cameahwait, made a short speech to the warriors. I gave him the flag, which I informed him was a symbol of peace among white men and was to be respected as a bond of union between us. On our arrival at their camp, all the women and children gathered around, we being the first white persons they had ever seen.

[Lewis, August 14, 1805]

I stayed in the Shoshone camp today to gather information. I communicated using the common language of signs, which seems to be understood by all the tribes we have yet met. This language is imperfect and prone to error, but much less so than one would expect. The major ideas are seldom mistaken. I asked the chief to instruct me as to the local geography. He informed me that, according to the pierced-nosed Indians who live below the Rocky Mountains, the river below runs a great way toward the setting sun and finally loses itself in a great lake of ill-tasting water.

I learned the Shoshone desperately desire guns and ammunition. Without these, they are defenseless and easy prey to their bloodthirsty neighbors—the Minnetarees of Fort de Prairie. The Minnetarees, who have guns, murder the Shoshone and steal their horses. To avoid them, the Shoshone spend most of the year in these mountains, where they suffer great hardships. "But this," added Cameahwait, with his fierce eyes and his face grown thin from hunger, "would not be the case if we had guns. We could then live in the country of buffalo and eat as our enemies do and not be forced to hide and live on roots and berries. We do not fear our enemies when placed on an equal footing with them."

I assured him that we would find a way to stop the Minnetarees from waging war against the Shoshone, that after we finally returned to our homes towards the rising sun, white men would come to them with plenty of guns and every other article necessary for their defense and comfort, and that they would be able to obtain these items in exchange for the skins of the beaver, otter, and ermine. Cameahwait expressed great pleasure at this information and said his tribe had been long anxious to see the white men that traded guns, and that we might rest assured of their friendship.

I asked the chief to persuade his people to go with me tomorrow to the forks of Jefferson's River, where a large party of white men awaited my return. There, we would trade with them for horses, confirm our plans for reaching the ocean, and discuss future trade possibilities. I told him that we had with us a woman of his nation who had been taken prisoner by the Minnetarees, and that by means of her I hoped to explain myself more fully than I could do by signs. He agreed with my request and made a lengthy speech to his village. His people agreed to accompany us, and I promised to reward them for their trouble.

[Lewis, August 15, 1805]

This morning, the chief had to address his people several times before they would move. They seemed reluctant to accompany me. I asked the chief why, and he told me that some foolish persons had suggested that we were in league with the Minnetarees and had come to lead the Shoshone into an ambush. He said that, for his part, he did not believe it. I perceived that our situation was somewhat dangerous, as the leap from suspicion to certainty would not be difficult in the minds of these ignorant people who view every stranger as an enemy.

I told Cameahwait that I was sorry his people had so little confidence in us, that I knew they were unfamiliar with white men, and therefore could forgive them, but that among white men it was considered disgraceful to lie or to trick an enemy. I told him if they continued to think meanly of us that no white men would ever come to trade with them or bring them guns and ammunition, and that I hoped there were still some among them brave enough to go with me and witness the truth of what I had said. He told me he was determined to go. He mounted his horse and spoke to his village a third time. Shortly after this, he was joined by six or eight warriors. Before we reached the creek, it appeared to me that all the men of the village and a number of women had joined us.

[Lewis, August 16, 1805]

Today, I sent Drewyer and Shields out to kill some meat. I asked the chief to keep his young men here, lest their noise alarm the game. This aroused their suspicions. Two parties of scouts immediately set out to watch the hunters and make sure they were not giving information to an enemy lying in wait. I did not try to convince them to stay, for I saw that would only confirm their suspicions.

When we arrived at the meeting place, I discovered that Clark's party had not arrived. The Indians slowed their pace. I now scarcely knew what to do. I was determined to restore their confidence, cost what it might, and therefore gave the chief my gun. I told him if his enemies were in the bushes that he could defend himself with my gun. I said that if he thought I had deceived him, he could use the gun as he thought proper. In other words, he could shoot me. My men also gave their guns to other Indians, which seemed to boost the Indians' confidence.

I now remembered the notes which I had posted for Clark at a spot nearby. I directed Drewyer to go with an Indian man and bring them to me. I had formed a plan. After reading the notes, which were the same I had left, I told the chief that Clark and I had agreed to send up word in the event his

party was delayed. I claimed that one of the notes had been left here today by one of Clark's men. In it, Clark informed me he was just below the mountains, coming up slowly, and that I should wait here for him. I said I would send a man to meet Clark and, if the Indians did not believe me, they might also send one of their young men. The rest of us would remain here. This plan was readily adopted and one of the young men offered his services. I promised to reward him for his confidence in us.

That night, the chief and five or six other warriors slept about my fire. The others hid in the willow brush to avoid the enemy they feared would attack them in the night. I knew that if the Indians left me they would hide themselves in the mountains, where it would be impossible to find them or pursue them. They would spread the alarm to all the nearby tribes, and we wouldn't have any luck getting horses. That would greatly slow our progress and increase the labor of our voyage. I feared it might so discourage the men as to defeat the expedition altogether. I slept but little, as might be expected, my mind dwelling on the state of the expedition, which I have always valued as equal to my own life, and the fate of which appeared at this moment to depend upon the whim of a few savages who were fickle as the wind.

[Lewis, August 17, 1805]

Drewyer and the Indian had been gone about two hours when a scout returned to camp and reported that the party of white men was coming. The Indians appeared transported with joy, and the chief gave me a brotherly hug. I felt as pleased by this information as they appeared to be. Soon, Captain Clark arrived with the interpreter Charbonneau and the Indian woman, who proved to be a sister of Chief Cameahwait. The meeting of those people was really affecting, particularly between Sacagawea and an Indian woman who had been taken prisoner at the same time with her, and who had afterwards escaped from the Minnetarees and rejoined her nation.

We once more found ourselves all together, now with a good chance of getting as many horses as we needed to undertake our voyage. Through Charbonneau and Sacagawea, we fully communicated to the Shoshone why we had come to this distant part of the country. We let them know that they were dependent on the will of our government for every type of merchandise, as well for their defense and comfort. We emphasized the strength of our government and its friendly disposition towards them. We claimed that the reason we were journeying to the western ocean was to find a more direct way to bring merchandise to them. Since no trade could take place before our return to our homes, we said, it was in their interest to help speed our voyage and our return. We explained that we needed their horses and a guide to lead us through the mountains, but that we fully intended to compensate them in return. The chief thanked us for our friendship towards himself and his nation and declared his wish to serve us in every respect.

1 Understanding the Reading. Answer the following questions in good sentence form.

1. Why does it matter that Sacagawea and Charbonneau are with Clark at the time Lewis encounters the Shoshone?

_____

_____

2. Name three actions that Lewis takes upon meeting the Shoshone women and warriors to prove that he means them no harm.

   a. _____

   b. _____

   c. _____

3. Lewis uses "the common language of signs" to communicate with the Shoshone. What does he consider to be the benefits and drawbacks of this language?

_____

_____

_____

4. What detail does Chief Cameahwait mention that suggests Lewis is on his way to reaching the Pacific Ocean?

_____

_____

5. According to Cameahwait, how would life change for the Shoshone if they had guns?

_____

_____

_____

6. Lewis and Clark made great steps towards peaceful relationships with many Native American tribes. However, Lewis makes several statements that suggest he has some prejudiced views of the Indians. What clues can you find in his journal entries to support that fact?

_____

_____

_____

7. Lewis tries to convince the Shoshone warriors that he is not leading them into an ambush. List four of the different strategies he uses, and explain what he hopes to accomplish with each.

a. _____

_____

b. _____

_____

c. _____

_____

d. _____

_____

8. Why is it so important that Lewis and Clark manage to get horses for the next part of their trip?

_____

_____

_____

9. Explain some of the strange connections that are discovered once Sacagawea rejoins Lewis's party. How does Sacagawea's own history support Cameahwait's account of the hardships facing the Shoshone?

_____

_____

_____

_____

2 What Do You Think? Journal entries present one person's point of view. The author's opinions shape the way he or she perceives and writes about an event. It is important to think about the event from other points of view. Keeping that in mind, answer the following questions about the reading.

1. Lewis writes that the Shoshone "view every stranger as an enemy." But the events he describes do not always support that opinion. What are some examples in the reading that weaken his claim?

   _____

   _____

   _____

2. Lewis suggests that the Indians fear strangers out of ignorance. The journal entry presents other reasons that could explain the Shoshone's distrust. What are some of those reasons? Can you think of any others?

   _____

   _____

   _____

3. Lewis makes several risky decisions, such as lying to the Shoshone about Clark's letters and giving the chief his gun. If these actions were interpreted in the wrong way, the results could have been very bad. Explain how these actions could have been misunderstood. What could have happened as a result?

   _____

   _____

   _____

4. In the final entry, Lewis tells the Shoshone how the white men and the government will help the Native Americans. If you were Chief Cameahwait, how would you feel about what Lewis has to say? Would you appreciate the offer or would you be suspicious?

   _____

   _____

   _____

5. Why do you think Lewis uses the word *claim* when he says "we claimed that the reason we were journeying to the western ocean . . ."? Do you think he is telling the truth? Explain.

   _____

   _____

   _____

3 Words in Context. The sentences below come from Clark's account of the meeting with Lewis and the Shoshone on August 17, 1805. Use context, along with the information you have already read, to figure out the meaning of the underlined words. For each sentence, write the letter of the correct answer on the line to the left.

_____ 1. I saw several Indians on horseback coming towards me. The underline interpreter and the Indian woman, who were ahead of me at some distance, danced for the joyful sight.
   a. scout   **b.** translator   **c.** guide   **d.** merchant

_____ 2. The chief who accompanied Captain Lewis met me with great cordiality.
   a. friendliness   **b.** fear   **c.** anger   **d.** suspicion

_____ 3. Captain Lewis informed me that he had persuaded those with him to come and meet us. They had been under great apprehension all the way.
   a. excitement   **b.** joyfulness   **c.** confusion   **d.** fear

_____ 4. Everything appeared to astonish those people: the appearance of our men, our guns, the canoes, the clothing.
   a. bore   **b.** startle   **c.** amaze   **d.** annoy

_____ 5. We spoke a few words to them in the evening respecting our route, intentions, want of horses, etc.
   a. needs   **b.** concerns   **c.** purposes   **d.** demands

_____ 6. The account they gave us of the surroundings was very unfavorable. They said that in most places the mountains were impenetrable.
   a. impassable   **b.** impossible   **c.** accommodating   **d.** accessible

_____ 7. They said the river abounded with great falls.
   a. lacked   **b.** required   **c.** acquired   **d.** had plenty of

_____ 8. They informed us that there wasn't enough timber on the river to make small canoes.
   a. skin   **b.** wood   **c.** rope   **d.** bark

_____ 9. The Indians were greatly pleased that our hunters had killed three deer, which we all ate in a short time—the Indians being so harassed and compelled to move about in those rugged mountains that they were half-starved.
   a. hassled and forced   **c.** worried and motivated
   b. tired and concerned   **d.** troubled and anxious

_____ 10. We decided to proceed as we had heretofore—I would go ahead and scout out the best route.
   a. once before   **b.** never before   **c.** repeatedly   **d.** up until now

4 Spelling Check. Lewis and Clark's journals are full of misspelled words. The sentences below are adapted from Lewis's journal and include the original misspellings. For each sentence, underline the misspelled words, and spell them correctly on the lines provided. There are as many blank lines as there are misspelled words. In some sentences, you might need to use context to help you figure out what word the author meant to use.

1. I scelected a fat buffaloe and shot him very well, through the lungs.

   _____

   _____

2. While I was gazeing on the poor anamal, having entirely forgotton to reload my rifle, a large white, or reather brown, bear had crept on me.

   _____

   _____

   _____

   _____

3. I drew up my gun to shoot, but at the same instant recolected that it was not loaded and that the bear was too near for me to hope to perform this opperation before he reached me, as he was then briskly advancing on me.

   _____

   _____

4. I thought of retreating in a brisk walk as fast as he was advancing untill I could reach a tree, but I had no sooner terned myself about than he pitched at me, open mouthed and at full speed.

   _____

   _____

5. The idea struk me to get into the water to such debth that I could stand and he would be obliged to swim; accordingly, I ran haistily into the water about waist deep.

   _____

   _____

   _____

6. The moment I put myself in an attitude of defence, he sudonly wheeled about as if frightened, declined the combat on such unequal grounds, and retreated.

   _____

   _____

7. I now began to reflect on this novil occurrence and indeavoured to account for this sudden retreat of the bear.

_____

_____

8. On examination, I saw the grownd toarn with his tallons immediately on the impression of my steps.

_____

_____

_____

9. The cause of his allarm still remains with me misterious and unaccountable.

_____

_____

10. So it was and I feelt myself not a little gratifyed that he had declined the combat.

_____

_____

11. My direction led me directly to an anamal of a brownish yellow colour, and when I approached it, it couched itself down like a cat as if it planned to spring on me.

_____

_____

_____

12. It now seemed to me that all the beasts of the neighborhood had made a league to distroy me, or that some fortune was disposed to amuse herself at my expence, for I had not proceded more than three hundred yards from the burrow of this tyger cat, before three bull buffaloe ran full speed towards me.

_____

_____

_____

_____

13. I then continued my rout homewards, not wanting to remain all night in this place that, due to the series of curious adventures I'd had, seemed almost inchanted.

_____

_____

_____

5 Powers of Observation. Part of Lewis and Clark's assignment involved describing native wildlife and plant life in great detail. The following brief passage by Clark gives an example of his powers of observation. He writes about finding a flounder, a fish he had never seen before. After reading the passage, look at the picture beneath it. Imagine you are seeing the animal and plants in the picture for the first time. Write a paragraph describing the scene. Include as much detail as possible.

[Clark, November 15, 1805]

We found a curious flat fish shaped like a turtle with fins on each side and a notched tail. The fish's features are all on one side, and the tail and fins lie flat. This fish, a flounder, has white on one side and lies flat to the ground.

_____

_____

_____

_____

_____

_____

_____

_____

_____

_____

Words for Study

floes	hedgerows	formidable	titanic	looming
gigantic	junctions	sufficiently	relentlessly	essential
jigsaw	volcano	icebergs	sentient	rudder
disarranged	corrugates	intruders	comparative	fragile
congested	strenuous	elementary	annihilating	precarious

LESSON 8
Endurance

Journeys to the North and South Poles involved much failure, loss of life, and hardship. They tested explorers' determination and leadership skills during critical and life-threatening emergencies.

In 1914, British explorer Sir Ernest Shackleton set out for the South Pole, hoping to become the first man to cross the Antarctic continent by land. Shackleton and a party of 27 men sailed across the Weddell Sea aboard the ship *Endurance*. However, the summer turned out to be unusually cold, causing the ocean "ice pack" to form early. The *Endurance* steered between giant sheets of ice, or floes, looking for channels of open water, or leads, that would allow safe passage. The ship eventually became trapped in the ice, drifting hopelessly. The focus of the expedition quickly turned to one of survival, as Shackleton's party struggled to endure the Antarctic winter and reach dry land.

The following passages are adapted from Shackleton's book *South*. They begin in December 1914, just as the ship becomes trapped.

* * *

December

I had been prepared for evil conditions in the Weddell Sea, but had hoped that in December and January the pack would be loose, even if no open water was to be found. What we were actually encountering was fairly dense pack of a very stubborn character. Pack ice might be described as a gigantic and endless jigsaw puzzle devised by nature. The parts of the puzzle in loose pack have floated slightly apart and become disarranged. In many places, they have pressed together again. As the pack gets closer, the congested areas grow larger and the parts are jammed harder together. Finally it becomes "close pack" when the whole of the jigsaw puzzle becomes jammed to such an extent that it can be crossed on foot. Where the parts do not fit closely there is, of course, open water, which freezes over in a few hours after giving off volumes of "frost-smoke." In obedience to renewed pressure, this young ice "rafts," forming double thicknesses. The opposing edges of heavy floes rear up in slow and almost silent conflict, until high "hedgerows" are formed. At the junction of several floes, jumbled areas of piled-up blocks and masses of ice are formed. Sometimes 5-foot to 6-foot piles of evenly shaped blocks of ice are seen so neatly laid that it seems impossible for them to be nature's work. A winding canyon may cut through icy walls 6 feet to 10 feet high, or a dome may be formed that under renewed pressure bursts upward like a volcano. All winter the drifting pack changes—grows by freezing, thickens by rafting, and corrugates by pressure. If, finally, in its drift it touches a coastline, such as the western shore of the Weddell Sea, terrific pressure is set up and a nightmare of ice-blocks, ridges, and hedgerows results, extending possibly for 150 or 200 miles off shore. This was the nature of the ice through which we pushed our way for many hundreds of miles.

February

On February 24, we ceased to observe ship routine, and the *Endurance* became a winter station. All hands were on duty during the day and slept at night, except a watchman who looked after the dogs and watched for any sign of movement in the ice. Seals appeared occasionally, and we killed all that came within our reach. They represented fuel as well as food for men and dogs. Orders were given for the stores to be checked, so that we might know exactly how we stood for a siege by an Antarctic winter. The dogs went off the ship on the following day. They seemed heartily glad and yelped loudly and joyously as they were moved to their new quarters. We had begun the training of teams, and the flat floes and frozen leads in the neighborhood of the

ship made excellent training grounds. Hockey and football on the floe were our chief amusements, and all hands joined in many a strenuous game. The care of the dog teams was our heaviest responsibility in those days. The movement of the floes was beyond all human control, and there was nothing to be gained by allowing one's mind to struggle with the problems of the future, though it was hard to avoid anxiety at times.

July

The drift of the *Endurance* in the grip of the ice pack continued without incident through June. By July, the ice pressure, which was indicated by distant rumblings and the appearance of formidable ridges, was increasingly a cause of anxiety. The noise resembled the roar of heavy, distant surf. Standing on the stirring ice, one could imagine it was disturbed by the breathing and tossing of a mighty giant below.

September

During the final days of September, the roar of the pressure grew louder, and I could see that the area of disturbance was rapidly approaching the ship. We were drifting into the congested area of the western Weddell Sea, the worst part of the worst sea in the world. The question for us was whether or not the ice would open sufficiently to release us, or at least give us a chance of release, before the drift carried us into the most dangerous area. There was no answer to be got from the silent icebergs and the grinding floes, and we faced the month of October with anxious hearts.

October

Frost-smoke from opening cracks appeared in all directions October 6. It had the appearance of a great prairie fire, rising from the surface and getting higher as it drifted off before the wind in heavy, dark, rolling masses. Elsewhere, the smoke columns gave the effect of warships steaming in line ahead.

Then on October 24, there came what for the *Endurance* was the beginning of the end. Throughout the day we watched the threatening advance of the floes. Huge blocks of ice, weighing many tons, were lifted into the air and tossed aside as other masses rose beneath them. We were helpless intruders in a strange world, our lives dependent upon the play of grim elementary forces that made a mock of our puny efforts. I scarcely dared hope now that the *Endurance* would live. We could see from the bridge that the ship was bending like a bow under titanic pressure. Almost like a living creature, she resisted the forces that would crush her; but it was a one-sided battle. Millions of tons of ice pressed relentlessly upon the little ship that had dared the challenge of the Antarctic.

The fateful day came on October 27. I wrote the following entry in my diary:

> "After long months of ceaseless anxiety and strain, after times when hope beat high and times when the outlook was black indeed, the end of the *Endurance* has come. It is hard to write what I feel. To a sailor his ship is more than a floating home, and in the *Endurance* I had centered ambitions, hopes, and desires. Now, straining and groaning, her timbers cracking and her wounds gaping, she is slowly giving up her sentient life at the very outset of her career. She is crushed and abandoned after drifting more than 570 miles during the 281 days since she became locked in the ice."

It was a sickening sensation to feel the decks breaking up under one's feet, the great beams bending and then snapping with a noise like heavy gunfire. Men and dogs descended and made their way to the comparative safety of an unbroken portion of the floe. Just before leaving, I stood on the ship's quivering deck. I cannot describe the impression of relentless destruction that was forced upon me as I looked down and around. The floes, with the force of millions of tons of moving ice behind them, were simply annihilating the ship.

We made camp for the night, but at about 7 p.m. the ice we were occupying became involved in the pressure and started to split and smash beneath our feet. I had the camp moved to a bigger floe, just beyond the bow of the ship. That night, the temperature dropped to −16°, and most of the men were cold and uncomfortable. For myself, I could not sleep. The destruction and abandonment of the ship was no sudden shock. The disaster had been looming ahead for many months, but the thoughts that came to me were not cheerful. The task now was to secure the safety of the party, and to that I must bend my energies and mental power and apply every bit of knowledge that experience of

the Antarctic had given me. The task was likely to be long and strenuous, and an ordered mind and a clear plan were essential if we were to come through without loss of life. A man must shape himself to a new mark directly after the old one goes to ground.

All night long an electric light gleamed from the dying *Endurance,* like a lamp in a cottage window. It braved the night, until in the early morning the ship received a particularly violent squeeze. There was a sound of breaking beams and the light disappeared. The connection had been cut.

April

There were twenty-eight men living on the floating cake of ice that we called "Patience Camp." The floe itself was steadily shrinking due to the wind, weather, and heavy swell. We had adjusted to life on the floe, but our hopes had been fixed all the time on some possible landing place. Our drifting home had no rudder to guide it, no sail to give it speed. We were dependent upon the whims of wind and current; we went wherever those irresponsible forces carried us. Occasionally a neighboring floe would hammer against the ice on which we were camped, and the lesson of these blows was plain to read.

The floe had been a good friend to us, but it was reaching the end of its journey, and it was liable at any time to break up and fling us into the sea.

We were standing by, with our preparations complete, when our floe suddenly split right across. Looking across the widening channel of water, I could see the spot where for many months my head and shoulders had rested when I was in my sleeping bag. How fragile and precarious had been our resting place! Yet usage had dulled our sense of danger. The floe had become our home, and during the early months of the drift we had almost ceased to realize that it was but a sheet of ice floating on tossing seas. Now our home was being shattered under our feet.

I noted with envy the calm, peaceful attitudes of two seals which lounged lazily on a rocking floe. They were at home and had no reason for worry or cause for fear. If they thought at all, I suppose they counted it an ideal day for a joyous journey on the tumbling ice. To us it was a day that seemed likely to lead to no more days. I do not think I had ever before felt the anxiety that belongs to leadership quite so keenly.

1 Understanding the Reading. Answer the following questions in good sentence form.

1. Explain some of the dangers the ice pack poses to the expedition as the floes freeze, break up, and melt.

   a. Freeze: _____

   _____

   _____

   b. Break up: _____

   _____

   _____

   c. Melt: _____

   _____

   _____

2. Once the *Endurance* becomes stuck in the ice, the men spend their time training the dogs and playing sports. The men are not simply goofing off. Think of several practical reasons why the men might have decided to spend their time in this way.

   _____

   _____

   _____

   _____

   _____

3. What worries Shackleton about the ship's drift through the ocean?

   _____

   _____

   _____

4. What two possibilities does the presence of "frost-smoke" indicate for the ship?

   _____

   _____

   _____

5. How does Shackleton describe his relationship to the *Endurance*?

   _____

   _____

   _____

6. What does Shackleton mean when he writes, "a man must shape himself to a new mark directly after the old one goes to ground"? What was Shackleton's "old mark"? How did it "go to ground"? What is his "new mark"?

_____

_____

_____

_____

7. Why do you think Shackleton watches the seals "with envy" in the final paragraph?

_____

_____

_____

_____

8. If you were part of Shackleton's crew, what would you consider to be some pros and cons of living onboard the ship and living on the ice floe? Think of factors such as temperature, exercise, boredom, danger, etc.

Ship

Pro _____   Con _____

Pro _____   Con _____

Pro _____   Con _____

Floe

Pro _____   Con _____

Pro _____   Con _____

Pro _____   Con _____

2 Comprehension Check. Match each term listed below with its correct definition.

Antarctic	drift	grinding	ice pack	loose pack
close pack	floe	hedgerows	ice pressure	rafting
corrugating	frost-smoke	iceberg	lead	young ice

_____ 1. Walls of ice resembling rows of shrubs formed when floes press together

_____ 2. Movement by which the ice pack travels through the ocean

_____ 3. Process by which floes rub against each other and wear each other down

_____ 4. Steam released from ice cracks when open water freezes

_____ 5. A great, jagged mountain of ice floating in the sea

_____ 6. Huge amount of force built up when floes jam together

_____ 7. Pathway of open water caused by a crack in the ice

_____ 8. A large ice sheet floating on the sea

_____ 9. Causing ridges and ripples to appear in ice

_____ 10. Term that describes the ice when floes are jammed together

_____ 11. Ice that is newly formed, thin

_____ 12. Term that describes the ice when floes are not touching or jammed together

_____ 13. Process by which young ice thickens

_____ 14. Region that includes the ocean and land mass surrounding the South Pole

_____ 15. Collection of ice floes that travel together

3 Shades of Meaning. As we know, a word can have more than one meaning. In Shackleton's account some words appear in unusual contexts, suggesting that a meaning other than the common meaning is intended. Look at the sentences below, and use context clues to help you determine the intended meaning of the underlined word. Write the letter of the correct answer on the line provided.

_____ 1. All <u>hands</u> were on duty during the day and slept at night, except a watchman who looked after the dogs.
  a. body parts **b.** cards **c.** workers **d.** skills

_____ 2. Orders were given for the <u>stores</u> to be checked, so that we might know exactly how we stood for a siege by an Antarctic winter.
  a. supplies **b.** shops **c.** goods **d.** storage

_____ **3.** Standing on the <u>stirring</u> ice, one could imagine it was disturbed by the breathing and tossing of a mighty giant below.

    a. waking   **b.** excited   **c.** mixing   **d.** shifting

_____ **4.** We were helpless intruders in a strange world, our lives dependent upon the play of grim <u>elementary</u> forces that made a mock of our puny efforts.

    a. natural and powerful   **c.** hungry and angry

    b. simple and easy   **d.** basic and early

_____ **5.** We could see from the bridge that the ship was bending like a <u>bow</u> under titanic pressure.

    a. tree   **c.** curved wood used to shoot arrows

    b. front of a ship   **d.** knot

_____ **6.** The floe itself was steadily shrinking due to the wind, weather, and heavy <u>swell</u>.

    a. bulge   **b.** surf   **c.** hill   **d.** slope

_____ **7.** The journeys to the <u>Poles</u> involved much failure, loss of life, and hardship.

    a. either ends of the earth's axis   **c.** areas in Europe

    b. ends of a trip   **d.** icy oceans

_____ **8.** The journeys tested explorers' determination and leadership skills during <u>critical</u> and life-threatening emergencies.

    a. fault-finding   **b.** analytical   **c.** logical   **d.** serious

_____ **9.** As the pack gets closer, the <u>congested</u> areas grow larger and the parts are jammed harder together.

    a. stuffy   **b.** traffic-filled   **c.** concentrated   **d.** overcrowded

_____ **10.** Where the parts do not fit closely there is, of course, open water, which freezes over in a few hours after giving off <u>volumes</u> of "frost-smoke."

    a. large amounts   **b.** loud sounds   **c.** long scrolls   **d.** noisy rolls

_____ **11.** We were dependent upon the whims of wind and <u>current</u>; we went wherever those irresponsible forces carried us.

    a. water power   **b.** electricity   **c.** water flow   **d.** money

_____ **12.** We had adjusted to life on the floe, but our hopes had been <u>fixed</u> all the time on some possible landing place.

    a. attached   **b.** focused   **c.** repaired   **d.** adjusted

4 Looking Closely at Language. Part A. Shackleton uses striking descriptions and comparisons throughout his account. Answer the following questions about his use of language.

1. Shackleton compares the pack ice to "a jigsaw puzzle." Explain how the two things are alike.

_____

_____

2. Shackleton writes: "Standing on the stirring ice one could imagine it was disturbed by the breathing and tossing of a mighty giant below." What is the mighty giant below the ice? What does the description suggest about the men's relationship toward their surroundings?

_____

_____

_____

3. Shackleton compares the appearance of the frost-smoke to what two things? What do all three things have in common, besides smoke?

_____

_____

_____

4. After abandoning the ship, Shackleton compares the light shining from the *Endurance* to a "lamp in a cottage window." What does the comparison suggest about his feelings toward the ship? What is the emotional effect of the light going out?

_____

_____

_____

5. In his account, Shackleton often "personifies" the *Endurance*. That means he describes the ship, a lifeless object, as if it were a living being. List three examples of how Shackleton personifies the ship.

_____

_____

_____

6. What is the effect of Shackleton's use of "personification"? How does it help the reader better understand Shackleton's feelings toward the ship and its loss?

_____

_____

7. When describing "Patience Camp," Shackleton compares the ice floe to a boat. List examples of how he does so. Why does it make sense that he compares the two objects, while also referring to the floe as a "home"?

_____

_____

_____

_____

_____

8. World War I broke out the very day the *Endurance* set sail, almost stopping the expedition before it began. The crew didn't hear any news about the war during the expedition. Some of the metaphors and descriptions that Shackleton uses to describe his ordeal suggest the war might have been on the explorer's mind. List four examples.

_____

_____

_____

_____

Part B. Imagine you are one of Shackleton's crew members, living on the ice floe that the crew named "Patience Camp." Write a paragraph describing your last day on the ice floe. Come up with your own comparisons and descriptions that help express what it is like to be trapped on the ice.

_____

_____

_____

_____

_____

_____

_____

_____

_____

_____

5 Labeling a Storyboard. A storyboard tells a story in pictures. Below are four photos showing different ordeals faced by the crew of the *Endurance*. Put the pictures in the correct order by labeling them with the month and year they most likely took place according to the reading. For each picture, write a caption on the lines provided that summarizes what is happening at that point in the story. Make sure to mention the month in which the events took place.

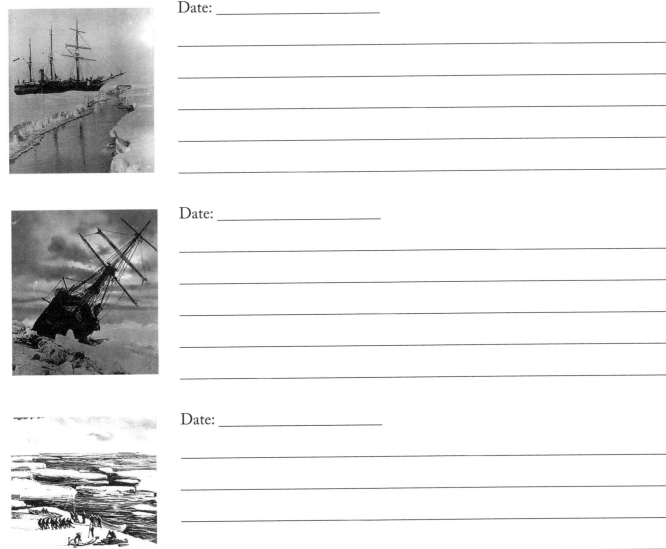

Date: _____

_____

_____

_____

_____

_____

Date: _____

_____

_____

_____

_____

_____

Date: _____

_____

_____

_____

_____

_____

Date: _____

_____

_____

_____

_____

_____

Words for Study

frigid	illumined	fossils	inadequate
diameter	ascent	submersibles	alliance
winch	suspended	maneuverable	riveted
luminescent	sediments	capable	submarines

LESSON 9
Exploring the Deep

Along the coastline of every continent lies a relatively shallow body of water. These waters may be as much as 500 feet deep. Just beyond these coastal waters, the sea floor drops away rapidly. This is the deep ocean, and it is thousands of feet deep. It covers about 70 percent of the earth's surface, and it is largely unknown, unmapped, and unexplored.

Most of the deep ocean hovers just a few degrees above freezing at a frigid 39°F, and little if any light reaches to the great depths. Every 250 feet, sunlight dims by about ten percent. At 1,600 feet, the light is just one-millionth as strong as on the surface; it's almost totally black. The pressure is intense. Much of the deep ocean has a pressure of between 3,000 and 9,000 pounds per square inch, about 100 to 300 times the air pressure in an automobile tire. At the bottom of the Mariana Trench, the deepest place on earth at 35,802 feet below sea level, the pressure is equal to the weight of 48 jumbo jets resting on an average-sized woman.

In 1930, William Beebe and Otis Barton descended into the darkness of the deep ocean, the first people ever to go deep into the sea. They had crammed themselves into a hollow steel ball measuring 4½ feet wide. They had designed the ball, or bathysphere as they called it, themselves. It weighed 2½ tons and had 1½-inch thick steel walls and two round windows 8 inches in diameter and 3 inches thick. Once they were inside, the steel door was bolted into place, and the hollow steel ball was lowered into the ocean from their ship, the ball dangling from a single steel cable.

Very, very slowly, the ball was lowered by a steam-powered winch into the depths of the ocean. The sea was relatively calm, but gentle waves rocked the ship, and as it rocked it first pulled on the cable supporting the ball, and then slackened, and then jerked the cable tight once more. Not only would it have made for a stomach-churning descent, but it added stress to the thin cable, which was Beebe and Barton's lifeline for returning to the surface. The bathysphere had no power of its own and it could not be steered. Beebe and Barton had oxygen tanks on board, but electricity for lights and telephone communication with the surface were carried to the bathysphere by a power cable.

At 1,400 feet, Barton casually observed that every square inch of the windows had a pressure of more than 650 pounds, and the windows were enduring a pressure of 9 tons. At 1,426 feet, the men were still thousands of feet from the bottom of the sea, but they had reached their planned depth. The surface crew began reeling the bathysphere back up. Beebe and Barton had reached a depth never before seen by humans.

Over the next few years, the two men made a series of dives to greater and greater depths. Then, in 1934, Beebe and Barton made a new record-breaking dive. When they reached 1,900 feet, Beebe observed that he could still see the "faintest hint of dead gray light," but at 2,000 feet it had gone. "The world was forever black," he later wrote. "The sun, source of all light and heat on the earth, has been left behind. It is only a psychological mile-post, but it is a very real one. We had no realization of the outside pressure but the blackness itself seemed to close in on us."

But although the ocean was black, there were lights everywhere, Beebe reported. Luminescent animals swam singly and in schools around them. There were fish, jellyfish, shrimp, and other animals. Many had never been seen before. At one point, he said, "I saw some creature, several feet long, dart toward the window, turn sideways and—explode. At the flash, which was so strong that it illumined my face and the inner sill of the window," he said, "I saw the great red shrimp and the outpouring fluid of flame."

They descended farther, for two hours altogether, until they reached a depth to 3,028 feet—more than

one-half mile. They lingered there just three minutes and then began their lengthy ascent.

Although the dives set records for diving never before approached by living humans, Beebe was not trying to set records. He was absorbed in the search for new life-forms and for clues to the geography of the deep sea. This same curiosity had fueled the efforts of other scientists for generations. These earlier explorers lacked the equipment to descend to such depths themselves, so they used other means to study the bottom of the ocean.

The first explorers used sounding weights to investigate the deep ocean. These were simple weights suspended from ropes and used to measure the depth of the ocean. Vessels cruised around the world, measuring ocean depth and mapping what they could of the sea bottom. By 1870, other tools, such as dredges, scoops, and nets, had been added to sounding weights. With these crude instruments, scientists were able to dig up sediments and capture some of the creatures that lived at depths up to three miles down. Many of the animals that were brought up were completely new to science. Some were animals that were known only from fossils. Scientists thought these animals had become extinct long ago.

The bathysphere that Beebe and Barton invented to study the ocean was a primitive device. It only went up and down and couldn't stay down for very long. Still, it provided a way to actually visit and observe life at great depths. Following Beebe and Barton's breakthrough explorations, others created new deep-sea submersibles.

The next generation of deep ocean submersibles was developed by the Swiss physicist Auguste Piccard in 1948. Unlike Beebe's bathysphere, Piccard's bathyscaphe, the *FNRS-2,* was not tied to a surface ship by a cable. It was more maneuverable than Beebe's submersible. It was also capable of greater depths. Unfortunately, the first trials of the *FNRS-2* were underfunded. An inadequate ship was provided that couldn't effectively manage the *FNRS-2* with its heavy weight of fuel. The submersible was almost lost at sea, and the mission ended. After the near disaster, investors lost confidence and funding was withdrawn. Later the French government purchased *FNRS-2* and rebuilt it, naming it *FNRS-3*. This submersible was highly successful, setting a record by diving to 13,287 feet in 1954. By that time, however, Auguste Piccard had begun his next project, another submersible that was named the *Trieste.* His son Jacques had obtained financing for the submersible, which was launched in 1953. In September of that year, Auguste and Jacques took the *Trieste* to the bottom of the Mediterranean, a depth of 10,392 feet.

The Piccards suffered through several years of low funding, but then formed an alliance with the U.S. Office of Naval Research. The ONR agreed to fund further research with the *Trieste.* The goal was to take the submersible to the floor of the Challenger Deep in the Mariana Trench in the Pacific Ocean. At 35,800 feet, it is the deepest part of the ocean.

In January 1960, the *Trieste* was towed by the U.S. Navy ship *Wandank* through rough seas to the location directly above the Challenger Deep. Then, on January 23, Jacques Piccard and Lieutenant Don Walsh of the U.S. Navy made the attempt. The descent took several hours. Nothing noteworthy occurred until the *Trieste* reached a depth of 32,500 feet when, without warning, "we heard and felt a powerful, muffled crack," according to Walsh, and "the sphere rocked as though we were on land and going through a mild earthquake." Walsh and Piccard checked all their instruments, but found nothing to account for the incident. Since everything looked secure, they continued their descent.

When their instruments told them they were nearly on the bottom, Piccard brought the *Trieste* to a stop. They floated in the sea just a few feet above the bottom. "Lying on the bottom just beneath us," Piccard said, "was some type of flatfish . . . about 1 foot long and 6 inches across." It was visible in the *Trieste*'s floodlight. "Even as I saw him, his two round eyes on top of his head spied us. Eyes? Why should he have eyes?" Piccard asked. What use were eyes in the total darkness of the trench?

More important than the question Piccard asked, however, was the answer that the flatfish gave to a question that had riveted scientists' attention since the beginning of deep ocean exploration: Could living things exist at the ocean's deepest depths? Clearly, the answer was "yes."

Then, as Piccard and Walsh studied the sea floor about them, Walsh made a discovery. "I see now what caused the shock at 30,000 feet!" he called. The rear porthole window had cracked under the extreme pressure of the sea. Now, water was seeping in. This was a serious situation, and the men decided not to linger at the bottom. The time had come to surface. They returned safely without further incident.

The *Trieste* was completely rebuilt by the Navy following its trip to the Challenger Deep, but its days as an ocean explorer were numbered. In the years that followed small submarines were developed that could reach those same great depths. These submarines were more maneuverable, lighter, and more easily transported than the previous generation of submersibles.

Although deep-diving submarines have brought the ocean even closer, allowing scientists to peer into places unknown fifty years ago, the deep ocean remains one of the great mysteries on earth. We have mapped in detail the surfaces of Venus, Mars, and the moon, but we know only 5 percent of Earth's ocean floor in comparable detail. We knew about as much about the ocean in 1950 as we did about our solar system in 1450. At that time, we didn't even know that the earth revolved around the sun. Our knowledge has advanced greatly since then, but we still live in considerable ignorance of the oceans. For all the exploration of the past one hundred years, the ocean remains Earth's last real frontier.

1 Understanding the Reading. Put the letter of the best answer on the line.

1. The deep ocean _____.
   a. covers one-half of the earth's surface
   b. may be as much as 500 feet deep
   c. is cold with a temperature of about 39°F
   d. has revealed most of its mysteries to scientists

2. With the bathysphere, Beebe and Barton _____.
   a. became the first men to descend into the depths of the deep ocean
   b. brought sediment and deep-ocean fish to the surface
   c. descended into the Mariana Trench, the deepest place on earth
   d. reached the Challenger Deep in the Pacific Ocean

3. Unlike Beebe's bathysphere, the *FNRS-2* _____.
   a. was suspended from a steel cable
   b. did not need to be transported by ship to begin exploring
   c. was built to sustain the intense pressures of the deep ocean
   d. could be maneuvered beneath the sea

4. The exploding fish with the "outpouring fluid of flame" that Beebe saw was a(n) _____.
   a. piece of driftwood that seemed to glow
   b. light placed in the water to light their descent
   c. deep-sea shrimp that glowed in the dark
   d. instrument left by earlier explorers to measure ocean depth

5. When scientists of the 1870s used dredges to explore the ocean floor, they _____.
   a. became the first humans to actually visit those depths
   b. discovered animals that they had thought were extinct
   c. could not prove that animals lived very far beneath the ocean surface
   d. were unable to reach more than a few hundred feet below the surface

6. What happened to the *FNRS-2* during one of its earliest tests? _____
   a. It set a record by descending deeper than any previous submersible.
   b. It was almost lost at sea due to the heavy weight of its fuel.
   c. It broke loose from its cable and nearly sank into the depths of the Mediterranean.
   d. It demonstrated how its maneuverability could help scientists examine the sea floor.

7. After building the *Trieste,* the Piccards formed an alliance with the _____.

    a. French government   **c.** Belgium government

    b. company owned by William Beebe   **d.** U.S. Office of Naval Research

8. What was the sound Piccard and Walsh heard in the *Trieste* as they descended to 32,500 feet? _____

    a. the glass in the rear porthole breaking

    b. a large creature that bumped into their submersible

    c. a warning sound made by the Navy ship the *Wandank*

    d. the explosion of a great red shrimp

9. When Piccard saw the flatfish lying on the bottom of the sea, it proved that _____.

    a. all deep-ocean fish glowed in the dark   **c.** animals can see in total darkness

    b. the pressure at those depths was not so great   **d.** animal life existed at the greatest depths

10. Submersibles like the *Trieste, FNRS-2,* and Beebe's bathysphere were replaced by _____.

    a. dredges   **b.** submarines   **c.** bathyscaphes   **d.** sounding weights

2 What Do You Think? Imagine that you have become an explorer. Write your answers to these questions in good sentence form.

1. Where would you go? _____

_____

2. How would you travel? _____

_____

3. How would you prepare for your journey? _____

_____

4. What would you take with you? _____

_____

5. What special skills would you need? _____

_____

6. What dangers might you face? _____

_____

7. What would you expect to see or discover? _____

_____

_____

3 Word Relationships. Write the letter of the answer that best completes each statement on the line.

1. Intense is to soothing as _____.
   a. listless is to restful
   b. illumined is to shadowy
   c. intent is to purposeful
   d. essential is to unreliable

2. Diameter is to sphere as _____.
   a. explore is to discover
   b. river is to ocean
   c. equator is to earth
   d. frigid is to arctic

3. ! is to exclamation point as _____.
   a. * is to asterisk
   b. ' is to contraction
   c. ? is to question
   d. " is to quotation

4. Luminous is to glowing as _____.
   a. particular is to general
   b. finite is to limited
   c. superior is to moderate
   d. intrepid is to cowardly

5. Incident is to event as _____.
   a. beginning is to completion
   b. success is to acceptance
   c. realization is to interest
   d. advance is to breakthrough

6. Lizard is to reptile as _____.
   a. vessel is to sea
   b. loner is to antisocial
   c. penicillin is to antibiotic
   d. sofa is to armchair

7. Forebear is to ancestor as _____.
   a. sailor is to mariner
   b. sediment is to beach
   c. waves are to current
   d. statesman is to dictator

8. Winch is to crane as _____.
   a. tornado is to breeze
   b. holiday is to celebration
   c. dollar is to cost
   d. landscape is to prairie

9. Thorn is to prickly as _____.
   a. error is to glaring
   b. interpretation is to abstract
   c. likelihood is to habit
   d. misconception is to faulty

10. Atlantic is to ocean as _____.
    a. book is to appendix
    b. lecture is to classroom
    c. *Titanic* is to ocean liner
    d. postscript is to letter

4 Still More Prefixes. From the list at the left, choose the word that best completes each sentence, and write it in the blank.

| concocted |
| concurred |
| conferred |
| conformed |

1. con: *with, together, jointly*

Hiram Emory and his companion Norah Pace were walking to a nearby coffee shop after attending a lecture. Although both _____ that the lecture had been a waste of time, their reasons for thinking so were quite different.

| professed |
| propelled |
| protested |
| provoked |

2. pro: *forward, before*

"What _____ me the most was how she kept harping on how important it is to live in the here and now," complained Norah Pace.

| adhere |
| adjoin |
| administer |
| adopt |

3. ad: *near to, to*

"You're absolutely right," exclaimed Hiram. "How can anyone _____ to such a foolish notion when reflecting on the good old days is what helps to make life bearable."

| contradiction |
| contradictory |
| contrary |
| contrast |

4. contra: *against, opposing, or contrary*

"On the _____," replied the shocked Ms. Pace, "people should put the past behind them. Everyone knows that planning ahead is absolutely essential!"

| ejected |
| elapsed |
| eluded |
| emitted |

5. e: *out, out of, from*

Hiram _____ a disapproving growl in spite of himself. "Are you suggesting that we spend all our time thinking about the future?"

| permissible |
| permissive |
| permanent |
| perpetual |

6. per: *through, throughout*

"Well, of course it's _____ to dwell on past events," retorted

Norah rather rudely, "if you have no ambition to be somebody!"

| supercharged |
| super-duper |
| superficial |
| supernatural |

7. super: *above, on, over*

"And I suppose, with all your plans for a _____ future, you

consider yourself a superior human being?" Hiram shot back in an equally rude voice.

| semicircle |
| semifinal |
| semiformal |
| semiprecious |

8. semi: *half*

"Have you ever considered that you've never made it to the _____

round at the club's tennis tournament because you're too busy thinking about what

a great athlete you were in high school?" Norah suggested smugly.

| subdivide |
| submerge |
| submit |
| subsist |

9. sub: *under*

"Don't expect me to _____ to such insults!" shouted Hiram

angrily. "The reason you've never once been promoted at the office is that you're

forever dreaming of next week, next month, next year!"

| circumference |
| circumstance |
| circumstantial |
| circumvent |

10. circum: *around*

This dispute was never resolved, for so absorbed were they in their argument that

they failed to _____ a giant pothole that lay directly in their

path. Hiram sprained his ankle, and their attention turned to getting him home

where he could soak it.

5 A Look Back. The sea has fascinated people from the beginning of time. In a poem written in 1798, Samuel Taylor Coleridge imagined the life of a sailor blown far off course.

from The Rime of the Ancient Mariner
by Samuel Taylor Coleridge

And now the Storm-blast came, and he
Was tyrannous and strong:
He struck with his o'ertaking wings,
And chased us south along.

With sloping masts and dipping prow,
As who pursued with yell and blow
Still treads the shadow of his foe,
And forward bends his head,
The ship drove fast, loud roar'd the blast,
The southward aye we fled.

And now there came both mist and snow,
And it grew wondrous cold:
And ice, mast-high, came floating by,
As green as emerald.

And through the drifts
   the snowy cliffs
Did send a dismal
   sheen:
Nor shapes of men
   nor beasts we ken*—   * saw
The ice was all between.

The ice was here, the ice was there,
The ice was all around:
It crack'd and growl'd, and roar'd and
   howl'd,
Like noises in a swound!*   * a fainting fit

1. What has happened to the ship the ancient mariner is on?

_____

_____

2. List two images, or pictures, of the wind that Coleridge uses.

   a. _____

   b. _____

3. List two images of the icy land the mariner finds himself in.

   a. _____

   b. _____

4. List two images you might use if you were to write a poem describing a storm as you experience it.

   a. _____

   b. _____

Words for Study

ponder	Cosmonaut	spectacular	debris
astronomers	lunar	millennium	catalogue
Aeronautics	probes	alien	gravity
hallmark	optic	Messenger	Observatory

LESSON 10
A Brief History of Space Exploration

Since the dawn of time, man has looked to the skies and wondered: "What's out there?" Some things, like the moon and stars, moved in patterns that even ancient sky watchers could follow and predict. Early Greek scholars worked to answer questions such as: Does the sun move around the planets? Is the Earth the center of the universe? Students and teachers would sit together. They would ponder these questions and others, discussing what the answers might be and how to arrive at them.

Aristotle, who lived from 384–322 BC, is one of the most famous early Greek astronomers. He is sometimes called the grandfather of modern science—for being one of the first scholars to study the planets and for his methods of doing so. More than 1,000 years later, Galileo Galilei was born. This Italian sky watcher is known as the father of modern science. He, too, was one of the great early astronomers. Galileo believed some of the early Greek theories that the Sun, not the Earth, was at the center of our universe. He made advances in telescope design that allowed him to see objects enlarged up to 20 times. He wrote about his work in 1610. Sir Isaac Newton, an English scientist born in 1642 (the year Galileo died), used a different method to advance the telescope. He built his first reflecting telescope in 1669. During the 1700s and 1800s, several space discoveries were made, including identification of the planet Uranus in 1781. Uranus was the first planet discovered past Saturn, which was thought by ancient astronomers to be the most distant planet. In 1846, another new planet—Neptune—was found.

In 1895, the first article on the possibility of space flight was published. During World War II, a team of German scientists developed the V-2 rocket, the first rocket-powered missile. It was first used in 1944. After the war ended, both the Soviet Union and the U.S. recruited scientists from the German team to work on their space programs.

In 1950, the U.S. launched NASA, the National Aeronautics and Space Administration. The U.S. was in a race against the Soviet Union to be the first country to explore space. In 1957, the Soviet Union launched *Sputnik 1* into orbit. It was the first artificial satellite ever launched into space. The U.S. launched its first satellite, *Explorer 1*, four months later. One of the hallmark moments of the space race between the U.S. and the Soviet Union was when Soviet Cosmonaut Yuri Gagarin became the first person to orbit the Earth. The incredible feat took place in April 1961. One month later, U.S. Astronaut Alan Shepard became the first American in space. In 1962, Astronaut John Glenn followed in the footsteps of Gagarin to become the first American to orbit the Earth.

From the mid- to late-1960s, both Soviet and American space programs worked to land unmanned spacecrafts on the moon. In 1966, the Soviet *Luna 9* made the first successful soft landing on the moon, putting the Soviets one step closer to winning the space race. Then, in 1969, the *Apollo 11* spacecraft touched down on the lunar surface. As Americans across the nation sat motionless before their TV sets and radios, Astronaut Neil Armstrong became the first man to set foot on the lunar surface—planting the American flag and winning the space race.

In 1971, the Soviet Union launched its first space station, *Salyut 1*, into orbit. It was followed by a series of space stations. *Mir*, the last station to be sent up by the Soviet Union, went into orbit in 1986. During the 1970s both the U.S. and the Soviet Union sent probes to several planets. These included Venus, Mars, Uranus, and Neptune. In the 1980s, a new type of spacecraft was developed. It was a reusable space shuttle, making space travel routine and eventually leading to the launch of an International Space Station. In 1990, the Hubble Space Telescope was launched using the space shuttle. The Hubble became the first optic telescope in orbit. Although it quickly developed mirror problems, a repair mission in 1993 let the telescope produce spectacular images of distant stars and galaxies.

Construction of the International Space Station began in 1998. The huge space station is a joint project among many countries including past space rivals the U.S. and Russia, the former Soviet Union.

The new millennium brought with it many new discoveries by U.S. space explorers. In 2000, the space shuttle *Endeavor* made a detailed global map of Earth. And that year, new evidence of water was found on Mars. In 2001, the *NEAR* Spacecraft made its first successful landing on an asteroid. And that same year, U.S. businessman Dennis Tito became the first tourist to fly into space. Tito paid the Russian space program 20 million dollars to go to the International Space Station.

In 2004, the *Cassini* probe arrived at Saturn. It spent the next four years photographing the planet and its many moons. The next year, the *Huygens* probe landed on Saturn's largest moon. It is the first-ever landing of a spacecraft on an alien moon. The *Huygens* sent photos back to Earth, giving scientists their first glimpse of the surface of a moon other than ours.

In 2006, Pluto lost its status as a planet. Known as the ninth planet since its discovery in 1930, Pluto was downgraded and is now called a *dwarf planet*. That means it is not considered a true planet. Pluto is not like the other planets. It is just a small, icy body. For many years, scientists believed that there were other icy bodies like Pluto at the fringe of our solar system. By 2003 and 2004, several of these had been found. So Pluto was reclassified.

In 2008, NASA's *Messenger* spacecraft passed just 124 miles above Mercury. It mapped never-before-seen parts of the planet. Also that year, the first-ever images of nearby solar systems were seen. One of the solar systems spotted is like ours in many ways. It has planets that circle around a center sun. One planet is about the same size as Jupiter. Another is about the same size as Saturn.

In 2009, experts charted more planets outside of our solar system. About 300 have been found so far. But scientists believe many more are out there. Also in 2009, the *IBEX* spacecraft began gathering data to build the first maps of the edge of our solar system. The first complete images are expected to tell scientists a great deal about the basic nature of the area mapped. It was a perfect project for 2009, which was proclaimed "The International Year of Astronomy" by the United Nations.

It seems there's no limit to what today's space explorers can accomplish. Some experts believe humans could set foot on Mars as early as 2014. Others think people could begin living in space by 2050.

Space Junk

Space. We've been there. We've explored. But we've also left things behind. What? Space junk. Officially called orbital debris, space junk includes any manmade item intentionally or accidentally left behind by humans during space exploration. This junk includes abandoned space probes, broken pieces of space shuttles, wreckage from satellite breakups and explosions, and much, much more—at last count there was about 100 tons of it orbiting the Earth. Experts say there are more than 600,000 objects larger than 1 centimeter. Each one is large enough to damage a satellite or space-based telescope.

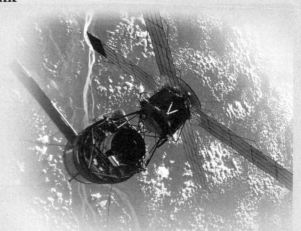

One U.S. space agency keeps a catalogue of about 13,000 pieces of such debris. But most space junk goes unwatched. There are millions of tiny harder-to-track objects such as flecks of paint and bits of plastic. Each piece of space junk is moving at tremendous speed—some faster than 17,000 miles per hour. The orbits of these objects differ in direction, angle, and exact speed. That means collisions are bound to happen!

The first collision with a piece of space debris happened in 1996. A bit of space junk tore off a piece of the French satellite *Cerise*. In 2009, a retired Russian satellite weighing 2,094 pounds collided 500 miles above Siberia with a commercial satellite weighing 1,235 pounds. The speed of impact was about 26,170 miles per hour. The collision destroyed both satellites and created a huge cloud of debris.

At some point, all space junk will return from space. Gravity will cause anything that has ever orbited the Earth to fall back home. Much of the space junk we've left behind will burn up in the Earth's atmosphere upon reentry. But some will land or has landed back on Earth. NASA says on average one piece of orbital debris returns to Earth each day. Only one person has ever been reported being hit by manmade debris falling from space. In 1997, an Oklahoma woman was hit on the shoulder by a 10- x 13-centimeter piece of a fuel tank from a rocket launched by a U.S. Air Force satellite in 1996. The woman was not injured.

The most fantastic reentry of a piece of space junk was *Skylab*. *Skylab* was the first U.S. space station put into orbit. It was launched in 1973 (two years after the Soviet Union put its first space station into orbit). Six years after *Skylab* was launched, the first and only U.S. space station tumbled back to Earth. Part of it splashed down in the Indian Ocean. Another part landed in Australia.

Space Discovery Time Line

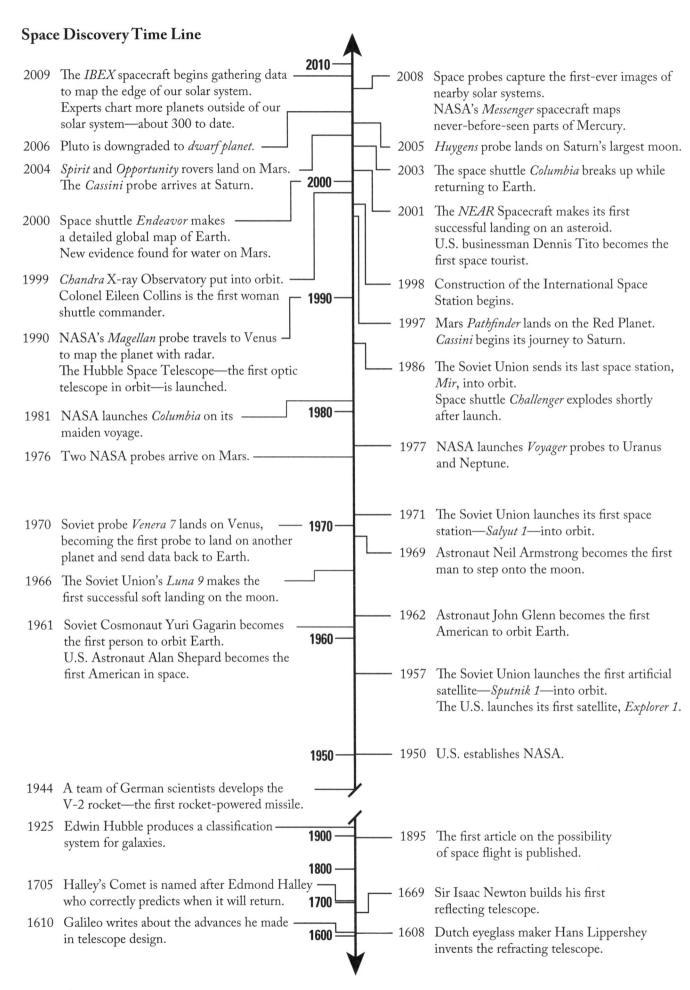

2010

2009 The *IBEX* spacecraft begins gathering data to map the edge of our solar system. Experts chart more planets outside of our solar system—about 300 to date.

2008 Space probes capture the first-ever images of nearby solar systems. NASA's *Messenger* spacecraft maps never-before-seen parts of Mercury.

2006 Pluto is downgraded to *dwarf planet.*

2005 *Huygens* probe lands on Saturn's largest moon.

2004 *Spirit* and *Opportunity* rovers land on Mars. The *Cassini* probe arrives at Saturn.

2000

2003 The space shuttle *Columbia* breaks up while returning to Earth.

2000 Space shuttle *Endeavor* makes a detailed global map of Earth. New evidence found for water on Mars.

2001 The *NEAR* Spacecraft makes its first successful landing on an asteroid. U.S. businessman Dennis Tito becomes the first space tourist.

1999 *Chandra* X-ray Observatory put into orbit. Colonel Eileen Collins is the first woman shuttle commander.

1990

1998 Construction of the International Space Station begins.

1990 NASA's *Magellan* probe travels to Venus to map the planet with radar. The Hubble Space Telescope—the first optic telescope in orbit—is launched.

1997 Mars *Pathfinder* lands on the Red Planet. *Cassini* begins its journey to Saturn.

1986 The Soviet Union sends its last space station, *Mir*, into orbit. Space shuttle *Challenger* explodes shortly after launch.

1981 NASA launches *Columbia* on its maiden voyage.

1980

1976 Two NASA probes arrive on Mars.

1977 NASA launches *Voyager* probes to Uranus and Neptune.

1970 Soviet probe *Venera 7* lands on Venus, becoming the first probe to land on another planet and send data back to Earth.

1970

1971 The Soviet Union launches its first space station—*Salyut 1*—into orbit.

1969 Astronaut Neil Armstrong becomes the first man to step onto the moon.

1966 The Soviet Union's *Luna 9* makes the first successful soft landing on the moon.

1961 Soviet Cosmonaut Yuri Gagarin becomes the first person to orbit Earth. U.S. Astronaut Alan Shepard becomes the first American in space.

1962 Astronaut John Glenn becomes the first American to orbit Earth.

1960

1957 The Soviet Union launches the first artificial satellite—*Sputnik 1*—into orbit. The U.S. launches its first satellite, *Explorer 1.*

1950

1950 U.S. establishes NASA.

1944 A team of German scientists develops the V-2 rocket—the first rocket-powered missile.

1925 Edwin Hubble produces a classification system for galaxies.

1900

1895 The first article on the possibility of space flight is published.

1800

1705 Halley's Comet is named after Edmond Halley who correctly predicts when it will return.

1700

1669 Sir Isaac Newton builds his first reflecting telescope.

1610 Galileo writes about the advances he made in telescope design.

1600

1608 Dutch eyeglass maker Hans Lippershey invents the refracting telescope.

1 Understanding the Reading. Answer the following questions in good sentence form.

1. Why do you think Aristotle is called "the grandfather of modern science" while Galileo is called "the father of modern science?"

   _____

2. After World War II, what do you think might have happened to the German scientists who worked on the V-2 rocket if they had refused to join the U.S. or Soviet space exploration teams? Why?

   _____

   _____

3. Pluto was discovered in 1930 and named the ninth planet. Then, in 2006, it lost its status as a planet and was renamed a *dwarf planet.* Why did scientists make the change?

   _____

4. In 2001, U.S. businessman Dennis Tito went to the International Space Station as a guest of Russian Cosmonauts. Why do you think the U.S. did not take Tito into space?

   _____

   _____

5. The year 2009 was proclaimed "The International Year of Astronomy" by the United Nations. Why do you think the U.N. might have made that proclamation?

   _____

   _____

6. "Space Junk" lists many of the objects that have been left in space and have become orbital debris. List two types of debris and where they came from.

   _____

   _____

7. Can you think of other unlisted manmade objects that might also be orbiting as space junk?

   _____

   _____

8. A statement in the article reads, "In the 1980s, a new type of spacecraft was developed. It was a reusable space shuttle, making space travel routine . . ." Why do you think that a reusable space shuttle would allow space travel to become routine?

   _____

   _____

2 What Do You Think? Answer the following questions in complete sentences. Be sure to include reasons that support your opinion.

1. In 2004, the first manned private space flight took place. Do you think private companies or individuals should be allowed to travel into space? Why or why not?

_____

_____

_____

_____

2. In 2000, new evidence was found for water on Mars. Why do you think scientists consider this an important find?

_____

_____

_____

3. Many scientists believe something should be done to reduce the amount of space debris that litters the solar system. Do you agree or disagree? What do you think should be done about space junk?

_____

_____

_____

4. If you were given a chance to be a space tourist, would you take it? Why or why not?

_____

_____

_____

_____

3 Synonym Review. From the choices listed, choose the best synonym for the word in bold-faced type, and write it on the line to the right.

1. **missile:**	ship	rocket	debris	shuttle
2. **ponder:**	question	imagine	calculate	consider
3. **cling:**	adapt	adhere	adopt	advance
4. **astray:**	alone	single	lost	easygoing
5. **frigid:**	weather	damp	icy	dangerous
6. **fragile:**	delicate	broken	glass	tiny
7. **debris:**	pieces	remains	explosions	satellites
8. **hallmark:**	characteristic	card	label	common
9. **ascend:**	drop	reach	swim	rise
10. **observe:**	follow	challenge	watch	criticize
11. **imperfect:**	normal	flawed	mistake	critical
12. **capable:**	available	reliable	necessary	competent
13. **collision:**	race	crash	debris	wreckage
14. **probe:**	submerse	climb	travel	explore
15. **status:**	title	position	office	quantity
16. **alien:**	familiar	fictional	foreign	fragile
17. **routine:**	narrative	expedition	technique	habit
18. **spectacular:**	skeptical	luxurious	significant	fantastic
19. **exploration:**	vacation	expedition	investigation	contraption

4 Put Events in Order. Put the following events in order, from earliest to most recent.

_____ U.S. establishes NASA.

_____ Sir Isaac Newton builds his first reflecting telescope.

_____ Soviet Cosmonaut Yuri Gagarin becomes the first person to orbit Earth.

_____ The first article on the possibility of space flight is published.

_____ The *IBEX* spacecraft begins gathering data to build the first maps of the edge of our solar system.

_____ The Hubble Space Telescope is launched into orbit using the space shuttle.

_____ Astronaut Neil Armstrong becomes the first man to step onto the moon.

_____ Pluto is downgraded to *dwarf planet*.

5 Make Your Own Time Line.

a. Take another look at the "Space Discovery Time Line." Choose ten events on the time line that you consider to be the most important. Write the events on the lines in time order below, from earliest to most recent.

Date	Item
1. _____	_____
2. _____	_____
3. _____	_____
4. _____	_____
5. _____	_____
6. _____	_____
7. _____	_____
8. _____	_____
9. _____	_____
10. _____	_____

b. Now decide which three of the ten events you chose are the most important. Write the events on the lines below, and then write about the significance of each event. What makes each event so important? Use good sentence form, and give reasons why the events are important to our history—or to our future.

1. _____

   _____

   _____

   _____

2. _____

   _____

   _____

   _____

3. _____

   _____

   _____

   _____

1 Definitions. Match the words listed below with the correct definitions.

administration	expedition	intruder	porthole
circumstance	exposition	mariner	pros and cons
disposition	generation	navigator	rudder
endurance	illumination	observatory	sepulcher

_____ 1. the ability to withstand hardship

_____ 2. a condition, fact, or event that accompanies another act or event

_____ 3. a person who steers or controls the course of a ship or aircraft

_____ 4. a group of people born in the same period

_____ 5. a public exhibition or show, as of artistic or engineering developments

_____ 6. an opening in the side of a ship or aircraft

_____ 7. a person's natural way of acting toward others; mood

_____ 8. a sailor or seaman; one who navigates a ship

_____ 9. a person who forces his or her way in uninvited

_____ 10. a place equipped with a telescope for viewing the stars and planets

_____ 11. a moveable flat blade at the back of a boat by which it is steered

_____ 12. management; the managing of a business or office

_____ 13. the act of lighting up

_____ 14. a tomb or burial place

_____ 15. the arguments for and against something

_____ 16. a journey undertaken by an organized group of people with a definite objective; a long march or voyage made by military forces to the scene of a battle

2 Vocabulary Review. Write the letter of the best answer on the line.

1. The _____ is a straight line that goes from one side to the other through the center of a circle.
   - **a.** arc
   - **b.** diameter
   - **c.** circumference
   - **d.** radius

2. On a trip to the Antarctic, one would probably see _____.
   - **a.** lobsters
   - **b.** elephants
   - **c.** whales
   - **d.** unicorns

3. Who would be most anxious about the location of reefs? _____.
   - **a.** mariner
   - **b.** explorer
   - **c.** astronaut
   - **d.** scavenger

4. A _____ situation is one that could change at any moment.
   - **a.** controversial
   - **b.** precarious
   - **c.** treacherous
   - **d.** formidable

5. An iceberg would most likely be found in the same area as a _____.
   - **a.** fossil
   - **b.** cactus
   - **c.** floe
   - **d.** volcano

6. The place where two things meet is called a _____.
   - **a.** junction
   - **b.** rudder
   - **c.** winch
   - **d.** rivet

7. Which of the following is a fictional beast? _____.
   - **a.** seal
   - **b.** elephant
   - **c.** unicorn
   - **d.** flatfish

8. A gryphon is part lion, part snake, and part _____.
   - **a.** eagle
   - **b.** hawk
   - **c.** owl
   - **d.** penguin

9. Lewis and Clark traveled _____ to explore the country.
   - **a.** eastward
   - **b.** westward
   - **c.** northward
   - **d.** southward

10. Bits of trash floating around in space are officially known as _____.
    - **a.** asteroids
    - **b.** sediments
    - **c.** space debris
    - **d.** flecks

11. The term *aeronautics* refers to _____.
    - **a.** aliens
    - **b.** flight
    - **c.** planets
    - **d.** air

12. Which of the following is *not* a type of currency? _____.
    - **a.** dollar
    - **b.** jewelry
    - **c.** peso
    - **d.** euro

13. A major function of NASA is to _____.
    - **a.** explore the U.S.
    - **b.** explore the deserts
    - **c.** explore space
    - **d.** explore the Poles

14. The word *lunar* means "of the _____."

  a. world   **b.** planet   **c.** moon   **d.** sun

15. Sacagawea traveled with _____.

  a. Lewis and Clark   **b.** Marco Polo   **c.** Sir Shackleton   **d.** Neil Armstrong

16. In the line, "An inadequate ship was provided," the word *inadequate* means _____.

  a. unusual   **b.** disarranged   **c.** impenetrable   **d.** unsatisfactory

3 Antonym Review. From the choices listed, choose the word that is the best antonym for the word in bold-faced type, and write it on the line to the right.

1.	**annihilate:**	explode	protect	construct	terrorize	
2.	**gigantic:**	jumbo	tiny	vast	enlarged	
3.	**emphasize:**	minimize	maximize	exaggerate	contradict	
4.	**sentient:**	attentive	permissive	unconscious	fierce	
5.	**formidable:**	sufficient	trivial	equal	unreliable	
6.	**comrade:**	enemy	ally	commander	competitor	
7.	**revere:**	ensure	despise	respect	harass	
8.	**capable:**	curious	incompetent	sociable	unreliable	
9.	**prey:**	hunt	victim	animal	predator	
10.	**disarranged:**	bulky	orderly	injured	irresponsible	
11.	**maneuverable:**	rudderless	immobile	inadequate	reusable	
12.	**strenuous:**	serious	effortless	prone	persistent	
13.	**resolved:**	anxious	definite	undecided	partial	
14.	**reluctant:**	hesitant	eager	fickle	weak	
15.	**sufficiently:**	disturbingly	particularly	adequately	inadequately	

4 Today's Explorers. Use the prefixes listed below to complete this information about modern explorers. The first one has been done to get you started.

dis	✓ex	under	sub	un

1. Robert Ballard is a sea ___**ex**___plorer who is famous for his historic _____covery of the sunken luxury ship, *Titanic*. The ship had been _____disturbed beneath the sea for decades. Ballard uses the most up-to-date technology to build _____marines that can take him deep into the _____sea world.

con	re	extra	dis	per

2. Carl Sagan was a 20th-century American astronomer well known for his belief in _____terrestrial life. Sagan _____tributed to many planetary _____coveries through his work with NASA. Sagan once said, "It is far better to grasp the Universe as it really is than to _____sist in delusion, however satisfying and _____assuring."

com	ex	re	ad	re

3. Richard Byrd learned to fly in the U.S. Navy during World War I. Byrd's first Antarctic _____pedition, begun in 1928, _____vived America's interest in exploring the poles, and he _____turned a hero. Byrd was the first explorer to use modern mechanics—airplane, aerial camera, snowmobile, and _____munications. Byrd traveled to the Antarctic four more times, _____vancing our knowledge of the area with each trip.

de	re	dis	de	un

4. British astronomer Jocelyn Bell Burnell _____covered pulsars while studying at Cambridge University in 1943. A pulsar is a type of star that is rapidly rotating and has a very strong magnetic field. Scientists can _____tect pulsars by listening for their _____peated radio signals which are aimed toward Earth. Dr. Burnell is still _____voted to studying the stars and hopes to _____cover more of their secrets.

en	self	de	en	inter

5. Humans aren't the only explorers. Robots go where humans cannot, yet. While today's robots analyze the solar system, NASA is busy _____visioning the future. NASA plans to _____ploy a new generation of _____-sufficient spacecrafts that control their own probes, rovers, and cameras with minimal human _____vention. Surveys show that many people become attached to the rovers they hear about in the news. And NASA is _____couraging this growing affection by having its spaceships send messages to online followers on Twitter.

5 Discovery Time Line. The time line on the next page relates to the articles and exercises in this unit. Fill in the missing dates and events. Look back at the readings to help you decide where the events belong. You may have to look up some events in an encyclopedia or on the Internet. Fill in events you think may happen on future dates.

982–986	1804	1492	1915	2014	1275	1961
1325–54	1914	1969	1806	1609–11	1805	

Beebe and Barton reach a record-breaking depth of 3,028 feet below sea level.

The *Messenger* spacecraft maps the surface of Mercury.

Eric the Red discovers Greenland.

Roald Amundsen reaches the South Pole.

Amerigo Vespucci discovers North and South America.

Leif Erikson is the first European to reach North America.

The *Cassini* probe reaches Saturn.

Zheng He travels throughout Southeast Asia, East Africa, and Arabia.

Vasco da Gama sails around the Cape of Good Hope and reaches India.

Robert Peary and Matthew Henson reach the North Pole.

Henry Hudson explores eastern coast of North America and Canada.

James Cook explores the Pacific, South Pacific, and Arctic Ocean.

Lewis and Clark return home to St. Louis.

Yuri Gagarin is the first person to orbit Earth.

St. Brendan sails the Atlantic Ocean.

Marco Polo begins his exploration of Asia, Mongolia, China, and Persia.

Auguste Piccard takes the *Trieste* submersible to a depth of 32,500 feet.

500 BC	Hanno sails down the northwestern coast of Africa.
AD 530	
1001–2	
1271	
	Ibn Battutah explores North Africa, the Middle East, India, and Asia.
1405–33	
	Christopher Columbus lands in San Salvador.
1497–98	
1497–1504	
1519–21	Ferdinand Magellan circumnavigates the world.
1768–1779	
	Lewis and Clark set out to explore the western territories of the U.S.
	Sacagawea gives birth to a son, Jean Baptiste.
1909	
1911	
	Sir Ernest Shackleton sets out across Antarctica toward the South Pole.
1934	
1960	
	Neil Armstrong is the first person to walk on the moon.
2004	
2008	
	Humans land on Mars?
2050	
3000	

The Good Earth

As you read in the last unit, one question that mankind has often asked is, "What will the future bring?" Many people are asking this question in relation to the natural environment—the land on which we live. In this unit, the readings explore various attitudes toward the earth in general and more specifically toward our natural resources.

"A Fable for Tomorrow," the reading for Lesson 11, describes the efforts of Rachel Carson, a famous American biologist and author, to warn us about what could happen if we were not more careful in protecting the Earth against environmental pollution.

"No Way to Treat a Forest," the reading for Lesson 12, explains why the Amazon rainforest is so important to humankind. The author also describes how the rainforest has become endangered and prescribes several possible solutions to the problem.

But just how to adapt our needs and desires to the needs of the natural environment is not a simple matter. In the reading for Lesson 13, "The Good Earth: Two Points of View," two experts on natural resources discuss this complex problem.

Lessons 14 and 15 feature the American short story "Antaeus" in which a boy encounters resistance as he attempts to express his special love for the good Earth.

Words for Study

abundance	withered	substantial	toxic
maladies	vegetation	specter	pallbearers
moribund	anglers	marine	Interior
pollination	granular	malaria	contamination

LESSON 11
A Fable for Tomorrow

by Rachel Carson

There was once a town in the heart of America where all life seemed to live in harmony with its surroundings. The town lay in the midst of a checkerboard of prosperous farms, with fields of grain and hillsides of orchards where, in spring, white clouds of bloom drifted above the green fields. In autumn, oak and maple and birch set up a blaze of color that flamed and flickered across a backdrop of pines. Then foxes barked in the hills and deer silently crossed the fields, half hidden in the mists of the fall mornings.

Along the roads laurel, viburnum and alder, great ferns and wildflowers delighted the traveler's eye through much of the year. Even in winter the roadsides were places of beauty, where countless birds came to feed on the berries and on the seed heads of the dried weeds rising above the snow. The countryside was, in fact, famous for the abundance and variety of its bird life, and when the flood of migrants was pouring through in spring and fall people traveled from great distances to observe them. Others came to fish the streams, which flowed clear and cold out of the hills and contained shady pools where trout lay. So it had been from the days many years ago when the first settlers raised their houses, sank their wells, and built their barns.

Then a strange blight crept over the area and everything began to change. Some evil spell had settled on the community: mysterious maladies swept the flocks of chickens; the cattle and sheep sickened and died. Everywhere was a shadow of death. The farmers spoke of much illness among their families. In the town the doctors had become more and more puzzled by new kinds of sickness appearing among their patients. There had been several sudden and unexplained deaths, not only among adults but even among children, who would be stricken suddenly while at play and die within a few hours.

There was a strange stillness. The birds, for example—where had they gone? Many people spoke of them, puzzled and disturbed. The feeding stations in the backyards were deserted. The few birds seen anywhere were moribund; they trembled violently and could not fly. It was a spring without voices. On the mornings that had once throbbed with the dawn chorus of robins, catbirds, doves, jays, wrens, and scores of other bird voices there was now no sound; only silence lay over the fields and woods and marsh.

On the farms the hens brooded, but no chicks hatched. The farmers complained that they were unable to raise any pigs—the litters were small and the young survived only a few days. The apple trees were coming into bloom but no bees droned among the blossoms, so there was no pollination and there would be no fruit.

The roadsides, once so attractive, were now lined with browned and withered vegetation as though swept by fire. These, too, were silent, deserted by all living things. Even the streams were now lifeless. Anglers no longer visited them, for all the fish had died.

In the gutters under the eaves and between the shingles of the roofs, a white granular powder still showed a few patches; some weeks before it had fallen like snow upon the roofs and the lawns, the fields and streams.

No witchcraft, no enemy action had silenced the rebirth of new life in this stricken world. The people had done it themselves.

This town does not actually exist, but it might easily have a thousand counterparts in America or elsewhere in the world. I know of no community that has experienced all the misfortunes I describe. Yet every one of these disasters has actually happened somewhere, and many real communities have already suffered a substantial number of them. A grim specter has crept upon us almost unnoticed, and this imagined tragedy may easily become a stark reality as we all shall know.

What has already silenced the voices of spring in countless towns in America? This book is an attempt to explain.

* * *

The author of "A Fable for Tomorrow" was Rachel Carson, an American biologist and writer. She is famous for her books on environmental pollution and on the natural history of the sea.

The book to which she refers is *Silent Spring* which was published in 1962. The fable is the first chapter of this widely read book.

Rachel Carson's own story began in Springdale, Pennsylvania, where she was born in the spring of 1907. The woods around her childhood home were where young Rachel first came into contact with the natural world that she was to defend all her life.

Wanting to become a writer, Miss Carson entered Pennsylvania State College for Women. When she took a required biology course, she decided that subject appealed to her more. Later she received her masters degree in biology from Johns Hopkins University and then studied marine biology at the Woods Hole Marine Biological Laboratory. Despite a long-felt love for the sea, Rachel Carson had never even seen a sea until she studied at Woods Hole, which is located on the Massachusetts coast.

The desire to write was still strong, however, and so after she finished her studies, she applied for a job with the United States Bureau of Fisheries as a writer and editor for its publications. She got the job and served with this agency for many years.

Her first book, *Under the Sea Wind*, was published on the eve of America's entry into World War II. Although the book did not sell well at the time, it was later reprinted and achieved great success.

It was during the war that Miss Carson had an opportunity to read many reports on scientific discoveries then being made. These reports included studies on substances used for pesticides, of which the best-known was DDT. DDT is the shortened form of dichloro-diphenyl-trichloro-ethane. Even as DDT was achieving its great breakthrough in combating malaria and other human diseases carried by insects, Rachel Carson was having serious second thoughts about the biological effects of DDT's widespread use. But her involvement during the wartime and postwar years was again with the sea.

In 1951 her second book, *The Sea Around Us*, was published and became a best seller. Suddenly the little-known Rachel Carson was a national celebrity. She hated it. A quiet person, she wanted mainly to be left alone to work and write. But even though the success of *The Sea Around Us* brought her unwanted fame, it also gave her the financial security she needed to make writing a full-time career.

It was in the 1950s that Rachel Carson was beginning to wonder what she might write to warn people about the harm that mankind was doing to the earth. Some scientists had expressed concerns as early as 1945 about the effects of DDT on the environment. Later, facts about DDT's ability to accumulate in fatty tissue of wildlife started to emerge. Houseflies were becoming immune to DDT. Birds that ate insects sprayed with DDT died. Scientists gradually became aware of the fact that they did not really know what the long-term effects of DDT might be. It was an area that cried out for scientific investigation.

On the other hand, DDT was cheap, plentiful, and effective for the purpose of controlling insects. Farmers, especially, used it in vast quantities. One of its "advantages" was that it persisted in its toxic state for many years, so that farmers needed to use it only occasionally. And of course, as we now know, this was the most serious disadvantage of DDT—it continues to be with us, with its harmful effects as well as its benefits, for years.

Rachel Carson started what became an effort of several years to gather all the scientific information available about chemical pesticides and insecticides. When her book was finally published in 1962 as *Silent Spring*, it drew an unbelievable amount of criticism from the chemical industry and from the Department of Agriculture. Nearly all the criticism was based on either a failure to read the book or a deliberate attempt to distort what Rachel Carson had actually written.

Critics of *Silent Spring* said, for example, that it called for the end of all insecticide use. It did not. Rachel Carson was roundly and frequently criticized as having dabbled in the field of science where she had no right to dabble. This particular criticism was indeed strange, for Rachel Carson was a respected biologist and *Silent Spring* contains the most careful records of the work of many hundreds of scientists.

Dr. Norman E. Borlaug, winner of a Nobel Peace Prize for his work in developing new strains of wheat, asserted that *Silent Spring* had failed to mention the importance of chemicals in producing and protecting food and fiber crops.

Yet Miss Carson had written: "All this is not to say there is no insect problem and no need of control. I am saying, rather, that control must be geared to realities, not to mythical situations, and that the methods employed must be such that they do not destroy us along with the insects . . .

"It is not my contention that chemical insecticides must never be used. I do contend that we have put poisonous and biologically potent chemicals indiscriminately into the hands of persons largely or wholly ignorant of their potential for harm.

"We have subjected enormous numbers of people to contact with these poisons, without their consent and often without their knowledge. If the Bill of Rights contains no guarantee that a citizen shall be secure against lethal poisons distributed either by private individuals or by public officials, it is surely only because our forefathers, despite their considerable wisdom and foresight, could conceive of no such problem.

"I contend, furthermore, that we have allowed these chemicals to be used with little or no advance investigation of their effect on soil, water, wildlife and man himself. Future generations are unlikely to condone our lack of prudent concern for the integrity of the natural world that supports all life."

Few of her readers, friends and critics alike, knew what a physical effort it had been for Rachel Carson to write *Silent Spring*. While the book was being debated up and down the land and giving birth to some forty pieces of state legislation to limit the use of pesticides, its author became increasingly ill. By the summer of 1963, Rachel Carson knew she was dying. Few people realized that she was sick because she tried to carry on the defense of her ideas. Her last public appearance was to testify before a U.S. Senate subcommittee headed by Connecticut's Senator Abraham Ribicoff. The topic was suggestions for the proper use of pesticides.

Rachel Carson died in the spring of 1964. Among the pallbearers at her funeral were Secretary of the Interior Stewart Udall and Senator Ribicoff. The Senator called Rachel Carson "this gentle lady who aroused people everywhere to be concerned with one of the most significant problems of mid-20th-century life—man's contamination of his environment."

1 Understanding the Reading. Write the letter of the best answer on the line.

1. "A Fable for Tomorrow" appears in _____.
   a. *The Sea Around Us*   b. *Silent Spring*   c. *The Edge of the Sea*   d. *Under the Sea Wind*

2. In the sentence ". . . and when the flood of migrants was pouring through in the spring and fall people traveled from great distances to see them," *migrants* refers to _____.
   a. birds   b. fish   c. tourists   d. workers

3. The "strange blight" mentioned in "A Fable for Tomorrow" refers to _____.
   a. DDT   b. malaria   c. pollination   d. witchcraft

4. Which word *least* describes the countryside after the "strange stillness"? _____.
   a. moribund   b. scenic   c. substantial   d. withered

5. Miss Carson probably wrote "A Fable for Tomorrow" _____.
   a. to emphasize how forces exist that are beyond our understanding
   b. to fulfill her ambitions as a writer
   c. to portray man's ability to destroy his environment
   d. to show what has happened to many American communities

6. When Miss Carson's findings on pesticides and insecticides were published, they were _____.
   a. instantly dismissed   b. severely criticized   c. universally praised   d. generally ignored

7. Which of these statements about DDT is false? _____
   a. DDT is an effective combatant against many diseases.
   b. DDT was first used during World War II.
   c. Miss Carson was the first scientist to recognize the dangers of DDT.
   d. The toxic effect of DDT persists for many years.

8. Which word best describes Miss Carson's personal habits? _____
   a. carefree   b. inconsistent   c. reclusive   d. sociable

9. Which of the following best indicates that Miss Carson succeeded in convincing people of the harm they are doing to the environment? _____
   a. Abraham Ribicoff's statement
   b. Dr. Borlaug's assertion
   c. forty pieces of state legislation
   d. testifying before the Senate subcommittee

2 What Do You Think? The following statement is from a letter that Chief Seattle wrote to President Franklin Pierce in 1854. Seattle was a Native American chief. Some say that the letter was forged, but the message is still powerful and relevant. Read the statement, and then answer the questions that follow in good sentence form. Be sure to offer reasons or examples to support your point of view.

"This we know: the earth does not belong to man; man belongs to the earth. This we know. All things are connected like the blood which unites one family. All things are connected. Whatever befalls the earth befalls the sons of the earth. Man did not weave the web of life: he is merely a strand in it. Whatever he does to the web, he does to himself."

1. Does Chief Seattle's statement support or contradict "A Fable for Tomorrow"? Explain.

   _____

   _____

   _____

2. Cite two things many Americans commonly do that suggest that they would agree with Chief Seattle's statement.

   a. _____

   b. _____

3. Cite two things many Americans commonly do that suggest that they would not agree with Chief Seattle's statement.

   a. _____

   b. _____

4. What is your reaction to Chief Seattle's statement?

   _____

   _____

   _____

   _____

3 What Is the Nobel Prize? It was mentioned in the reading that one of Miss Carson's critics had won a Nobel Prize. Use the words listed at the left to complete this information about Nobel prizes.

anniversary
distinction
economics
enrichment
substantial

1. Awarded each year on December 10, the _____ of Alfred Nobel's death, Nobel Prizes are given to men and women who have achieved _____ in the fields of medicine, physics, literature, chemistry, peace, and _____, and have made a(n) _____ contribution for the _____ of humanity.

accumulated
distinguished
estate
massive
portion

2. Born in Sweden in 1833, Alfred Nobel was a(n) _____ inventor who _____ a(n) _____ fortune from the manufacture of dynamite and other explosives. When he died in 1896, he left the major _____ of his _____ (about $8.5 million) for the institution of the Nobel Prizes.

abundance
capable
fateful
incident
tragedy

3. Nobel's innovations in the field of explosives brought him an _____ of wealth, but they also brought him personal _____. One _____ day in 1864, for example, just after the _____ chemist had begun making nitroglycerin, the factory blew up. Nobel's youngest brother and four others were killed in this disastrous _____.

determinedly
indignant
minimize
rebuild
reliable

4. Denounced by _____ Swedes as a "mad scientist" and public enemy, and forbidden to _____ his factory, Nobel _____ continued his experiments on a barge, seeking a(n) _____ way to _____ the danger of handling nitroglycerin.

ambitions
ample
dedicated
exertion
inevitable

5. Many will concur that no matter how _____ a person is in pursuing his _____, it is more often than not a(n) _____ dose of good fortune rather than personal _____ that makes success _____.

discredited
patents
precisely
reclusive
sociable

6. And this is _____ what happened in the case of Alfred Nobel who, through a chance discovery, perfected the explosive he named dynamite for which he was granted exclusive _____ in 1867 and 1868. The man who had been _____ as a "mad scientist" was now rich and famous. The fame, at least, must have burdened Nobel who was _____ rather than _____ by nature.

4 Global Warming. Read the information about global warning below and in the table, and then answer the questions on the next page in **Parts A** and **B**.

Global warming is the gradual average increase in the earth's temperature. Global warming causes climate changes such as increases or decreases in rainfall, changes in storm patterns, and changes in snow and ice cover. Scientists all over the world study and track weather and climate changes in an effort to predict how our environment might change in the future. The table shows some of the effects of climate change that scientists believe are likely to occur over the next century.

Projected Impacts of Climate Change

Projected Change	Projected Impact			
	Agriculture and Forestry	**Water Resources**	**Human Health**	**Industry and Society**
Warmer day and night temperatures over land areas	Increased yields in colder regions; decreased yields in warmer regions	Less water available from snow melt	Fewer deaths from extreme cold	Reduced energy demand for heating; increased demand for cooling; declining urban air quality
Increased frequency of warm spells and heat waves	Reduced yields in warmer regions; increased danger of fire	Increase in water demand; decrease in water quality	Increased risk of heat-related deaths	Reduced quality of life in warm regions without air conditioning; reduced efficiency of thermoelectric power production
Increased frequency of heavy precipitation events	Damage to crops; soil erosion; decrease in soil quality	Decrease in quality of surface and groundwater; water contamination	Deaths, injuries, infection, and allergies from floods and landslides	Disruption of settlements, transportation, and commerce due to flooding
More areas affected by drought	Decrease in soil quality; lower yields; crop damage; livestock deaths	Widespread stress on water resources	Increased risk of food and water shortage; increase in wildfires; increased risk of diseases spreading	Water shortages for people and industry; reduced hydropower generation; possible population migration
Increase in intense tropical cyclones	Crop damage, tree damage	Power outages disrupt water supply	Increased risk of food and water shortage; increased risk of diseases spreading	Disruption by floods and high winds
Increase in incidents of extreme high sea level	Salinization of irrigation and well water	Decrease in available fresh water	Increase in drowning deaths; increase in stress-related diseases	Increased costs for coastal protection

Table based on information from the Intergovernmental Panel on Climate Change Fourth Assessment Report (IPCC, 2007) located online at the United States Environmental Protection Agency website: www.epa.gov.

Part A Read the predictions below. If a prediction is likely to be true based on the information in the table, write **T** on the line to the left. If the prediction is likely to be false, write **F**. If you cannot determine the answer from the information in the table, write a **?**.

_____ **1.** Canada should see an increase in crops in areas that receive sufficient rain.

_____ **2.** Coastal areas in tropical regions will be hard hit by crop damage, decrease in water quality, and increase in deaths and diseases.

_____ **3.** An increase in high sea level incidents may cause coastal damage and wildfires.

_____ **4.** Regions that suffer either a water shortage or an increase in heavy rain will see a decrease in harvest and a decrease in available drinking water.

_____ **5.** In areas affected by frequent, severe drought, people will build fewer homes.

_____ **6.** A warm region that has an increased incidence of drought and heat waves may see a reduced quality of life, a rise in heat-related deaths, and an increase in hydropower generation.

_____ **7.** The biggest negative impact on human health is caused by warmer land temperatures.

_____ **8.** In areas seriously affected by drought, people may have to move in order to maintain their quality of life.

Part B Answer these questions in good sentence form. Support your answers with information from the table.

1. Based on the information in the table, what do you think life will be like in your hometown one hundred years from now? Describe the agriculture, water, health, and community situation. How will it be different from today?

_____

_____

_____

_____

2. Where would you want to live one hundred years from now? Choose a city, country, continent, or climate region, and describe why you would want to live there.

_____

_____

_____

_____

5 Names in Nature. Choose the best answers for these brief word histories.

_____ 1. This plant got its name because, as Captain John Smith wrote in 1624, "The Poysoned weed is much in shape like our English ivy."

    a. dandelion   **b.** poison ivy   **c.** poison oak   **d.** ragweed

_____ 2. The ancient Roman colony Tarentum gave its name to this fearsome-looking, hairy bug.

    a. moth   **b.** tarantula   **c.** tick   **d.** yellow jacket

_____ 3. The explorer Hernando de Soto didn't realize this animal was actually a bison when he gave it the Spanish name meaning "wild ox" in 1544.

    a. antelope   **b.** buffalo   **c.** bull   **d.** steer

_____ 4. First recorded in 1682, this animal's name also comes from the Spanish—_el lagarto_, which means lizard.

    a. alligator   **b.** crocodile   **c.** Gila monster   **d.** turtle

_____ 5. From two Spanish words, both of which mean "having no master" comes the name of this wild, or half-wild animal.

    a. burro   **b.** camel   **c.** mustang   **d.** muskrat

_____ 6. Named after the garden herb, this is so abundant in the western plains that by 1894 it became the nickname for the state of Nevada.

    a. cactus   **b.** crabgrass   **c.** sagebrush   **d.** tumbleweed

_____ 7. This word derived from the French means "large meadow."

    a. glen   **b.** prairie   **c.** range   **d.** valley

_____ 8. The first major Louisiana French word to enter American English, this word—which the French borrowed from the Choctaw Indians—means "creek."

    a. bayou   **b.** bog   **c.** delta   **d.** stream

_____ 9. From the Greek word meaning "sprout," our 18th-century ancestors referred to this vegetable as "sparrow-grass."

    a. artichoke   **b.** asparagus   **c.** broccoli   **d.** cauliflower

_____ 10. When this bird was discovered, it was named after certain officials in the Roman Catholic Church because its color was the same as their hats.

    a. blackbird   **b.** blue jay   **c.** cardinal   **d.** yellowthroat

Words for Study

rainforest	Protocol	feasible	incentives
deforestation	notable	monitor	intertwined
anesthetic	emissions	induced	intact
decompose	pharmaceutical	diversifying	biodiversity

LESSON 12

No Way to Treat a Forest

The Amazon rainforest stretches across the heart of South America. Most of it is in Brazil, but large parts of the forest extend into Venezuela, Colombia, Peru, and other surrounding nations. The Amazon rainforest is the world's largest wilderness. But today, this vast area is in danger. Huge swaths of the forest have been harvested as lumber or cut or burned down to make way for farms, ranches, roads, pipeline construction, and mining. Experts estimate that more than 20 percent of the rainforest is already gone, and the rate of deforestation is increasing.

Why should anyone care? One answer is because the Amazon rainforest may be the most ecologically important area on earth. There are, for example, about 2,500 species of trees in the Amazon and around 30,000 plant species altogether. That's about 30 percent of those in the whole world. Scientists don't know all of the benefits that this vast biological diversity may have for humankind, but many economic and social benefits are evident.

We know, for example, that many of our medicines come from native plants. At least 120 of those in use today were originally developed from plants. Among them is quinine, a product of the South American cinchona tree. Quinine is used to treat malaria. Novocaine, from the coca plant, is used as a local anesthetic, often by dentists. Turbocuarine

is used as a muscle relaxant during surgery. It is also used to treat muscle disorders such as multiple sclerosis and Parkinson's disease.

The fact that native plants are a major source of modern medicines is well known. However, only five percent of the plants in the rainforest have been studied for possible medicinal value. So we need to care about these forests. We should worry that they're disappearing. We should act to protect these forests so we have a chance to find the cures hidden in them.

We should also care about these vast forests because of the impact they have on the carbon cycle and global warming. Carbon dioxide is one of the greenhouse gases that cause global warming and climate change. Plants lock up carbon dioxide that floats free in the atmosphere. About 10% of the earth's carbon is stored in plants in the Amazon rainforest. When forests are cut down and the land is cleared, the plants are burned or rot. As they decompose, the stored carbon is released back into the atmosphere where it becomes a greenhouse gas. Currently, Brazil is one of the world's largest producers of greenhouse gases. Most of it comes from logging and burning the rainforest.

A third reason to preserve the rainforest is to save the cultures that have thrived there for hundreds of years. These native peoples live in small bands scattered through the forest. They have gathered vast knowledge of the forest and of the medicinal values of plants. These people are disappearing as the forest is sliced by roads and the trees are cut down. At least 90 different groups have disappeared since 1900. Helping these people sustain their cultures in the years to come is an important goal.

So what can we do to preserve the Amazon rainforest? The answer is not easy to find, but we must search for it. There are numerous proposals.

One possibility is the use of the "carbon credits" that are part of the Kyoto Protocol. This is an international agreement sponsored by the United Nations. More than 160 nations are working together to reduce global warming. (The United States is a notable non-participant.) Carbon credits are a way to limit development of projects that add carbon dioxide to the air. Countries that want to build projects that produce carbon dioxide could pay for the right by buying carbon credits. The credits would be sold by other countries that are, in effect, willing to give up building carbon-producing projects of their own. For example, imagine that a German company wanted to build a coal-fired power plant. The plant would produce carbon emissions. Laws would prevent the company from building the plant unless it can purchase carbon credits to offset its carbon dioxide production. So the German company purchases carbon credits from Brazil. When it sells the credits, Brazil is being paid not to produce carbon dioxide. One way it might get these credits is by preserving a section of rainforest rather than logging it.

Another interesting solution is ecotourism. This is a form of tourism that promotes traveling to wild areas. Ecotourism can be a huge economic benefit because of the money tourists spend. As such, it is an alternative to more destructive industries, such as agriculture, mining, and lumbering. Tourism helps local peoples become invested in protecting resources. They can see a direct connection between the forests and their standard of living.

Establishing parks and conservation areas can preserve large blocks of the rainforest. But these lands have to contribute to the economy of the communities and nations where they exist. Ecotourism is one logical way to get an economic benefit from wilderness preserves. Another way is to work with pharmaceutical companies to promote bio-prospecting. Bio-prospecting is the search for plants that can be used to produce medicine. This kind of program has already been implemented in the rainforests of Costa Rica in Central America. The pharmaceutical giant Merck signed an agreement with Costa Rica. It paid the government $1 million for help in identifying plants that may be useful in producing new medicines. If a marketable drug is found, the Costa Rican government shares in the royalties from sales of the medicine. Plans such as this one are being explored by other countries. This may provide another way to help make the protection of rainforests economically feasible.

Commercial logging is responsible for a large part of the rainforest's destruction. Timber companies send crews into the forest to harvest the best trees. To reach them, they bulldoze roads through the forest. Many of the trees are not marketable, of course. Most are too small or of the wrong kind. The vines and bushes and other plants are worthless. After taking out what they want, the timber companies cut down or bulldoze and burn much of what's left. Or they leave the rubbish piled in large mounds or scattered across the floor of what was once the rainforest. Logging is supposed to be strictly controlled through licensing. In practice, though, much of the logging—and the destruction—is illegal. Timber is a valuable product and loggers sometimes cut without a license, or they exceed their limits. The solution here is mainly enforcement.

Other strategies that should be promoted are selective cutting combined with low-impact harvesting techniques. Trees with commercial value are taken out while leaving the rest of the forest as undisturbed as possible. Low-impact harvesting requires careful planning before timber cutting to reduce damage to the forest that will remain. This might, for instance, involve deciding where to build roads to limit erosion. Given the great expanse of the rainforest, however, it's easy for illegal harvesting to continue. So it comes back to enforcement. Governments must take additional steps to monitor the forests. They must enforce laws to end illegal cutting.

Despite the real benefits of agriculture, it is another major cause of forest destruction. It can also be part of the solution. Modern farming techniques follow methods used in places like North America and Europe. There the land is cleared and a single crop is planted in fields. This process doesn't work well in the Amazon. Although the forest is fertile, the land itself is not. The first few years after the trees are cleared away the land can be highly productive. But then the fertility of the land declines. Soon it is exhausted and nearly worthless. Then the farmers move on and clear another stretch of rainforest. So the clearing and burning continue. Each year many more thousands of acres of forest are destroyed. An alternative approach is possible and has been successful in the Amazon for centuries. Farmers there once farmed without cutting the forests. Instead they managed the forests to favor crops that grew there naturally. For example, they might promote the growth of fruit trees, palm forests, and Brazil nut trees. These crops can thrive even though they grow in a forest. So the land is productive. Farmers can earn a living. And the forest is largely preserved.

Another way to protect the rainforest is to make better use of land that has already been cleared. It may or may not be possible to restore some of this land as rainforest, but much of it can be better used than it is at present. For example, many acres of rainforest are cleared each year by farmers who do not own the land. When the land is exhausted, they abandon it and clear new fields. If they can be induced to restore and use the already-cleared land instead of moving on, less additional forest would be lost. Several steps can be taken in this regard.

First, farmers might be given ownership of the land they farm. If they own it, they will be more likely to care for the land and to make it productive. Government or private agencies can assist them by helping them learn about and plant new crops. Diversifying crops and adding new ones that help rebuild soil can help farmers keep the land productive. These new crops can also provide farmers with new sources of income. In addition to these incentives, outside organizations might help farmers to market their produce.

The objective of these steps is to improve the financial well-being of people whose lives are intertwined with the health of the rainforests. If the people prosper and the lands they farm prosper, the remaining forests may be left intact.

There are other solutions as well that can help preserve the remaining Amazon rainforest. It will probably take a combination of solutions to really make a difference. But the key is to begin now and to apply as many of these solutions as it takes to stem the destruction. These forests help protect our world from the threat of global warming. And their incredible biodiversity holds the key to many known and unknown benefits for humankind. The Amazon rainforest is far too important to the people of the world to allow it to disappear.

1 Understanding the Reading: Part 1. Put the letter of the best answer on the line.

1. The Amazon rainforest _____.
   a. covers most of the northwestern part of the U.S.
   b. stretches across much of Central America
   c. covers much of central Africa
   d. is mostly in Brazil, Venezuela, Colombia, and Peru

2. The Amazon rainforest is home to about _____ of the plants in the entire world.
   a. 10 percent   b. 20 percent   c. 30 percent   d. 40 percent

3. According to the author, people should work to preserve the Amazon rainforest because _____.
   a. scientists have only studied 5 percent of the plants to see if they have medicinal value
   b. it is one of our most important sources for timber and minerals
   c. native peoples cannot survive without periodically clearing new lands for farming
   d. the clearing and burning of the forest help offset the buildup of greenhouse gases

4. The plants of the Amazon rainforest lock up about 10 percent of the earth's _____.
   a. oxygen   b. fresh water   c. carbon   d. greenhouse gases

5. Countries of the Amazon rainforest can help preserve the forest by _____.
   a. selling carbon credits to other nations
   b. encouraging construction of coal-fired power plants
   c. resisting policies proposed by the Kyoto Protocol
   d. buying carbon credits from other nations

6. A family travels to Venezuela to visit parks and reserves and to learn about the Amazon rainforest. Their trip is an example of _____.
   a. conservation   b. ecotourism   c. ecology   d. bio-prospecting

7. Trees and other plants return carbon to the atmosphere when they _____.
   a. grow   b. decompose   c. absorb light   d. produce seeds

8. Scientists who do bio-prospecting in the rainforest are _____.
   a. searching for sources of carbon dioxide
   b. looking for ways to improve agricultural practices
   c. trying to learn how the rainforest absorbs greenhouse gases
   d. hunting for plants with medicinal value

9. After people have farmed for several years land that was once rainforest, the land _____.
   a. rewards their efforts in clearing the land   c. becomes exhausted and infertile
   b. begins to recover its fertility   d. slowly becomes more productive

10. When farmers *diversify* their crops, they _____.
    a. grow different kinds of crops   c. grow crops that can be sold
    b. grow one or two crops   d. grow crops that feed people, not animals

2 Understanding the Reading: Part 2. Answer the following questions in good sentence form. Be sure to include information from the reading to support your answers.

1. Why is it important that any preserves that are created contribute in some way to the financial well-being of the people living nearby?

   _____

   _____

   _____

2. How can the better use of land that has been previously cleared of rainforest help to preserve the remaining forest?

   _____

   _____

   _____

3. List three reasons why people who do not live near the rainforest should care what happens to it?

   a. _____

   b. _____

   c. _____

What do you think? Do you think people are doing enough to protect the natural ecosystems of the world? Explain.

_____

_____

_____

_____

_____

_____

3 Synonyms and Antonyms. Choose a synonym to fill in the first blank in each sentence. Choose an antonym to fill in the second blank.

Synonyms
abundant
affirm
contaminate
decompose
dismiss
harmony
inducement
noteworthy
observe
practical
prosperous
withered

Antonyms
deny
deterrent
develop
employ
ignore
impossible
insignificant
needy
purify
skimpy
strife
thriving

1. Ample and _abundant_ are antonyms for _skimpy_.

2. Monitor and _observe_ are antonyms for _ignore_.

3. Decay and _decompose_ are antonyms for _thriving_.

4. Discharge and _dismiss_ are antonyms for _employ_.

5. Incentive and _____ are antonyms for _____.

6. Agreement and _____ are antonyms for _deny_.

7. Pollute and _contaminat_ are antonyms for _purify_.

8. Profess and _affirm_ are antonyms for _deny_.

9. Notable and _noteworthy_ are antonyms for _insignific_.

10. Shriveled and _____ are antonyms for _____.

11. Feasible and _____ are antonyms for _____.

12. Thriving and _prosperian_ are antonyms for _deternen_.

4 Two Environmentalists. Use the words listed at the left to complete this information about famous environmentalists.

career
conservation
submit
century
ecologists

1. **Rachel Carson** was one of the great _ecologist_ of the twentieth _century_. She began her _career_ as a biologist with the U.S. Bureau of Fisheries, but she had always wanted to be a writer. During her time with the bureau, she would sometimes _submit_ articles about _conservation_ to newspapers.

regulate
environment
well-being
inconvenient
advocate

2. Carson held strong opinions about people's relationship with the _environ_. She emphasized the need to _regulate_ the "forces of destruction." She was referring to our approach to managing nature by killing whatever was _inconvenient_ for us, such as insects. She became an _advocate_ for wildlife management who looked after the _well-being_ of the "fish as well as that of the fisherman."

controversial
latter
culmination
enabled
devoted

3. Carson published her first book, *Under the Sea-Wind,* in 1941, and a second called *The Sea Around Us* in 1951. The _latter_ was so successful, it _enabled_ Carson to leave her government job. She _devoted_ her time to writing. Her most famous as well as her most _controversial_ book was *Silent Spring,* in 1962. It marked the _culmination_ of her career.

pesticides
consciousness
forbidding
condemned
comprehend –

4. In *Silent Spring,* Carson _condemned_ the overuse of _pesticides_. She drew a _forbidding_ picture of a world poisoned by chemicals. Her words were written clearly, so people who were not scientists could _comprehend_ the significance of what was happening. Her words pushed this issue into people's _consciousness_, and set off a storm of protest. She is sometimes called the mother of the modern environmental movement.

5. **Edward Abbey** is a(n) _intriguing_ character whose impact on the environmental movement may have been as great as Carson's. However, his public _persona_ stands in _stark_ contrast to hers. He was a(n) _rebel_ and he seemed to relish such a(n) _characterization_.

Word bank: stark, personality, characterization, rebel, intriguing

6. Abbey always claimed to love writing, but it wasn't always _obvious_ while he was in school. Twice he _flunked_ his _journ[alism]_ class in high school. His interests seemed to _gravitate_ more toward social action than writing. In _graduate_ school, his master's thesis was titled "Anarchism and the Morality of Violence."

Word bank: gravitate, journalism, obvious, flunked, graduate

7. Although Abbey liked writing and was naturally _inclined_ toward social _activism_, his real love was for the American Southwest. He first saw it in 1948 when he _hitchhiked_ through the region. His life thereafter was _inseparable_ from that _passion_.

Word bank: hitchhiked, activism, inclined, passion, inseparable

8. Abbey's books and essays show a(n) _uncomp[romising]_ devotion to the Southwest. They _evoke_ his joy in exploring the _canyons_ and mountains of the region. They also show a(n) _commit[ment]_ to protecting it against every action that might spoil it. His words _inspired_ generations of devoted environmental activists.

Word bank: evoke, canyons, inspired, commitment, uncompromising

Words for Study

Cascade	penalizing	traversed	caches
lode	consolation	detritus	succulent
transcendent	terrain	macabre	aftermath
precedence	ravine	bestrewn	hydraulic

The Good Earth: Two Points of View

by John McPhee

Most people will agree that measures need to be taken to conserve our precious natural resources. The issue that people disagree about is—what measures should be taken?

The writer, John McPhee, once climbed the mountains in the Cascade Range, an area rich in copper which is situated in the Western United States. With him were two men whose ideas about the uses of natural resources were quite different. One of these men was David Brower, the leader of a conservation organization called Friends of the Earth. The other was Charles Park, a mineral engineer.

As you read Mr. McPhee's description of this expedition, notice the different viewpoints presented by Brower and Park.

* * *

Near the southern base of Plummer Mountain and in the deep valley between Plummer Mountain and Glacier Peak—that is, in the central foreground of the view that we were looking at from Cloudy Pass—was the lode of copper that Kennecott would mine, and to do so the company would make an open pit at least two thousand four hundred feet from rim to rim.

Park said, "A hole in the ground will not materially hurt this scenery."

Brower stood up. "None of the experts on scenic resources will agree with you," he said.

"This is one of the few remaining great wildernesses in the lower forty-eight. Copper is not a transcendent value here."

"Without copper, we'd be in a pretty sorry situation."

"If that deposit didn't exist, we'd get by without it."

"I would prefer the mountain as it is, but the copper is there."

"If we're down to where we have to take copper from places this beautiful, we're down pretty far."

"Minerals are where you find them. The quantities are finite. It's criminal to waste minerals when the standard of living of your people depends upon them. A mine cannot move. It is fixed by nature. So it has to take precedence over any other use. If there were a copper deposit in Yellowstone Park, I'd recommend mining it. Proper use of minerals is essential. You have to go get them where they are. Our standard of living is based on this."

"For a fifty-year cycle, yes. But for the long term, no. We have to drop our standard of living, so that people a thousand years from now can have any standard of living at all."

A breeze coming off the nearby acres of snow felt cool but not chilling in the sunshine, and rumpled the white hair of the two men.

"I am not for penalizing people today for the sake of future generations," Park said.

"I really am," said Brower. "That's where we differ."

"Yes, that's where we disagree. In 1910, the Brazilian government said they were going to preserve the iron ore in Minas Gerais, because the earth would run short of it in the future. People— thousands and thousands of people in Minas Gerais—were actually starving, and they were living over one of the richest ore deposits in the world, a fifteen-billion-ton reserve. They're mining it now,

and people there are prospering. But in the past it was poor consolation to people who were going hungry to say that in the future it was going to be better. You have to use these things when you have them. You have to know where they are, and use them. People, in the future, will go for the copper here."

"The kids who are in Congress in the future should make that decision, and if it's theirs to make I don't think they'll go for the copper here," Brower said.

"Sure they will. They'll have to, if people are going to expect to have telephones, electric lights, airplanes, television sets, radios, central heating, air-conditioning, automobiles. And you *know* people will want these things. I didn't invent them. I just know where the copper is."

Brower swung his pack up onto his back. "Pretend the copper deposit down there doesn't exist," he said. "Then what would you do? What are you going to do when it's gone?"

"You're trying to make everything wilderness," Park said.

"No, I'm not. I'm trying to keep at least two percent of the terrain as wilderness."

"Two percent is a lot."

"Two percent is under pavement."

"Basically, our difference is that I feel we can't stop all this—we must direct it. You feel we must stop it."

"I feel we should go back, recycle, do things over again, and do better, even if it costs more. We mine things and don't use them again. We coat the surface of the earth—with beer cans and chemicals, asphalt and old television sets."

"We *are* recycling copper, but we don't have enough."

"When we knock buildings down, we don't take the copper out. Every building that comes down could be a copper mine. But we don't take the copper out. We go after fresh metal. We destroy that mountain."

"How can you ruin a mountain like Glacier Peak?" Park lifted his pick toward the mountain. "You *can't* ruin it," he went on, waving the pick. "Look at the Swiss mountains. Who could ruin *them*? A mine would not hurt this country—not with proper housekeeping."

Brower started on down the trail. We retrieved our packs and caught up with him. About five hundred feet below us and a mile ahead was another pass—Suiattle Pass—and to reach it we had to go down into a big ravine and up the other side. There were long silences, measured by the sound of boots on the trail. From time to time, the pick rang out against a rock.

Brower said, "Would America have to go without much to leave its wilderness unspoiled?"

We traversed a couple of switchbacks and approached the bottom of the ravine. Then Park said, "Where they are more easily accessible, deposits have been found and are being—or have been—mined."

We had seen such a mine near Lake Chelan, in the eastern part of the mountains. The Howe Sound Mining Company established an underground copper mine there in 1938, built a village and called it Holden. The Holden mine was abandoned in 1957. We had hiked past its remains on our way to the wilderness area. Against a backdrop of snowy peaks, two flat-topped hills of earth detritus broke the landscape. One was the dump where all the rock had been put that was removed before the miners reached the ore body. The other consisted of tailings—crushed rock that had been through the Holden mill and had yielded copper. What remained of the mill itself was a macabre skeleton of bent, twisted, rusted beams. Wooden buildings and sheds were rotting and gradually collapsing. The area was bestrewn with huge flakes of corrugated iron, rusted rails, rusted ore carts, old barrels. Although there was no way for an automobile to get to Holden except by barge up Lake Chelan and then on a dirt road to the village, we saw there a high pile of gutted and rusted automobiles, which themselves had originally been rock in the earth and, in the end, in Holden, were crumbling slowly back into the ground.

Park hit a ledge with the pick. We were moving up the other side of the ravine now. The going was steep, and the pace slowed. Brower said, "We saw that at Holden."

I counted twenty-two steps watching the backs of Brower's legs, above the red tops of gray socks. He was moving slower than I would have. I was close behind him. His legs, blue-veined, seemed less pink than they had the day before. They were sturdy but not athletically shapely. Brower used to put food caches in various places in the High Sierra and go from one to another for weeks at a time. He weighed two hundred and twelve pounds now, and he must have wished he were one-eighty.

Park said, "Holden is the sort of place that gave mining a bad name. This has been happening in the West for the past hundred years, but it doesn't have to happen. Poor housekeeping is poor housekeeping wherever you find it. I don't care if it's a mine or a kitchen. Traditionally, when mining companies finished in a place they just walked off. Responsible groups are not going to do that anymore. They're not going to leave trash; they're not going to deface the countryside. Think of that junk! If I had enough money, I'd come up here and clean it up."

I thought how neat Park's house, his lawn, and his gardens are—his roses, his lemon tree, his two hundred varieties of cactus. The name of the street he lives on is Arcadia Place. Park is a member of the Cactus and Succulent Society of America. He hit a fallen tree with the hammer end.

"It's one god-awful mess," Brower said.

"That old mill could be cleaned up," Park said. "Grass could be planted on the dump and the tailings."

Suiattle Pass was now less than a quarter mile ahead of us. I thought of Brower, as a child, on his first trip to the Sierra Nevada. His father drove him there from Berkeley in a 1916 Maxwell. On the western slopes, they saw both the aftermath and the actual operations of hydraulic mining for gold. Men with hoses eight inches in diameter directed water with such force against the hillsides that large parts of the hills themselves fell away as slurry.

"Holden was abandoned in 1957, and no plants of any kind have caught on the dump and the tailings," Brower said.

Holden, in its twenty years of metal production, brought out of the earth ten million tons of rock— enough to make a hundred thousand tons of copper, enough to wire Kansas City.

Park said, "You could put a little fertilizer on— something to get it started."

When we reached the pass, we stood for a moment and looked again at Glacier Peak and, far below us, the curving white line of the Suiattle. Park said, "When you create a mine, there are two things you can't avoid: a hole in the ground and a dump for waste rock. Those are two things you can't avoid."

Brower said, "Except by not doing it at all."

1 Understanding the Reading. Answer the following questions. Where appropriate, use good sentence form and information from the reading to support your answers.

1. With the help of context clues and a dictionary, write a brief definition for each of the italicized words below.

   a. ". . . we had to go down into a big *ravine* and up the other side."

   _____

   b. "We traversed a couple of *switchbacks* . . ."

   _____

   c. ". . . two flat-topped hills of earth *detritus* broke the landscape."

   _____

   d. "Men with hoses eight inches in diameter directed water with such force against the hillsides that large parts of the hills themselves fell away as *slurry*."

   _____

2. What is the setting for this reading? _____

_____

3. What is about to happen in this setting? _____

_____

4. What is David Brower's occupation? _____

5. What is Charles Park's occupation? _____

6. Why does Park use the example of Minas Gerais? _____

_____

_____

7. Explain how Brower and Park agree in their comments about Holden.

_____

_____

_____

_____

8. Explain the basic disagreement between Brower and Park in their viewpoints on the uses of natural resources.

_____

_____

_____

_____

_____

What do you think? What is your point of view about this discussion of natural resources?

_____

_____

_____

_____

_____

_____

2 The Earth: A Cartoonist's Point of View. Study the cartoon, and answer the questions that follow.

"You take a left by that tire, then bear right by the sunken rowboat 'til you come to an abandoned shopping cart by a large pile of beer cans...."

1. How would David Brower probably respond to this cartoon?

_____

_____

2. How would Charles Park probably respond to this cartoon?

_____

_____

3. Describe your response to this cartoon.

_____

_____

3 Word Families. Use the words listed at the left to complete each sentence correctly.

vigor
vigorous

1. As the _____ early American settlers worked to tame and exploit the American wilderness, little did they realize that their great-grandchildren would, with equal _____, have to resolve problems they had created.

prosper
prosperous
prosperity

2. "We cannot continue our style of _____" claims a respected environmentalist, adding the warning that to _____ at the expense of our precious resources is the least _____ of courses in the long run.

consistent
inconsistent
consistently
consistency

3. "_____ is the key to self-mastery," another _____ reminds audiences attending her lectures. "And it is tragic that we have been so _____ in exploiting the land for our own selfish gain and so _____ in our attempts to remedy this disastrous situation."

emphasize
emphasis
emphatic

4. It may be true that public education and the media _____ environmental issues more than they ever have; but ecologists like David Brower are _____ in their assertion that this _____ isn't strong enough.

probable
improbable
probability

5. Even though ecologists stress the strong _____ that we will exhaust our natural resources, many Americans assume this possibility to be _____ because they believe that scientific solutions to environmental questions are highly _____.

complicate
complicated
complication

6. Many ecologists agree that protecting the environment is further _____ because the interests of different groups vary; these groups _____ the basic issues and entangle environmental discussions in one _____ after another.

4 America's Resources. Use a dictionary or the Internet to help you complete these descriptions of some of America's beautiful resources.

1. Located in southern _____, the Everglades, one of the world's largest swamps, was uninhabited until the Seminole Indians fled to the area in 1842 after wars with U.S. troops and white settlers.

2. Niagara Falls consists of two main falls, the Canadian or _____ Falls and the American Falls. In 1683 a Roman Catholic priest wrote: "These waters foam and boil in a fearful manner."

3. _____, _____, _____, _____, and _____ form the largest group of freshwater lakes in the world. Called the Great Lakes, they occupy an area of 94,710 square miles on either side of the U.S.-Canadian border.

4. The Spanish explorer _____ de Soto was the first European to travel on the Mississippi River. He crossed the river in 1541 while searching for gold. The word *Mississippi* comes from an Indian word meaning "big river."

5. Situated in the state of _____, the Mesabi Range is a chain of hills that was once one of the great iron ore regions of the world. *Mesabi* is an Indian word meaning "hidden giant."

6. Situated in southwestern _____ and northeastern Wyoming, the Sioux Indians called them the Black Hills because the pine forests covering the slopes looked black when seen from the plains. In these hills is the town of Lead, home of the largest gold mine in the United States.

7. In the year _____, Congress established Yellowstone National Park. This is the oldest national park and is noted for its scenic beauty, wildlife, and geysers.

8. Located in northwestern _____, Great Salt Lake is a natural wonder of the world. Although fed by freshwater streams, this inland sea is saltier than the ocean.

9. A gorge formed by the _____ River, the Grand Canyon was named by John Wesley Powell, an American geologist who led an expedition through the vast canyon in 1869.

10. Located in central _____, the Painted Desert is a brilliantly colored region extending about 200 miles along the Little Colorado River. This region is particularly beautiful at sunrise and sunset.

11. Located on the island of _____, Mauna Loa is the world's largest volcano. Its longest eruption, which occurred in 1855–56, lasted for 18 months.

12. Named after _____ McKinley, the twenty-fifth president of the United States, Mount McKinley is often called "the top of the continent" because it has the highest summit in North America. Mount McKinley is situated in central Alaska.

5 Can You Crack the Code? Copper is a valuable metal that was mentioned in the reading. Can you crack the code of this puzzle and identify some other valuable metals? The code is the same for all the metals. When you have guessed a metal, fill in the letters and use these letters for the other metals until you have cracked the code for the entire group. Use the facts about the metals to help you crack the code. The first one is done to get you started.

C O P P E R
‾A‾ ‾E‾ ‾Z‾ ‾Z‾ ‾T‾ ‾F‾

1. An excellent conductor of heat and electricity, this metal is widely used for electrical wiring and water piping.

___ ___ ___ ___
K E D J

2. One of the first known metals, the possession of this attractive bright yellow metal has been a mark of wealth for thousands of years.

___ ___ ___
Y C M

3. Because it can easily be formed into complex shapes, this metal is used in the manufacture of a variety of products such as cans, paper clips, safety pins, and utensils.

___ ___ ___ ___
C F E M

4. One of the cheapest and most useful metals, this metal is the basic material of steel.

___ ___ ___ ___
D T I J

5. In spite of its usefulness, if too much of this metal builds up in the body, poisoning results. Thus, the U.S. government now restricts the amount of this metal in paint and gasoline, as well as the amount that can be released into the air.

___ ___ ___ ___ ___ ___
W T F A G F Q

6. Named for the swift messenger of the gods in Roman mythology, this metal is also called quicksilver because, unlike any other metal, it is a liquid at room temperature.

___ ___ ___ ___ ___ ___
O C D B T F

7. Harder than gold but softer than copper, this metal is used in jewelry and tableware. Despite the advancements in digital photography, this is still used in coating and developing film.

___ ___ ___ ___ ___ ___ ___
A X F E W C G W

8. Hard, brittle, and gray, this metal is used to plate automobile bumpers, door handles, and trim.

___ ___ ___ ___ ___ ___ ___ ___
W I M K I M T O T

9. A plentiful element found throughout much of the earth's crust, this metal is used in the manufacture of dry cell batteries and many dyes.

___ ___ ___ ___ ___ ___
A E H I D Y

10. A rare metal, one of its most widely known uses is for the treatment of cancer and the diagnosis of certain diseases.

Words for Study

Antaeus	initials	domain	enterprises
sedan	resolute	vacant	laborious
parapet	bale	contemplate	dilating
robust	stolid	distracted	toilsome

LESSON 14
Antaeus: Part I

by Borden Deal

This was during the wartime, when lots of people were coming North for jobs in factories and war industries, when people moved around a lot more than they do now and sometimes kids were thrown into new groups and new lives that were completely different from anything they had ever known before. I remember this one kid, T.J. his name was, from somewhere down South, whose family moved into our building during that time. They'd come North with everything they owned piled into the back seat of an old-model sedan that you wouldn't expect could make the trip, with T.J. and his three younger sisters riding shakily on top of the load of junk.

Our building was just like all the others there, with families crowded into a few rooms, and I guess there were twenty-five or thirty kids about my age in that one building. Of course, there were a few of us who formed a gang and ran together all the time after school, and I was the one who brought T.J. in and started the whole thing.

The building right next door to us was a factory where they made walking dolls. It was a low building with a flat, tarred roof that had a parapet all around it about head-high and we'd found out a long time before that no one, not even the watchman, paid any attention to the roof because it was higher than any of the other buildings around.

So my gang used the roof as a headquarters. We could get up there by crossing over to the fire escape from our own roof on a plank and then going on up. It was a secret place for us, where nobody else could go without our permission.

I remember the day I first took T.J. up there to meet the gang. He was a stocky, robust kid with a shock of white hair, nothing sissy about him except his voice—he talked in this slow, gentle voice like you never heard before. He talked different from any of us and you noticed it right away. But I liked him anyway, so I told him to come on up.

We climbed up over the parapet and dropped down on the roof. The rest of the gang were already there.

"Hi," I said. I jerked my thumb at T.J., "He just moved into the building yesterday."

He just stood there, not scared or anything, just looking, like the first time you see somebody you're not sure you're going to like.

"Hi," Blackie said. "Where are you from?"

"Marion County," T.J. said. We laughed. "Marion County?" I said. "Where's that?"

He looked at me for a moment like I was a stranger, too. "It's in Alabama," he said, like I ought to know where it was.

"What's your name?" Charley said.

"T.J.," he said, looking back at him. He had pale blue eyes that looked washed-out but he looked directly at Charley, waiting for his reaction. He'll be all right, I thought. No sissy in him—except that voice. Who ever talked like that?

"T.J.," Blackie said. "That's just initials. What's your real name? Nobody in the world has just initials."

"I do," he said. "And they're T.J. That's all the name I got."

His voice was resolute with knowledge of his rightness and for a moment no one had anything to say. T.J. looked around at the rooftop and down at the black tar under his feet. "Down yonder where I come from," he said, "we played out in the woods. Don't you-all have no woods around here?"

"Naw," Blackie said. "There's the park a few blocks over, but it's full of kids and cops and old women. You can't do a thing."

T.J. kept looking at the tar under his feet. "You mean you ain't got no fields to raise nothing in?—no watermelons or nothing?"

"Naw," I said scornfully. "What do you want to grow something for? The folks can buy everything they need at the store."

He looked at me again with that strange, unknowing look. "In Marion County," he said, "I had my own acre of cotton and my own acre of corn. It was mine to plant and make ever' year."

He sounded like it was something to be proud of, and in some obscure way it made the rest of us angry. "Jesus!" Blackie said. "Who'd want to have their own acre of cotton and corn? That's just work. What can you do with an acre of cotton and corn?"

T.J. looked at him. "Well, you get part of the bale offen your acre," he said seriously. "And I fed my acre of corn to my calf."

We didn't really know what he was talking about, so we were more puzzled than angry; otherwise, I guess, we'd have chased him off the roof and wouldn't let him be part of our gang. But he was strange and different and we were all attracted by his stolid sense of rightness and belonging, maybe by the strange softness of his voice contrasting our own tones of speech into harshness.

He moved his foot against the black tar. "We could make our own field right here," he said softly, thoughtfully. "Come spring we could raise us what we want to—watermelons and garden truck and no telling what all."

"You'd have to be a good farmer to make these tar roofs grow any watermelons," I said. We all laughed.

But T.J. looked serious. "We could haul us some dirt up here," he said. "And spread it out even and water it and before you know it we'd have us a crop in here." He looked at us intently. "Wouldn't that be fun?"

"They wouldn't let us," Blackie said quickly.

"I thought you said this was you-all's roof," T.J. said to me. "That you-all could do anything you wanted to up here."

"They've never bothered us," I said. I felt the idea beginning to catch fire in me. It was a big idea and it took a while for it to sink in but the more I thought about it the better I liked it. "Say," I said to the gang. "He might have something there. Just make us a regular roof garden, with flowers and grass and trees and everything. And all ours, too," I said. "We wouldn't let anybody up here except the ones we wanted to."

"It'd take a while to grow trees," T.J. said quickly, but we weren't paying any attention to him. They were all talking about it suddenly, all excited with the idea after I'd put it in a way they could catch hold of it. Only rich people had roof gardens, we knew, and the idea of our own private domain excited them.

"We could bring it up in sacks and boxes," Blackie said. "We'd have to do it while the folks weren't paying any attention to us, for we'd have to come up to the roof of our building and then cross over with it."

"Where could we get the dirt?" somebody said worriedly.

"Out of those vacant lots over close to the school," Blackie said. "Nobody'd notice if we scraped it up."

I slapped T.J. on the shoulder. "Man, you had a wonderful idea," I said, and everybody grinned at him, remembering that he had started it. "Our own private roof garden."

He grinned back. "It'll be ourn," he said. "All ourn." Then he looked thoughtful again. "Maybe I can lay my hands on some cotton seed, too. You think we could raise us some cotton?"

We'd started big projects before at one time or another, like any gang of kids, but they'd always petered out for lack of organization and direction. But this one didn't—somehow or other T.J. kept it going all through the winter months. He kept talking about the watermelons and the cotton we'd raise, come spring, and when even that wouldn't work he'd switch around to my idea of flowers and grass and trees, though he was always honest enough to add that it'd take a while to get any trees started. He always had it on his mind and he'd mention it in school, getting them lined up to carry dirt that afternoon, saying in a casual way that he reckoned a few more weeks ought to see the job through.

Our little area of private earth grew slowly. T.J. was smart enough to start in one corner of the building,

heaping up the carried earth two or three feet thick, so that we had an immediate result to look at, to contemplate with awe. Some of the evenings T.J. alone was carrying earth up to the building, the rest of the gang distracted by other enterprises or interests, but T.J. kept plugging along on his own and eventually we'd all come back to him again and then our own little acre would grow more rapidly.

He was careful about the kind of dirt he'd let us carry up there and more than once he dumped a sandy load over the parapet into the areaway below because it wasn't good enough. He found out the kinds of earth in all the vacant lots for blocks around. He'd pick it up and feel it and smell it, frozen though it was sometimes and then he'd say it was good growing soil or it wasn't worth anything and we'd have to go on somewhere else.

Thinking about it now, I don't see how he kept us at it. It was hard work, lugging paper sacks and boxes of dirt all the way up the stairs of our own buildings, keeping out of the way of the grown-ups so they wouldn't catch on to what we were doing. They probably wouldn't have cared, for they didn't pay much attention to us, but we wanted to keep it secret anyway. Then we had to go through the trap door to our roof, teeter over a plank to the fire escape, then climb two or three stories to the parapet and drop down onto the roof. All that for a small pile of earth that sometimes didn't seem worth the effort.

But T.J. kept the vision bright within us, his words shrewd and calculated toward the fulfillment of his dream; and he worked harder than any of us. He seemed driven toward a goal that we couldn't see, a particular point in time that would be definitely marked by signs and wonders that only he could see.

The laborious earth just lay there during the cold months, inert and lifeless, the clods lumpy and cold under our feet when we walked over it. But one day it rained and afterward there was a softness in the air and the earth was live and giving again with moisture and warmth. That evening T.J. smelled the air, his nostrils dilating with the odor of the earth under his feet.

"It's spring," he said and there was a gladness rising in his voice that filled us all with the same feeling. "It's mighty late for it, but it's spring. I'd just about decided it wasn't never gonna get here at all."

We were all sniffing at the air, too, trying to smell it the way that T.J. did, and I can still remember the sweet odor of the earth under our feet. It was the first time in my life that spring and spring earth had meant anything to me. I looked at T.J. then, knowing in a faint way the hunger within him through the toilsome winter months, knowing the dream that lay behind his plan. He was a new Antaeus, preparing his own bed of strength.

"Planting time," he said. "We'll have to find us some seed."

1 Understanding the Story. Put the letter of the best answer on the line.

1. The narrator of "Antaeus" is _____.
   a. a member of the gang.
   b. Blackie
   c. T.J.
   d. Charlie

2. "Antaeus" takes place during _____.
   a. the Gay Nineties
   b. the Roaring Twenties
   c. the Great Depression
   d. World War II

3. The gang used the doll factory roof for their headquarters because _____.
   a. it was near everyone's home
   b. it was protected by a parapet
   c. the building was deserted
   d. no one bothered them there

4. Which word *least* describes T.J.? _____.
   a. robust
   b. resolute
   c. sissy
   d. stocky

5. What does the narrator find most unusual about T.J.? _____
   a. his background
   b. his cowardice
   c. his voice
   d. his name

6. What does T.J. find most unusual about his new environment? _____
   a. the harshness of the people
   b. the lack of open land
   c. the number of policemen
   d. the pace of city life

7. The gang's initial reaction to T.J.'s description of his crops is _____.
   a. admiration
   b. jealousy
   c. anger
   d. worry

8. The narrator _____ T.J.'s idea of creating a garden.

    a. disagrees with

    b. rejects

    c. questions

    d. supports

9. Which of the following indicates that T.J. knows something about farming? _____

    a. He rejects some of the dirt.

    b. He avoids adults while carrying dirt to the roof.

    c. He successfully organizes the gang to carry dirt to the roof.

    d. He works harder than the other gang members.

10. *Antaeus* is the name of a figure in Greek mythology. Based on what happens in the first part of the story, which description of Antaeus is correct? _____

    a. the god of the underworld and dispenser of earthly riches

    b. a giant whose strength was renewed by contact with the earth

    c. a fabled king whose power enabled him to turn everything he touched to gold

    d. a hero noted for his great strength and for having accomplished twelve gigantic tasks imposed upon him

2 What Do You Think? Answer the following questions in good sentence form. Use details from the story and personal explanations to support your answers.

1. What qualities does T.J. have that help to make the gang's project a success?

    _____

    _____

    _____

    _____

    _____

2. What reasons do you think the boys have for continuing to work on the project?

    _____

    _____

    _____

    _____

    _____

3 Word Relationships. On the line, write the letter of the answer that best completes each statement.

1. Omnivore is to bear as _____.
   a. carnivore is to hippopotamus
   b. parasite is to flea
   c. herbivore is to spider
   d. shark is to scavenger

2. Switzerland is to Europe as _____.
   a. Berkeley is to the United States
   b. Brazil is to Central America
   c. Egypt is to Africa
   d. Holland is to Scandinavia

3. Sand is to granular as _____.
   a. lead is to toxic
   b. Gila monster is to mythical
   c. parapet is to obscure
   d. crabgrass is to brackish

4. Malaria is to malady as _____.
   a. angler is to mariner
   b. boulder is to detritus
   c. mineral is to organism
   d. copper is to metal

5. Hunter is to game as _____.
   a. lode is to miner
   b. pallbearer is to funeral
   c. predator is to prey
   d. tarantula is to habitat

6. Laborious is to toilsome as _____.
   a. dilated is to compressed
   b. determined is to resolute
   c. robust is to stolid
   d. toxic is to moribund

7. Cascade is to waterfall as _____.
   a. canyon is to estuary
   b. glen is to meadow
   c. mountain is to range
   d. ravine is to gorge

8. Distracted is to attentive as _____.
   a. accessible is to remote
   b. fearsome is to fearless
   c. improbable is to impossible
   d. predatory is to instinctive

9. Seattle is to Washington as _____.
   a. Carson City is to Montana
   b. New Orleans is to Louisiana
   c. Charleston is to North Carolina
   d. Pittsburgh is to Virginia

10. Consolation is to comfort as _____.
    a. DDT is to contamination
    b. domain is to terrain
    c. enterprise is to undertaking
    d. pollination is to predation

4 From the Earth. To identify the plants that match the following descriptions, *choose one* word from **List A**, and add a word from **List B** to it. Refer to a dictionary or the Internet for those items that give you difficulty. The first one is done to get you started.

List A

arrow

buck

fox

golden

hearts

✓hem

horse

penny

spear

sun

List B

ease

flower

glove

✓lock

mint

radish

rod

root

royal

wheat

_____ **hemlock** _____

1. T.J. and his friends would not have chosen this poisonous herb for their garden. Unfortunately, this plant strongly resembles parsley, and children have been poisoned when they made whistles or peashooters from its hollow stems.

2. Grown as a field crop for its seeds, these seeds are then ground into flour, mostly for pancake mixtures.

3. This mint plant has clusters of small, purplish flowers and yields an oil which is used in perfumes, medicines, candy, and chewing gum.

4. Only soybeans yield more vegetable oil than this plant which has showy yellow flowers. Its seeds are used in making margarine, cooking oil, and snack foods.

5. The leaves of this poisonous plant, when dried, are the source of the drug digitalis—a medicine that is useful for certain heart ailments.

6. Some Americans have suggested that this plant with its clusters of small yellow flowers should be proclaimed our national flower. Thomas A. Edison devised a method for extracting rubber from this plant, but it proved too costly for commercial use.

7. The root of this common, tropical plant is used to make a light starch which serves as an ingredient in puddings, pie fillings, and other desserts. American Indians used this root to absorb poison from arrow wounds.

8. The shredded or grated root of this coarse plant is often preserved in vinegar in order to keep its sharp, biting odor and taste.

9. This herb of the mint family yields an oil that is used to make various medicines, perfumes, and mosquito repellents.

10. This lovely pansy has several other romantic names such as "kiss-me-at-the-garden-gate," "love's idleness," and "Johnny-jump-up."

5 Arbor Day. Use the words listed at the left to complete the paragraphs below about Arbor Day.

pioneers
agriculture
necessity
territory

1. In 1854, J. Sterling Morton and his wife moved from Detroit to the Nebraska _____. Morton was a journalist who used his position as newspaper editor to spread information about _____ and trees. To the _____, trees were a(n) _____—for shelter from the wind and sun and also for building materials.

encouraged
observe
participating
proposed

2. Morton _____ people to plant trees and _____ a tree-planting holiday. More than a million trees were planted in Nebraska on the first Arbor Day in April of 1872. In the coming years, other states passed laws to _____ Arbor Day, and by 1882 schools all across the nation were _____.

region
national
research
beautify

3. _____ Arbor Day is the last Friday in April, but many states observe Arbor Day on different dates. Do you know when Arbor Day is in your state? Do you know your state tree? Before you plant a tree, make sure you are planting the right tree in the right place. Trees do more than just _____ your yard. Do some _____ at the library or online to find out what types of trees grow best in your _____.

essential
ecologist
pollutants
diversity
activist

4. You don't have to be a(n) _____ or a(n) _____ to plant trees. Trees are _____ for life on Earth. Just one acre of trees produces enough oxygen each day for 18 people. Trees help to cleanse the air of _____ and pollens. Trees are also good for local wildlife—the greatest _____ in bird population is in areas where there are many large trees of different varieties.

deforestation
habitats
serious
recovering
worldwide

5. Tree-planting can help to reverse some of the damage from _____. There are _____ organizations that plant trees where they are needed. Other areas ripe for tree-planting include former farm fields, forests _____ from wildfires, areas that have suffered _____ storm damage, war-torn cities, and natural wildlife _____.

Words for Study

hesitant	desecrated	levied	infinitely
ventilators	violation	sterile	sterility
sowing	principles	finality	contemplation
bravado	esoteric	frenzied	anonymous

LESSON 15
Antaeus: Part II

by Borden Deal

"What do we do?" Blackie said. "How do we do it?"

"First we'll have to break up the clods," T.J. said. "That won't be hard to do. Then we plant the seed and after a while they come up. Then you got you a crop." He frowned. "But you ain't got it raised yet. You got to tend it and hoe it and take care of it and all the time it's growing and growing, while you're awake and while you're asleep. Then you lay it by when it's growed and let it ripen and then you got a crop."

"There's those wholesale seed houses over on Sixth," I said. "We could probably swipe some grass seed over there."

T.J. looked at the earth. "You-all seem mighty set on raising some grass," he said. "I ain't never put no effort into that. I spent all my life trying not to raise grass."

"But it's pretty," Blackie said. "We could play on it and take sun baths. Like having our own lawn. Lots of people got lawns."

"Well," T.J. said. He looked at the rest of us, hesitant for the first time. He kept on looking at us for a moment. "I did have it in mind to raise some corn and vegetables. But we'll plant grass."

He was smart. He knew where to give in. And I don't suppose it made any difference to him, really. He just wanted to grow something, even if it was grass.

"Of course," he said, "I do think we ought to plant a row of watermelons. They'd be mighty nice to eat while we was a-laying on that grass."

We all laughed. "All right," I said. "We'll plant us a row of watermelons."

Things went very quickly then. Perhaps half the roof was covered with the earth, the half that wasn't broken by ventilators, and we swiped pocketfuls of grass seed from the open bins in the wholesale seed house, mingling among the buyers on Saturdays and during the school lunch hour. T.J. showed us how to prepare the earth, breaking up the clods and smoothing it and sowing the grass seed. It looked rich and black now with moisture, receiving of the seed, and it seemed that the grass sprang up overnight, pale green in the early spring.

We couldn't keep from looking at it, unable to believe that we had created this delicate growth. We looked at T.J. with understanding now, knowing the fulfillment of the plan he had carried alone within his mind. We had worked without full understanding of the task but he had known all the time.

We found that we couldn't walk or play on the delicate blades, as we had expected to, but we didn't mind. It was enough just to look at it, to realize that it was the work of our own hands, and each evening the whole gang was there, trying to measure the growth that had been achieved that day.

One time a foot was placed on the plot of ground— one time only, Blackie stepping onto it with sudden bravado. Then he looked at the crushed blades and there was shame in his face. He did not do it again. This was his grass, too, and not to be desecrated. No one said anything, for it was not necessary.

T.J. had reserved a small section for watermelons and he was still trying to find some seed for it. The wholesale house didn't have any watermelon seed and we didn't know where we could lay our hands on them. T.J. shaped the earth into mounds, ready to receive them, three mounds lying in a straight line along the edge of the grass plot.

We had just about decided that we'd have to buy the seed if we were to get them. It was a violation of our principles, but we were anxious to get the watermelons started. Somewhere or other, T.J. got

his hands on a seed catalogue and brought it one evening to our roof garden.

"We can order them now," he said, showing us the catalogue. "Look!"

We all crowded around, looking at the fat, green watermelons pictured in full color on the pages. Some of them were split open, showing the red, tempting meat, making our mouths water.

"Now we got to scrape up some seed money," T.J. said, looking at us. "I got a quarter. How much you-all got?"

We made up a couple of dollars between us and T.J. nodded his head, "That'll be more than enough. Now we got to decide what kind to get. I think them Kleckley Sweets. What do you-all think?"

He was going into esoteric matters beyond our reach. We hadn't even known there were different kinds of melons. So we just nodded our heads and agreed that Yes, we thought the Kleckley Sweets, too.

"I'll order them tonight," T.J. said. "We ought to have them in a few days."

"What are you boys doing up here?" an adult voice said behind us.

It startled us, for no one had ever come up here before, in all the time we had been using the roof of the factory. We jerked around and saw three men standing near the trap door at the other end of the roof. They weren't policemen, or night watchmen, but three men in plump business suits, looking at us. They walked toward us.

"What are you boys doing up here?" the one in the middle said again.

We stood still, guilt heavy among us, levied by the tone of voice, and looked at the three strangers.

The men stared at the grass flourishing behind us. *"What's this?"* the man said. *"How did this get up here?"*

"Sure is growing good, ain't it?" T.J. said conversationally. "We planted it."

The men kept looking at the grass as if they didn't believe it. It was a thick carpet over the earth now, a patch of deep greenness startling in the sterile industrial surroundings.

"Yes sir," T.J. said proudly. "We toted the earth up here and planted that grass." He fluttered the seed catalogue. "And we're fixing to plant us some watermelon."

The man looked at him then, his eyes strange and faraway. "What do you mean, putting this on the roof of my building?" he said. *"Do you want to go to jail?"*

T.J. looked shaken. The rest of us were silent, frightened by the authority of his voice. We had grown up aware of adult authority, of policemen and night watchmen and teachers, and this man sounded like all the others. But it was a new thing to T.J.

"Well, you wan't using the roof," T.J. said. He paused a moment and added shrewdly, "So we just thought to pretty it up a little bit."

"And sag it so I'd have to rebuild it," the man said sharply. He started turning away, saying to another man behind him, "See that all that junk is shoveled off by tomorrow."

"Yes sir," the man said.

T.J. started forward. *"You can't do that,"* he said. *"We toted it up here and it's our earth. We planted it and raised it and toted it up here."*

The man stared at him coldly. "But it's my building," he said. "It's to be shoveled off tomorrow."

"It's our earth," T.J. said desperately. *"You ain't got no right!"*

The men walked on without listening and descended clumsily through the trap door. T.J. stood looking after them, his body tense with anger, until they had disappeared. They wouldn't even argue with him, wouldn't let him defend his earth-rights.

He turned to us. "We won't let 'em do it," he said fiercely. "We'll stay up here all day tomorrow and the day after that and we won't let 'em do it."

We just looked at him. We knew that there was no stopping it. He saw it in our faces, and his face wavered for a moment before he gripped it into determination.

"They ain't got no right," he said. "It's our earth. It's our land. Can't nobody touch a man's own land."

We kept on looking at him, listening to the words but knowing that it was no use. The adult world had descended on us even in our richest dream and we knew there was no calculating the adult world, no fighting it, no winning against it.

We started moving slowly toward the parapet and the fire escape, avoiding a last look at the green beauty of the earth that T.J. had planted for us— had planted deeply in our minds as well as in our experience. We filed slowly over the edge and down the steps to the plank, T.J. coming last, and all of us could feel the weight of his grief behind us.

"Wait a minute," he said suddenly, his voice harsh with the effort of calling. We stopped and turned, held by the tone of his voice, and looked up at him standing above us on the fire escape.

"We can't stop them?" he said, looking down at us, his face strange in the dusky light. "There ain't no way to stop 'em?"

"No," said Blackie with finality. "They own the building."

We stood still for a moment, looking up at T.J., caught into inaction by the decision working in his face. He stared back at us and his face was pale and mean in the poor light, with a bald nakedness in his skin like cripples have sometimes.

"They ain't gonna touch my earth," he said fiercely. *"They ain't gonna lay a hand on it! Come on!"*

He turned around and started up the fire escape again, almost running against the effort of climbing. We followed more slowly, not knowing what he intended. By the time we reached him, he had seized a board and thrust it into the soil, scooping it up and flinging it over the parapet into the area below. He straightened and looked at us.

"They can't touch it," he said. *"I won't let 'em lay a dirty hand on it!"*

We saw it then. He stooped to his labor again and we followed, the gusts of his anger moving in frenzied labor among us as we scattered along the edge of the earth, scooping it and throwing it over the parapet destroying with anger the growth we had nurtured with such tender care. The soil carried so laboriously upward to the light and the sun cascaded swiftly into the dark areaway, the green blades of grass crumpled and twisted in the falling.

It took less time than you would think—the task of destruction is infinitely easier than that of creation. We stopped at the end leaving only a scattering of loose soil, and when it was finally over a stillness stood among the group and over the factory buildings. We looked down at the bare sterility of black tar, felt the harsh texture of it under the soles of our shoes, and the anger had gone out of us, leaving only a sore aching in our minds like overstretched muscles.

T.J. stood for a moment, his breathing slowing from anger and effort, caught into the same contemplation of destruction as all of us. He stooped slowly, finally, and picked up a lonely blade of grass left trampled under our feet and put it between his teeth, tasting it, sucking the greenness out of it into his mouth. Then he started walking toward the fire escape, moving before any of us were ready to move, and disappeared over the edge.

We followed him but he was already halfway down to the ground, going on past the board where we crossed over, climbing down into the areaway. We saw the last section swing down with his weight and then he stood on the concrete below us, looking at the small pile of anonymous earth scattered by our throwing. Then he walked across the place where we could see him and disappeared toward the street without glancing back, without looking up to see us watching him.

They did not find him for two weeks. Then the Nashville police caught him just outside the Nashville freight yards. He was walking along the railroad tracks; still heading south, still heading home.

As for us, who had no remembered home to call us—none of us ever again climbed the escape way to the roof.

1 Understanding the Story. Answer the following questions in good sentence form.

1. What does the gang want to plant in their roof garden? How does T.J. respond to this?

_____

_____

_____

_____

2. What does Blackie do with "sudden bravado"? How do the other members of the gang respond to this?

_____

_____

_____

3. What are the boys doing just before they are confronted by the owner of the building?

_____

_____

_____

4. Describe the mood of the owner. Explain the reason for his mood.

_____

_____

_____

_____

5. In what way is T.J.'s response to the owner's demands different from that of the other boys?

_____

_____

_____

_____

6. What actions are taken to follow up T. J.'s claim: "They ain't gonna touch my earth"?

_____

_____

_____

2 What Do You Think? Answer the following questions in good sentence form. Be sure to include reasons to support your answers.

1. If you had been the owner of the building, how would you have approached the boys about their grass garden?

   _____

   _____

   _____

   _____

2. Why does T.J. run away? Do you think he will eventually settle into the routines of city life, or will he probably run away again?

   _____

   _____

   _____

   _____

3 Which Word Does Not Fit? Choose the word in each row that does not fit, and write it on the line.

1.	Atlas	Jupiter	Mars	Mercury	Neptune	_____
2.	stamp	stomp	trample	traverse	tread	_____
3.	Shoshone	Minnetaree	Polynesian	Seminole	Sioux	_____
4.	despair	abandon	disappear	leave	desert	_____
5.	abstain	confine	limit	restrain	restrict	_____
6.	gap	gorge	gully	ravine	switchback	_____
7.	doubtful	hesitant	humble	skeptical	wavering	_____
8.	chromium	cobalt	laurel	manganese	mercury	_____
9.	crinkle	crumple	rumple	wriggle	wrinkle	_____
10.	lurch	stagger	stumble	teeter	waddle	_____
11.	bale	chunk	clod	hunk	lump	_____
12.	Brazil	Peru	Chile	Arcadia	Columbia	_____
13.	confer	contemplate	ponder	reflect	study	_____
14.	blemish	deface	disfigure	mutilate	wither	_____
15.	joined	intertwined	junction	connected	tangled	_____

4 Homonym Review. For each set, identify the homonyms that match the definitions. The first one is done to get you started.

doe	**1.** A female deer, hare, or kangaroo
dough	A mixture of liquid, flour, and other dry ingredients
_____	**2.** The capital of Italy
_____	To wander about aimlessly
_____	**3.** Any creature hunted or caught for food; a victim
_____	To make an earnest request to God
_____	**4.** A hole or tunnel dug in the ground by a small animal
_____	A small donkey, especially one used as a pack animal
_____	**5.** An elected or appointed group who advises or governs
_____	To recommend, advise, or offer guidance
_____	**6.** A passage between a row of seats as in an auditorium
_____	A small island
_____	**7.** A heavy burden; a supported weight or mass
_____	A vein of mineral ore; a rich source or supply
_____	**8.** To make, repair, or fasten with a needle and thread
_____	To scatter seed over the ground for growing
_____	**9.** A basic truth; a rule or standard of good behavior
_____	The head of an elementary school or high school
_____	**10.** A large bound package of raw or finished materials
_____	Money exchanged for the release of an arrested person; to empty water out of a boat by scooping or dipping

5 A Logic Problem. Four other children were more successful in growing a roof garden than were T.J. and his friends. Each of the four children planted a different vegetable. From the four clues, find the full name of each child and the vegetable he or she planted.

Clue 1: Neither the Nguyen child nor the Lane child planted cauliflower.

Clue 2: Juanita did not plant cauliflower and her last name is neither Nguyen nor Lane.

Clue 3: One child planted artichokes and another child's last name is Jones. The other two children are Alan and Juanita. (Note that all four children are mentioned in this clue.)

Clue 4: Neither Lucy nor the Kelly child nor the Nguyen child planted asparagus.

Use the chart on this page to solve this logic problem. Enter all information obtained from the clues, using an N to indicate a definite no and a Y to show a definite yes. The information from Clue 1 has been entered to get you started. Remember: Once you enter a definite yes (Y), you can place a no (N) in the other three boxes in both that row and that column in that section of the chart. You will probably have to read the clues several times to complete the puzzle. Fill in the sentences at the bottom as you figure out the answers.

	Jones	Kelly	Lane	Nguyen	artichokes	asparagus	broccoli	cauliflower
Alan								
Juanita								
Dennis								
Lucy								
artichokes				
asparagus				
broccoli				
cauliflower			N	N

_____ Jones planted _____.

_____ Kelly planted _____.

_____ Lane planted _____.

_____ Nguyen planted _____.

1 Definitions. Match the words listed below with the correct definitions.

anonymous	diagnosis	levy	swath
bravado	diverse	resolve	terrain
cache	emphatic	sediment	vegetation
capability	estimate	substantial	vigor

_____ **1.** different; composed of distinct elements or qualities

_____ **2.** a long, broad strip

_____ **3.** a region; a particular geographical area; ground

_____ **4.** active physical or mental strength; healthy energy

_____ **5.** false bravery; a swaggering show of courage

_____ **6.** having an unknown or withheld name

_____ **7.** solidly built; ample; actual; real

_____ **8.** bold and definite in expression or action

_____ **9.** the plants of an area or region

_____ **10.** to impose and collect (a tax, for example)

_____ **11.** material that settles to the bottom of a liquid

_____ **12.** a determination or decision; fixed purpose; to make a firm decision about

_____ **13.** ability; the capacity to be used, treated, or developed for a specific purpose

_____ **14.** a rough guess; an opinion or judgment of the nature or quality of a person or thing

_____ **15.** the process of recognizing a disease by its symptoms; a conclusion based on analysis

_____ **16.** a hole or similar hiding place for concealing or storing something

2 Using Context Clues: Part 1. Use the context clues to determine which pair of words best completes each sentence. Write the pair in the blanks.

1. The _____ carved his initials on a nearby _____ to mark the site of his triumphant catch.
   a. angler—alder   b. infielder—foxglove   c. Marine—laurel   d. predator—hemlock

2. David Brower, founder of Friends of Earth, _____ reminds his audiences that the _____ of our environment cannot continue.
   a. astonishingly—contamination   c. laboriously—sterility
   b. consistently—desecration   d. modestly—radiation

3. The conversation in the checkout line became _____ as the shoppers bemoaned how prices had _____ in just the past few months.
   a. distracted—cascaded   c. spirited—skyrocketed
   b. emphatic—teetered   d. frenzied—dilated

4. Huddled behind the _____, the combatant's former bravado gave way to outright cowardice as he _____ his fate.
   a. crater—abandoned   b. delta—diagnosed   c. parapet—pondered   d. ravine—resolved

5. When asked how she happened to know so much about the gold market, Molly replied casually, "Oh, I like to _____ in _____."
   a. contemplate—luxury   b. dabble—economics   c. excel—jewelry   d. probe—mineralogy

6. The ambassador was _____ because of his _____ remark about his host country.
   a. exploited—emphatic   c. recommended—turbulent
   b. trampled—ruthless   d. recalled—insulting

7. "Your _____ to this company has _____ improved our chances of beating the competition," beamed the supervisor as he proudly awarded the prize to Ajay.
   a. consistency—intently   c. dedication—inevitably
   b. contribution—infinitely   d. self-mastery—independently

8. _____ by cycles of chills, fever, and sweating, malaria is _____ by the bite of an infected female mosquito.
   a. Characterized—transmitted   c. Complicated—transformed
   b. Classified—transfixed   d. Contaminated—transacted

9. That she had tried to follow her _____ was Diana's only consolation as she bid farewell to the members of the town _____ for the last time.
   a. principals—council   b. principals—counsel   c. principles—council   d. principles—counsel

3 Using Context Clues: Part 2. As we know, a word can have more than one meaning. All the definitions for each underlined word are correct, but only one matches the word as it is used in the sentence. Write the letter of the correct definition on the line.

_____ 1. Anxious about her brother who sulked in front of the TV night after night, Rachel said, "Are you going to underline{vegetate} in that armchair forever just because your girlfriend jilted you?"

    a. to produce vegetation

    b. to grow or sprout as a plant does

    c. to lead a humdrum existence without exertion of body or mind

_____ 2. "If you want to know how to enjoy your life more," advised the counselor gently, "you've got to examine your underline{interior} life more closely rather than putting all the blame on outer circumstances."

    a. of or relating to one's mental or spiritual being

    b. situated away from a coast or border

    c. the inner portion or area of something

_____ 3. When underline{distractions} did not calm down the screaming baby, the frantic baby-sitter decided she had better call the parents immediately.

    a. anything that draws attention away, especially an amusement

    b. extreme mental or emotional disturbance

    c. the act of being pulled in conflicting directions

_____ 4. Upon being asked by the reporter if working the soil gave him a sense of belonging to the land, the farmer replied gruffly, "Son, today farming's nothing but another underline{enterprise}."

    a. energy or spirit for starting a new or difficult undertaking

    b. a business or undertaking, especially one of some risk

    c. boldness

_____ 5. Ernst was looking forward to the concert tonight when he could just underline{abandon} himself to the music and forget about the problems at work.

    a. to desert

    b. to surrender one's claim or right to

    c. to yield oneself completely, as to an emotion

_____ 6. In Mrs. Kennecott's underline{capacity} as hostess, she tried to make sure that none of the guests at her Christmas party felt left out.

    a. the position in which one functions

    b. the maximum amount that can be contained

    c. the ability to receive, hold, or absorb

_____ 7. Having dozed off for a few moments in the underline{niche}, the bandit awoke with a start as he heard the sound of approaching horses in the canyon.

    a. a recess in a wall for holding a statue or other ornament

    b. an area within a habitat occupied by an organism

    c. any steep, shallow recess, as in a rock or hill

4 Save the Earth: Go Green! Read the sentences below to learn how you can protect the environment by making simple changes. Number the sentences so that they appear in the order you would do them.

1. Recycling

_____ Take your recyclables to a recycling center or leave at the curb for pickup.

_____ Purchase products made from recycled materials.

_____ Manufacturers use recycled material to make new containers.

_____ Recyclables are sent to a recovery facility where they are sorted by material.

_____ Save and clean used bottles and cans, and stack used newspapers.

2. Composting

_____ Build the compost pile by layering food scraps and yard waste.

_____ Turn the pile with a pitchfork or shovel every few weeks to aerate.

_____ Save fruit and vegetable rinds and scraps and put in a sealed container.

_____ Find a spot in your yard or get a bin for your compost pile.

_____ Cover your compost pile, but water it occasionally to keep it moist.

_____ Set aside lawn clippings, leaves, and garden waste.

3. Packing a Green Lunch

_____ Put your beverage in a reusable thermos bottle.

_____ Put real silverware and a cloth napkin inside the lunch bag.

_____ Save leftover lunch waste for your compost pile.

_____ Find or purchase a reusable lunch container or bag.

_____ Pack sandwiches or other food in washable, reusable containers.

4. Green Floor Cleaning

_____ Pour green cleaner or white vinegar into a bucket of hot water.

_____ Use the mop to cover the floor with the cleaner and let it soak.

_____ Dunk a washable cloth mop in the bucket of cleaner.

_____ Use the mop and water to rinse floor well and let dry.

_____ Dump cleaner outside and refill bucket with water.

_____ Sweep up and throw away dust and debris.

_____ While the floor soaks, scrub any stains.

5 A Poet's Point of View. Read the poem below, and then answer the questions that follow.

The Forecast
by Dan Jaffe

Perhaps our age has driven us indoors.
We sprawl in the semi-darkness, dreaming sometimes
Of a vague world spinning in the wind.
But we have snapped our locks, pulled down our shades,
Taken all precautions. We shall not be disturbed.
If the earth shakes, it will be on a screen;
And if the prairie wind spills down our streets
And covers us with leaves, the weatherman will tell us.

1. According to the poet, what kind of relationship do most of us have with nature?

_____

_____

_____

_____

_____

2. What "forecast" does the poet seem to be making about mankind's relationship with the earth?

_____

_____

_____

_____

_____

_____

3. In a paragraph or poem, offer your own forecast about mankind's relationship with the earth.

_____

_____

_____

_____

_____

_____

_____

_____

_____

_____

_____

_____

_____

UNIT 4
Change

Change—especially for us living in the twenty-first century—is one thing of which we can be certain. It is everywhere. We change; our friends change; inventions and events change the world we live in. Sometimes we welcome these changes and sometimes we don't. In this last unit, you will have the opportunity to explore five writers' thoughts on various aspects of the concept of *change*.

In the reading for Lesson 16, entitled "Life without Furnace, Pipe, or Wire," the author presents a glimpse of what our everyday lives might be like if certain changes had *not* taken place.

In Lesson 17, an excerpt from Anton Chekhov's one-act play "A Marriage Proposal" portrays a change that has always been of interest to writers—a change of heart.

Times have changed the way we think about change and the way we go about making changes in the world. Lesson 18, "Digital Activism: The New Change Agent," tells about how new technologies are allowing people all over the world to inspire and support change.

In Lesson 19, "The Face of Change," the 44th President of the United States, Barack Obama, talks to Americans about change. In excerpts from three of his speeches, Obama tells about America's past progress and his plans for the country's future.

Finally, in "Heir to Tradition," the reading for Lesson 20, the author explores the importance of tradition in our rapidly changing world.

Words for Study

Heraclitus	hearth	suction	canopy
figment	thermostats	centralized	intervals
arduous	lavatories	sewers	tendency
blatant	chamber	extensively	prestige

LESSON 16
Life without Furnace, Pipe, or Wire

Centuries before the birth of Christ, the Greek philosopher Heraclitus wrote, "Nothing endures but change."

Quite often people's first reaction to change is one of doubt, suspicion, or even fear. Perhaps one way to approach change in a more positive light is to imagine what our daily lives would be like if certain changes had never taken place.

One instrument of change with which we are familiar is the invention. In this reading, an American historian presents a picture of life in a typical American home of the nineteenth century where many of the comforts we take so much for granted were no more than a figment of some inventor's imagination.

* * *

No matter how widely they varied, all homes in the early nineteenth century had one big thing in common: none of them could boast a furnace, a pipe, or a wire. Simple life functions, such as keeping warm, taking a bath, or getting set for the night, were pretty much the same in every kind of house. Life was everywhere arduous.

In every process, in each piece of equipment, there was a blatant need for improvement.

The open fireplace was still the main source of heat. And it was an exasperating kind of heat. Standing in front of the fire on a cold January night, the householder broiled in front and froze behind. Turning around, he quickly froze in the face and became uncomfortably hot in the seat, Walking fifteen feet to the washstand, he might find the water frozen in the china pitcher.

In every room the furnishings reflected this heating problem. A favorite parlor chair, for example, was the wing chair, with its high back and sides, or "wings." Sitting in it, the householder was exposed only in the front, and, of course, he usually chose to face the fire. Another common object was the foot warmer, a small iron box with a lid and handles. The householder would fill it with glowing coals from the fireplace and carry it elsewhere to use as a hot footstool.

Foot warmers

The men and boys in the house had the enormous and never-ending task of sawing and splitting wood, building and tending fires, lugging out the ashes. Summer was the best time for getting ahead on the winter fuel supply, but even then the kitchen fire had to be kept ablaze.

To start a fire, the householder filled a tinderbox with dry, crumbling wood. With a small steel bar, he would strike a piece of flint stone until sparks fell into the tinder. Then, blowing vigorously, he hoped that the tinder would begin to smolder. Not much better than the caveman's rubbing of sticks, this nineteenth-century process could actually take, even on a dry day, fifteen minutes to produce a fire.

An improved tinderbox, which worked much like a modern cigarette lighter, made the operation somewhat faster and easier to control. It had a steel sparking wheel at one end that would strike the flint several times whenever it was turned. But building up a big hearth fire from a chance spark was still such hard work that the householder seldom risked letting the fire go out.

The first "striking match" was not invented until 1836. Alonzo Phillips, its inventor, would make a wagonload of his phosphorous matches in his factory in Springfield, Massachusetts, and then ride around selling them from door to door. Needless to say, flint and steel were still widely used well into the 1840s.

Not until the 1870s could a person expect his home to be kept reasonably warm by a furnace of some kind. Even then, in the chill early morning, he had to go down cellar, shake down the ashes, poke the clinkers from the grates, pour fresh coal on the fire, and open the draft. For this was still the age of hand-shoveled coal. There would be no thermostats, oil burners, gas furnaces, or electric panels for another half century.

Tinderbox

With no plumbing, of course, there were no toilets and lavatories, in the modern sense of the words. Most of the time people used the outhouse, a sheltered seat built over an open pit. When the pit was filled, the males in the family would drag the outhouse to another spot over a new hole and cover up the old one. On a cold night, the ladies and children usually preferred to use a chamber pot, kept under the bed.

The average home had no special room for bathing. A bath, as a matter of fact, was so much trouble that during the work week most people just washed the parts of the body that showed, hoping for a full bath on Saturday night—if not this one, then surely the next.

The first step, and often the hardest, was to get a large enough supply of water to fill a tub. Even in the city, the typical house had its own dug well, surrounded by a latticed well house. One oaken bucket hung at either end of a rope, which ran over a pulley suspended from the ridgepole of the well-house roof. As he pulled up one bucket full of water, the householder was letting the other, empty one down. Or he might own a chain pump, which carried many small cups fastened along an endless chain. As he turned a crank handle, cups descended upside-down into the water, filled up, ascended right side up, tilted at the top, and spilled their contents into a spout as they resumed their endless journey.

Suction pumps were not manufactured for general use until later in the century. Yet even this invention had its drawbacks. In freezing weather a suction pump always had to be thawed out before it would work at all, and the well-water still had to be carried indoors, a bucket or two each trip.

Endless-chain pump

If he had domestic help, a person might have his big tin tub lugged up from the cellar or shed into his bedroom. But most people took their baths in the kitchen, always the warmest room and nearer to the well. Some families might use a sitz bath, which required less water, or in a pinch, just the regular wooden washtub.

Bathwater was heated in an iron kettle dangling from the kitchen fireplace crane, and the eager bather had to pour it, a bucket at a time, into his tub. In many homes, everybody bathed in the same water, mother first, then the girls, then father, and, finally, the dirtiest of all—the little boys. They used homemade soft soap.

Of course, after the Saturday-night bath, the females mopped up the kitchen floor, the males emptied the tub, a bucket at a time, out the kitchen door, and returned the tub to its storage place.

Nobody knows who deserves the credit for first piping water inside a house in the United States. What is known is that by the middle of the nineteenth century, health hazards forced cities to provide centralized water supplies and sewers.

Even getting ready for bed was hard work in "the good old days." The family retired early for four very good reasons. Illumination was poor because the crude oil lamps and the open fire did not provide much light, and candles were too expensive to be used very extensively on ordinary nights; everybody had to begin work at sunup; bed was the best place to keep warm; and getting there took so long that it was best to begin early.

First there was the serious problem of making sure there would be a fire in the morning. The householder added a "night log" to every fireplace and let it get a good start. In the meantime, he put some live coals and wood chips into a curfew—a small iron pan with a long handle and a cone-shaped tin cover—and set it inside the fireplace. Thus he had a small reserve fire in case the big open fire went out. Then he put more live coals into a long-handled brass pan called a bed warmer. And he banked the big fire with ashes, hoping it would last out the night.

The lady of the house, who had probably been filling the water pitcher on each washstand, now took the bed warmer, slid it slowly up and down between the sheets of each bed, and returned the pan to the hearth. In the late fall in many houses the sheets were replaced by cotton blankets as being less icy to the touch. Older children who could be entrusted with such dangerous tasks might help with the bed warming and the night logs.

About to retire, they put their outer garments away, not in a closet—there were no closets—but in a wardrobe, clothes press, or cupboard. They re-dressed in nightshirts, nightcaps, even night socks.

If people could afford it, they preferred to sleep in what was called a tester bed, with four high posts, a canopy across the top, and curtains that could be closed all around. This was no coil-spring bedstead. That would come later, inspired by the spring seats which carriage builders used in the more elegant buggies.

Rather, it was a cord-type bedstead. Holes were bored at eight-inch intervals through the foot, head, and side rails; sturdy rope was laced through these holes to make a web. A mattress stuffed with hay, straw, or maybe even corn shucks was placed on top of this crisscross rope.

When new, the cord bed was fairly comfortable, but the rope had a distressing tendency to sag with age, forming a kind of hammock, which made things increasingly difficult for occupants of a double bed.

Typical of hundreds of inventions aimed at making life less arduous was the bedstead-cord pin-with-a-crank, patented by John Beyer of Hainsville, Missouri, in 1859. With this gadget the householder could tune up his cord bed, much as he tuned up a banjo, until alas, the cords broke altogether.

Notice that hired help was almost a necessity for the nineteenth century homeowner. A large establishment with several teams of horses and vehicles required a coachman and often a groom, who lived in their own quarters over the coach house. Many families would keep a cow and a few chickens, and maybe hire a farm hand to help with a kitchen garden or an orchard of apple, peach, cherry, and pear trees.

When immigrants were arriving in large numbers, domestic live-in jobs attracted many of them. But with the spread of the factory system, young girls preferred to work in the mills; mill work paid better, allowed more personal freedom, and gave one higher social prestige. With the opening of new territories, domestic work in the East seemed even less attractive as lower-class families sought their own property and fortune in the West. Household servants became harder to find.

Even families not accustomed to having help looked forward to freedom from mere existence chores. In an "open society," in which anyone with ability could improve himself and enjoy life, everybody wanted time to learn, read, plan, relax.

The result was a continuous quest for laborsaving devices. Fortunately, the Industrial Revolution, which had introduced machine methods of production and made money available for research and inventions, could now help to improve home technology.

1 Understanding the Reading. An *outline* is a way to organize what we have read so that we can recall information more rapidly. Use the items listed below to complete this outline of information presented in "Life without Furnace, Pipe, or Wire." Note that in an outline, the first word of each item is capitalized.

Baths	Curfew	Night log	Tinderbox
Bed warmer	Fuel supply	Open fireplace	Water
Coal furnace	Kitchen	Outhouse	Water pitcher

Difficulties of Living in the 19ᵗʰ Century

I. Heating Problems

   A. _____ : failed to heat rooms evenly

   B. _____ : needed constant replenishing

   C. _____ : an ineffective piece of equipment which required patience and luck to start a fire

   D. _____ : an improvement over the fireplace as a source of heat but still required daily attention

II. Inconveniences resulting from lack of indoor plumbing

   A. _____ : typical toilet facility before indoor plumbing

   B. _____ : such a nuisance that they were taken only on Saturday

      1. _____ : had to be carted from wells and heated

      2. _____ : used because, even though it didn't offer much privacy, it was the warmest room in the house

III. The routine followed in getting set for the night

   A. _____ : needed to be started in every fireplace

   B. _____ : had to be prepared in case the big open fire went out

   C. _____ : had to be filled on each washstand

   D. _____ : had to be filled and taken to each bed to warm it

2 What Do You Think? Answer these questions in good sentence form. Be sure to include well-developed reasons to support your point of view.

1. Of all the inventions you can recall, which invention do you think has contributed most to improving the quality of life?

_____

_____

_____

_____

_____

_____

_____

_____

2. Which invention do you think has contributed the least to improving the quality of life?

_____

_____

_____

_____

_____

_____

_____

_____

3 Using Context Clues. Use the words listed at the left to complete each of these famous quotations about change.

all
endures
nothing

1. "_____ is flux, _____ stands still. Nothing _____ but change." (Heraclitus, Greek philosopher, 6th–5th century BC)

nature
silly
trial

2. "Human _____ will not change. In any future great national _____, compared with the men of this, we shall have as weak and as strong, as _____ and as wise, as bad and as good." (Abraham Lincoln, 16th U.S. president, 1809–1865)

actually
believe
consist
constantly

3. "Nothing changes more _____ than the past; for the past that influences our lives does not _____ of what _____ happened, but of what men _____ happened." (Gerald White Johnson, American writer, 1890–1980)

fact
human
pace

4. "The basic _____ of today is the tremendous _____ of change in _____ life." (Jawaharlal Nehru, Indian statesman, 1889–1964)

caused
institutions
organized
wars

5. "_____ are not 'acts of God.' They are _____ by man, by man-made _____, by the way in which man has _____ his society. What man has made, man can change." (Fred M. Vinson, American jurist, 1890–1953)

matters
refrain
reverse
years

6. "You are young, my son, and as the _____ go by, time will change and even _____ many of your present opinions. _____ therefore awhile from setting yourself up as a judge of the highest _____." (Plato, Greek philosopher, 427?–347 BC)

change
sensible
inevitable
dominant

7. "It is _____, continuing change, _____ change, that is the _____ factor in society today. No _____ decision can be made any longer without taking into account not only the world as it is, but the world as it will be." (Isaac Asimov, Russian-born American author, 1920–1992)

change
remain
same

8. "The more things _____, the more they _____ the _____." (Alphonse Karr, French journalist and writer, 1808–1890)

4 Writing about Change. Select one of the quotations from Exercise 3 and copy it on the lines below. Then, in a well-developed paragraph, write your thoughts about this quotation.

Quote: _____

_____

_____

_____

_____

_____

_____

_____

_____

_____

5 Inventors and Their Inventions. Use a dictionary or encyclopedia as necessary to complete these sentences about American inventors. The first one is done to get you started.

Alexander Graham Bell	George Eastman	Cyrus McCormick
William Burroughs	Thomas Edison	Samuel F. B. Morse
George W. Carver	✓Robert Fulton	Ransom E. Olds
Samuel Colt	Charles Goodyear	George Westinghouse
Lee DeForest	Elias Howe	Eli Whitney

1. Inventor and civil engineer, __**Robert Fulton**__ designed and built the *Clermont,* the first practical and financially successful steamboat, which ushered in a new age in the history of transportation in the early 1800s.

2. _____ enjoys two claims to fame. His cotton gin, invented in 1793, helped to make the United States the largest cotton producer in the world; and his method of manufacturing guns using machinery made him the father of mass production in the United States.

3. After many years of struggle, _____ received the necessary funds to string a telegraph line from the Capitol Building in Washington, D.C., to Baltimore, Maryland, in 1844. His famous message, "What hath God wrought," proved to be the beginning of many years of wealth and fame.

4. While in prison for his debts, _____ made his first efforts to change natural rubber into a useful product. Plagued by poor health and financial problems, his eventual perfection of this process brought him little in the way of worldly gain.

5. _____ is a good example of the good fortune that can come from being in the right place at the right time. Although not a brilliant or original device, his reaping machine came at a time when the rich prairie wheatlands were ready for development, and the inventor became a millionaire before he had reached forty.

6. _____ developed the first successful repeating pistol, which was patented in England in 1835. After his death, the company he had founded manufactured the famous six-shooters that were used throughout the West.

7. _____, having heard that whoever produced a workable sewing machine would make a fortune, patented one in 1846. After an arduous battle to protect his patent, this inventor finally saw the prediction come true.

8. _____, the organizer of more than 50 companies and president of 30 corporations, still managed to find time to invent new products. Among the inventions patented by this remarkably energetic man were the air brake for trains, the gas meter, and a system of pipes for safely conducting natural gas into homes.

9. _____ once remarked to his family that he would rather be remembered as a teacher of the deaf than as the inventor of the telephone, which he patented in 1876 at the age of 29.

10. _____, "the wizard of Menlo Park," stated that the phonograph, which he invented in 1878, was his favorite invention, even though the electric light is usually cited as his greatest invention.

11. _____, having invented a machine for coating glass plates in cameras, perfected flexible roll films and produced a light camera which sold for $1 in 1900, enabling millions to enjoy photography as a pastime.

12. His work as a bank clerk made _____ recognize the importance of laborsaving devices in accounting; in 1888, he patented an adding machine that was far more reliable than earlier models.

13. Among his many distinctions, _____ gained international fame for his research with agricultural products. He successfully developed more than 300 products from peanuts, including a milk substitute, soap, printer's ink, and face powder.

14. A pioneer automobile inventor and manufacturer, _____ was producing cars in 1901 which sold for $650. His success attracted others to the infant automobile industry and helped to make the automobile popular with the public.

15. A pioneer in radio broadcasting, _____ obtained patents on more than 300 inventions. His vacuum tube, patented in 1907, was basic to the development of long-distance radio and television communication, and has often been called as great an invention as the radio itself.

Words for Study

meditates	peculiar	architect	vulgar
palpitation	merciful	glutton	famine
gorgeously	intriguer	swindler	tuberculosis
inherited	dipsomaniac	disciplinarian	unabridged

LESSON 17
A Marriage Proposal
by Anton Chekhov

One change that has been particularly popular with writers throughout the centuries is a change of heart. In this excerpt from a one-act play by the Russian writer Anton Chekhov, note the changes in the characters' attitudes and the reasons for them.

* * *

Scene: The reception room in Stepan Stepanovitch Tscubukov's home. Ivan Vassiliyitch Lomov enters, wearing a dress suit.

Stepan: (*going toward Ivan and greeting him*) Who is this I see? My dear fellow! Ivan Vassiliyitch! I'm so glad to see you! (*Shakes hands*) But this is a surprise! How are you?

Ivan: Thank you! And how are you?

Stepan: Oh, so-so, my friend. Please sit down. It isn't right to forget one's neighbor. But tell me, why all this ceremony? Dress clothes, white gloves and all? Are you on your way to some engagement, my good fellow?

Ivan: No, I have no engagement except with you, Stepan Stepanovitch.

Stepan: But why in evening clothes, my friend? This isn't New Year's!

Ivan: You see, it's simply this, that—(*composing himself*) I have come to you, Stepan Stepanovitch, to trouble you with a request. It is not the first time I have had the honor of turning to you for assistance, and you have always, that is—I beg your pardon, I am a bit excited! I'll take a drink of water first, dear Stepan Stepanovitch. (*He drinks.*)

Stepan: (*aside*) He's come to borrow money! I won't give him any! (*To Ivan*) What is it then, dear Lomov?

Ivan: You see—dear—Stepanovitch, pardon me, Stepan—Stepan—dearvitch—I mean—I am terribly nervous, as you will be so good as to see—! What I mean to say—you are the only one who can help me, though I don't deserve it, and—and I have no right whatever to make this request of you.

Stepan: Oh, don't beat about the bush, my dear fellow. Tell me!

Ivan: Immediately—in a moment. Here it is, then: I have come to ask for the hand of your daughter, Natalia Stepanovna.

Stepan: (*joyfully*) Angel! Ivan Vassiliyitch! Say that once again! I didn't quite hear it!

Ivan: I have the honor to beg—

Stepan: (*interrupting*) My dear, dear man! I am so happy that everything is so—everything! (*Embraces and kisses him*) I have wanted this to happen for so long. It has been my dearest wish!

(*He represses a tear.*) And I have always loved you, my dear fellow, as my own son! May God give you His blessings and His grace and—I always wanted it to happen. But why am I standing here like a blockhead? I am completely dumbfounded with pleasure, completely dumbfounded. My whole being—I'll call Natalia—

Ivan: Dear Stepan Stepanovitch, what do you think? May I hope for Natalia Stepanovna's acceptance?

Stepan: Really! A fine boy like you—and you think she won't accept on the minute? Lovesick as a cat and all that—! (*He goes out.*)

Ivan: I'm cold. My whole body is trembling as though I was going to take my examination! But the chief thing is to settle matters! If a person meditates too much, or hesitates, or talks about it, waits for an ideal or for true love, he never gets it, Brrr! It's cold! Natalia is an excellent housekeeper, not at all bad looking, well educated—what more could I ask? I'm so excited my ears are roaring! (*He drinks water.*) And not to marry, that won't do! In the first place, I'm thirty-five—a critical age, you might say. In the second place, I must live a well-regulated life. I have a weak heart, continual palpitation, and I am very sensitive and always getting excited. My lips begin to tremble and the pulse in my right temple throbs terribly. But the worst of all is sleep! I hardly lie down and begin to doze before something in my left side begins to pull and tug, and something begins to hammer in my left shoulder—and in my head, too! I jump up like a madman, walk about a little, lie down again, but the moment I fall asleep I have a terrible cramp in the side. And so it is all night long!

(*Enter Natalia Stepanovna.*)

Natalia: Ah! It's you. Papa said to go in: there was a dealer in there who'd come to buy something. Good afternoon, Ivan Vassiliyitch.

Ivan: Good day, my dear Natalia Stepanovna.

Natalia: You must pardon me for wearing my apron and this old dress: we are working today. Why haven't you come to see us more often? You've not been here for so long! Sit down. (*They sit down.*) Won't you have something to eat?

Ivan: Thank you, I have just had lunch.

Natalia: Smoke, do, there are the matches. Today it is beautiful and only yesterday it rained so hard that the workmen couldn't do a stroke of work. How many bricks have you cut? Think of it! I was so anxious that I had the whole field mowed, and now I'm sorry I did it, because I'm afraid the hay will rot. It would have been better if I had waited. But what on earth is this? You are in evening clothes! The latest cut! Are you on your way to a ball? And you seem to be looking better, too—really. Why are you dressed up so gorgeously?

Ivan: (*excited*) You see, my dear Natalia Stepanovna—it's simply this: I have decided to ask you to listen to me—of course it will be a surprise, and indeed you'll be angry, but I—(*Aside*). How fearfully cold it is!

Natalia: What is it? (*A pause*) Well?

Ivan: I'll try to be brief. My dear Natalia Stepanovna, as you know, for many years, since my childhood, I have had the honor to know your family. My poor aunt and her husband, from whom, as you know, I inherited the estate, always had the greatest respect for your father and your poor mother. The Lomovs and the Tscubukovs have been for decades on the friendliest, indeed the closest, terms with each other, and furthermore my property, as you know, adjoins your own. If you will be so good as to remember, my meadows touch your birch woods.

Natalia: Pardon the interruption. You said "my meadows"—but are they yours?

Ivan: Yes, they belong to me.

Natalia: What nonsense! The meadows belong to us—not to you!

Ivan: No, to me! Now, my dear Natalia Stepanovna!

Natalia: Well, that is certainly news to me. How do they belong to you?

Ivan: How? I am speaking of the meadows lying between your birch woods and my brick-earth.

Natalia: Yes, exactly. They belong to us.

Ivan: No, you are mistaken, my dear Natalia Stepanovna, they belong to me. It is all a matter of record, my dear Natalia Stepanovna. It is true that at one time the title to the meadows was disputed, but now everyone knows they belong to me. There is no room for discussion. Be so good as to listen: my aunt's grandmother put these meadows, free from all costs, into the hands of your father's father's grandfather's peasants for a certain time while they were making bricks for my grandmother. These people used the meadows free of cost for about forty years, living there as they would on their own property. Later, however, when—

Natalia: There's not a word of truth in that!

Ivan: I'll show you the papers, Natalia Stepanovna.

Natalia: No, either you are joking, or trying to lead me into a discussion. That's not at all nice! We have owned this property for nearly three hundred years, and now all at once we hear that it doesn't belong to us. Ivan Vassiliyitch, you will pardon me, but I really can't believe my ears. So far as I am concerned, the meadows are worth very little. In all they don't contain more than five acres and they are worth only a few hundred roubles, say three hundred, but the injustice of the thing is what affects me. Say what you will, I can't bear injustice.

Ivan: Only listen until I have finished, please!

Natalia: And if you keep on explaining it for two days, and put on five suits of evening clothes, the meadows are still ours, ours, ours! I don't want to take your property, but I refuse to give up what belongs to us!

Ivan: Natalia Stepanovna, I don't need the meadows, I am only concerned with the principle. If you are agreeable, I beg of you, accept them as a gift from me!

Natalia: But I can give them to you, because they belong to me! That is very peculiar, Ivan Vassiliyitch! Until now we have considered you as a good neighbor and a good friend; only last year we lent you our threshing machine so that we couldn't thresh until November, and now you treat us like thieves! You offer to give me my own land. Excuse me, but neighbors don't treat each other that way. In my opinion, it's a very low trick—to speak frankly—

Ivan: The meadows are mine, do you understand? Mine!

Natalia: Really, you needn't scream so! If you want to scream and snort and rage you may do it at home, but here please keep yourself within the limits of common decency.

Ivan: My dear lady, if it weren't that I were suffering from palpitation of the heart and hammering of the arteries in my temples, I would deal with you very differently! (*In a loud voice*) The meadows belong to me!

Natalia: Us!

Ivan: Me!

(*Enter Stepan.*)

Stepan: What's going on here? What is he yelling about?

Natalia: Papa, please tell this gentleman to whom the meadows belong, to us or to him?

Stepan: My dear fellow, the meadows are ours.

Ivan: But, merciful heavens, Stepan Stepanovitch, how do you make that out? You at least might be reasonable. My aunt's grandmother gave the use of the meadows free of cost to your grandfather's peasants; the peasants lived on the land for forty years and used it as their own, but later when—

Stepan: Permit me, my dear friend. You forget that your grandmother's peasants never paid, because there had been a lawsuit over the meadows, and everyone knows that the meadows belong to us. You haven't looked at the map.

Ivan: I'll prove to you that they belong to me!

Natalia: The meadows belong to us and I won't give them up! I won't give them up! I won't give them up!

Ivan: We'll see about that! I'll prove in court that they belong to me.

Stepan: In court! You may sue in court, sir, if you like! Oh, I know you, you are only waiting to find an excuse to go to law! You're an intriguer, that's what you are! Your whole family were always looking for quarrels. The whole lot!

Ivan: Kindly refrain from insulting my family. The entire race of Lomov has always been honorable! And never has one been brought to trial for embezzlement, as your dear uncle was!

Stepan: And the whole Lomov family were insane!

Natalia: Every one of them!

Stepan: Your grandmother was a dipsomaniac, and the younger aunt ran off with an architect.

Ivan: And your mother limped. (*He puts his hand over his heart.*) Oh, my side pains! My temples are bursting! Lord in Heaven! Water!

Stepan: And your dear father was a gambler—and a glutton!

Natalia: And your aunt was a gossip like few others!

Ivan: And you are an intriguer. Oh, my heart! And it's an open secret that you cheated at the elections—my eyes are blurred! Where is my hat?

Natalia: Oh, how low! Liar! Disgusting thing!

Ivan: Where's the hat—? My heart! Where shall I go? Where is the door—? Oh—it seems—as though I were dying! I can't—my legs won't hold me—(*He goes to the door.*)

Stepan: (*following him*) May you never darken my door again!

Natalia: Bring your suit to court! We'll see! (*Lomov staggers out.*)

Stepan: (*angrily*) The devil!

Natalia: Such a good-for-nothing! And then they talk about being good neighbors!

Stepan: Loafer! Scarecrow! Monster!

Natalia: A swindler like that takes over a piece of property that doesn't belong to him and then dares to argue about it!

Stepan: And to think that this fool dares to make a proposal of marriage!

Natalia: What? A proposal of marriage?

Stepan: Why, yes! He came here to make you a proposal of marriage.

Natalia: Why didn't you tell me that before?

Stepan: That's why he had on his evening clothes! The poor fool!

Natalia: Proposal for me? Oh! (*Falls into an armchair and groans*) Bring him back! Bring him back!

Stepan: Bring whom back?

Natalia: Faster, faster, I'm sinking! Bring him back! (*She becomes hysterical.*)

Stepan: What is it? What's wrong with you? I'm cursed with bad luck! I'll shoot myself! I'll hang myself!

Natalia: I'm dying! Bring him back!

Stepan: Bah! In a minute! Don't bawl! (*He rushes out.*)

Natalia: (*groaning*) What have they done to me? Bring him back! Bring him back!

Stepan: (*Comes running in*) He's coming at once! The devil take him! Ugh! Talk to him yourself, I can't.

Natalia: (*groaning*) Bring him back!

Stepan: He's coming, I tell you! Oh, Lord! What a task it is to be the father of a grown daughter!

1 Understanding the Play. Answer the following questions in good sentence form.

1. What does Stepan *first* believe to be the reason for Ivan's visit?

_____

2. What is the real reason for Ivan's visit?

_____

3. Why do Ivan and Natalia begin to quarrel?

_____

4. Does their argument pertain to serious or trivial matters? Be sure to include evidence from the play to support your answer.

_____

_____

_____

5. How does Ivan intend to resolve the quarrel?

_____

_____

6. Why does Natalia soon regret Ivan's sudden departure?

_____

7. Why does Stepan remark, "What a task it is to be the father of a grown daughter!"?

_____

8. Do you think this play is intended to be *serious* or *humorous*? Cite evidence from the play which supports your answer.

_____

_____

_____

_____

_____

2 You Be the Playwright. The scene you have just read is only the first part of a one-act play. Based on what you have learned about the characters thus far, write a relatively detailed description of how you think the play should end. If you wish, use your own paper to actually write the dialogue. If you include stage directions, be sure to enclose them in parentheses.

_____

_____

_____

_____

_____

_____

_____

_____

_____

_____

_____

_____

_____

_____

_____

_____

3 More about Anton Chekhov. Use the words listed at the left to complete these sentences correctly.

monotony
monotonous
monotonously

1. Anton Chekhov, the author of "A Marriage Proposal," was born in 1860 in a province in southern Russia where many of the townspeople complained _____ about the _____ of their lives, which must have made their daily routines seem even more _____.

inspired
uninspired
inspiration

2. _____ by his life in the small town, Anton found his _____ in swimming and fishing. On one of his outings, he became quite ill and was nursed back to health by a kindly doctor who is said to have _____ the young Chekhov's own choice of a medical career.

severe
severely
severity

3. Known for his _____, his father, who was a grocer, _____ scolded his six children for wrongdoings; but Anton's brother wrote that their father was _____ only when absolutely necessary and beat the children only in "exceptional cases."

reliably
unreliable
reliability

4. Although Anton's father was _____ strict as a disciplinarian, he was _____ as a grocer. After he went bankrupt, the family moved to Moscow where they counted on Anton's strength and _____ to pull them through their hardships.

wretched
wretchedly
wretchedness

5. In the 1880s, Chekhov began to write plays that, at first, audiences found _____ immature. But since he was his own worst critic Chekhov always had the last word on _____, and he described his successful one-act play "A Marriage Proposal" as "a _____, vulgar, boring little skit."

irritate
irritation
irritable

6. Actors and actresses could _____ Chekhov a great deal. Actresses, whom he described as cows, made him _____, and his _____ with actors caused him to state that they should never be allowed to speak their opinions because they were so boring.

176   Lesson 17

**censor
censorship
uncensored**

7. Another nuisance for Chekhov was _____. The duty of a(n) _____ was to tone down material that might provoke thought. *Famine,* for example, which was a very stark reality for many Russian people, was supposed to be called a "temporary food shortage," and Chekhov was astonished when this word remained _____ in one of his stories.

**modest
modesty
immodest**

8. Chekhov may have been _____ in his remarks, but he reacted with utmost _____ to the fact that, by the late 1880s, he was honored as a national celebrity even though the income from his plays and stories was still quite _____ and barely covered his expenses.

**mortal
mortally
immortal
immortality**

9. In 1904, Chekhov lay _____ ill from tuberculosis, a disease that had plagued his _____ being for many years. As his wife pressed an ice pack against his heart, Chekhov perhaps realized his writing might achieve _____ but that he himself was not _____, for he remarked to his wife, "You don't put ice on an empty heart."

4 Foreign Currency. In "A Marriage Proposal," the characters spoke of the worth of the meadow in terms of *roubles.* With the help of a dictionary or the Internet, match the currencies listed below with the correct country. (HINT: In most unabridged dictionaries, the entries *currency* or *money* provide this information.)

dinar	dong	krone	peso	rand	rouble	shekel	yen
dollar	euro	kwacha	pound	ringgit	rupee	won	yuan

_____ **1.** Australia

_____ **2.** China

_____ **3.** Denmark

_____ **4.** Egypt

_____ **5.** Eurozone

_____ **6.** India

_____ **7.** Iraq

_____ **8.** Israel

_____ **9.** Japan

_____ **10.** Korea

_____ **11.** Malawi

_____ **12.** Malaysia

_____ **13.** Mexico

_____ **14.** Russia

_____ **15.** South Africa

_____ **16.** Vietnam

5 Synonym Review. From the choices given, choose the best synonym for the word in bold-faced type, and write it on the line to the right.

1. **hazard:**   complication   danger   darkness   setback   _____

2. **basis:**   figment   foundation   hearth   objective   _____

3. **meditate:**   determine   fascinate   ponder   profess   _____

4. **reap:**   cultivate   harvest   shuck   sow   _____

5. **intrigue:**   fantasy   imposition   motive   scheme   _____

6. **interval:**   extension   pause   postponement   recurrence   _____

7. **flexible:**   adaptable   motivated   objective   vigorous   _____

8. **ascend:**   circumvent   climb   elevate   hoist   _____

9. **tendency:**   conception   instinct   leaning   motivation   _____

10. **prestige:**   dedication   influence   precedence   profession   _____

11. **elegant:**   enormous   expressive   honorable   splendid   _____

12. **domestic:**   household   personal   professional   public   _____

13. **arduous:**   alien   difficult   dishonorable   unreasonable   _____

14. **palpitate:**   cascade   collapse   dilate   flutter   _____

15. **blatant:**   contradictory   distorted   improbable   obvious   _____

16. **flux:**   abundance   flow   tremor   vigor   _____

Words for Study

third world	petitions	oriented	sustainability
momentum	advocacy	like-minded	micro-philanthropy
prominently	demographic	nonprofit	optimist
rants	compiled	myriad	pessimist

LESSON 18
Digital Activism: The New Change Agent

Are you interested in advocating for animal rights? Does global warming stir you to action? Or, do you feel compelled to fight for human rights in third-world countries? No matter what your favorite cause is, you can find a way to voice your opinions through digital activism.

Digital activism began during the computer and Internet revolution of the 1990s, and it is really gaining momentum in the 21st century. Unlike activists of the past who marched and picketed, wrote letters, or knocked on doors, today's activists are using the latest technology to promote social, political, and environmental change. This technology includes the Internet, blogs, and mobile phones, . . . so far.

Digital activists use social networking tools to get their causes noticed. You can find their views posted prominently on their Facebook pages, and you can view their rants on YouTube. Activists also use e-mail to spread the word about favorite causes to family, friends, and people of influence. Not too long ago, people would write their representatives with pen and paper. Today, they can submit letters to congressmen, congresswomen, senators, and even the White House via e-mail. And instead of coming to your door to get your signature, activists circulate Internet petitions calling for change and ask for digital signatures.

Who is today's typical digital activist? In 2009, researchers at DigiActive conducted the first survey of people who use digital tools for activism and advocacy. They collected basic data about this new demographic. The Digital Activism Survey 2009 looked at people who use digital tools like blogs, social networking outlets such as Facebook or YouTube, e-mail, and digital mobile technology. The survey presented 21 questions. Of these, most were multiple choice. The results showed that most digital activists were adult males. Here is a sample of the data compiled.

Information about survey respondents who use digital tools for activism:	
Age	Most were adults between the ages of 26 and 50, with the largest number being between ages 31 and 50 (49%).
Gender	In North America, the number of male responders was almost exactly the same as the number of females. But outside North America, males who responded to the survey outnumbered female responders 7 to 3.
Geography	North America accounted for 47% of survey responders, while 20% were from Asia, and 13% were from Western Europe. This distribution is consistent with global Internet access figures.
Economics	Frequent use was an important factor in digital activism. Responders were more likely than the general population of their areas to have high-speed Internet access from home. And they were more likely to work in white-collar jobs where the Internet is also available. Multiple site access is important because 98% of survey responders were online more than once each day.
Access	The amount of Internet use, not merely simple access to the Internet, is what characterized digital activists. And since high use is only possible for people who can afford home access to the Internet, digital activists are most commonly from the global middle class.
Mobiles	Survey responders who had more than four features on their mobile phones, such as Internet access, video, camera, or GPS, were more likely to use their phones for digital activism.
Causes	No matter where survey responders were located, "rights" were by far the most popular cause. Of the 21 rights listed, human rights and women's rights were the most common. The most named causes aside from rights were environmental causes, poverty, and peace/nonviolence.

Since this is the first survey of its kind, we have a lot more to learn as digital activism continues to spread. Based on this study, we do know that digital activists have access to the Internet, and they use it often. In the U.S., Internet access is open to everyone. Many people have access from their homes, workplaces, or schools. People can also log on for free at local libraries.

Is reading about digital activism inspiring you to get involved? One of the easiest places to start is with a change-oriented website. There are countless websites that you can access for information on issues. Just type a cause that interests you into a search engine, like Google. You'll get hundreds of links to sources of information or sites where you can get involved. There is probably a website for every cause you could imagine. Some sites give the latest advocacy news or the most recent legal changes. Others connect you with like-minded people who want to work for change in specific areas of interest. Some sites also offer listings of nonprofit organizations that are looking for volunteers or donations to support a cause.

One of the largest activist sites is Change.org. The site asks users to choose or write in the causes they are interested in. Then it connects people who are interested in the same causes. It gives users a place to work together to address issues, to exchange information, and to find ways to make a difference.

One of Change.org's most important features is that it works to change the way people interact with nonprofit groups. In the past, people who wanted to get involved in a cause had few choices about how they worked toward making a change. Usually they had to contact a nonprofit's local office by phone. They could make donations or speak with a volunteer coordinator who would let them know what volunteer jobs were available. Volunteers might stuff envelopes, take petitions door-to-door, or take part in local bake sales or food drives. But this process worked best for very general kinds of help.

Change.org is helping to change the way we change the world. Now you can get involved in national, international, or global causes—no matter where you live. Anyone from anywhere can participate in activities taking place on the other side of the country or the other side of the world. Change.org offers a database of information about approximately one million nonprofit agencies. It profiles some of the better known ones. For each of the nonprofits profiled on the site, Change.org displays background information, user reviews, photos, videos, and a community blog. There is also a profit page for each. There visitors can donate money to help fund special projects or can make general donations to a group. People can also get involved at a local level. They can donate time instead of money by helping to coordinate events on a group's action page. These pages offer volunteer opportunities, events, and activities based on the user's zip code.

Digital activism is an exciting new way to work toward positive changes in the world. And with access to the Internet, you can learn about the myriad causes spanning the globe. No matter what cause you select or how you choose to make a difference, what is most important is that you *act*. Isn't it time you got involved?

digital activism websites of interest

- **change.org**
  An outstanding site that works to connect like-minded people and to change how activists get involved with nonprofit groups. It offers a database of information about approximately one million nonprofit groups from around the globe.

- **care2.com**
  This is the largest social change-oriented community site, with over six million active members.

- **fivelimes.com**
  This social change-oriented community site focuses on environmental and social sustainability.

- **treehugger.com**
  This is another environmentally focused, community-oriented site.

- **firstgiving.com**
  This is a website that helps anyone create a free, personalized fund-raising page that can then be promoted through e-mail, your blog, or various other social networking outlets such as Facebook, MySpace, etc.

- **donorschoose.org**
  This site calls what it does *micro-philanthropy*. It allows individuals to request limited grants for specific projects.

- **takingitglobal.org**
  This site has been the leader in tackling youth global issues in the social networking arena since 1999.

- **volunteersolutions.org**
  The volunteer opportunities presented on this site have been reviewed by local volunteer centers to ensure quality.

- **changingthepresent.org**
  This is an outstanding website for helping to make a difference in a very specific way. It offers lots of information about nonprofits and lets you choose precisely what you want to accomplish.

1 Understanding the Reading. Put the letter of the best answer on the line.

1. Digital activism was inspired during the computer and Internet revolution of the _____.
   a. 1960s
   b. 1970s
   c. 1980s
   d. 1990s

2. Technology used so far by today's activists include _____.
   a. the Internet
   b. blogs
   c. mobile phones
   d. all of the above

3. Not too long ago, people would write their representatives using pen and paper. Now they _____.
   a. write blogs to congress
   b. circulate Internet petitions
   c. e-mail their congressman, congresswomen, and senators
   d. go door-to-door

4. The results of the 2009 DigiActive study found that most digital activists were _____.
   a. adults
   b. children
   c. teenage girls
   d. seniors

5. Change.org does *not* _____.
   a. ask users to choose the causes they are interested in
   b. give users a place to work together to make a difference
   c. connect people who are interested in the same causes
   d. fund special projects only in the U.S.

6. Change.org offers a database of information about approximately one million _____.
   a. causes
   b. celebrity activists
   c. nonprofit agencies
   d. retail stores

7. This is the largest social change-oriented community site. _____
   a. treehugger.com
   b. care2.com
   c. firstgiving.com
   d. donorschoose.org

8. This website helps anyone create a free, personalized fund-raising page.
   a. treehugger.com
   b. care2.com
   c. firstgiving.com
   d. donorschoose.org

2 Optimists and Pessimists. An *optimist* looks on the brighter side of any situation. His opposite—the *pessimist*—has eyes only for the gloomy side. An activist might be an optimist ("We can really make the world better!") or a pessimist ("There are so many things wrong in the world that we can never fix them all."). Decide how an optimist and a pessimist might respond to the following quotes about change, and write your answers in the space provided. The first one is done to get you started.

1. "Technological change is like an axe in the hands of a pathological criminal." *Albert Einstein*

   a. Optimist: <u>I believe that technological change will pave the way to a brighter</u> <u>future for us all.</u>

   b. Pessimist: <u>I agree wholeheartedly with Einstein. Technology is dangerous.</u>

2. "No person is your friend who demands your silence, or denies your right to grow." *Alice Walker*

   a. Optimist: _____

   _____

   b. Pessimist: _____

   _____

3. "It is not the strongest of the species that survives, nor the most intelligent, but the one most responsive to change." *Charles Darwin*

   a. Optimist: _____

   _____

   b. Pessimist: _____

   _____

4. "How wonderful it is that nobody need wait a single moment before starting to improve the world." *Anne Frank*

   a. Optimist: _____

   _____

   b. Pessimist: _____

   _____

5. "Change will not come if we wait for some other person or some other time. We are the ones we've been waiting for. We are the change that we seek." *Barack Obama*

   a. Optimist: _____

   _____

   b. Pessimist: _____

   _____

3 Antonym Review. From the choices listed, choose the best antonym for the word in bold-faced type and write it on the line to the right.

1. **advocate:** opponent   backer   believer   cause   _____

2. **involuntary:** attentive   meditated   predictable   willful   _____

3. **specific:** pointed   general   clear   easy   _____

4. **myriad:** few   different   numerous   active   _____

5. **accustomed:** arduous   consistent   inflexible   unusual   _____

6. **irritable:** pleasant   pretentious   reliable   stately   _____

7. **positive:** glaring   open   plus   negative   _____

8. **volunteer:** employee   unpaid   donate   time   _____

9. **individuals:** man   groups   woman   singles   _____

10. **active:** costly   busy   healthy   passive   _____

11. **social:** relative   friendly   society   antisocial   _____

12. **pessimistic:** adaptable   optimistic   prosperous   unknowing   _____

13. **hazardous:** exposed   permissible   primitive   safe   _____

14. **global:** worldwide   local   systemic   change   _____

4 Signs of Change. Match the changes below with the person who would be most likely to recognize them.

activist	economist	grocer	navigator	sociologist
ecologist	environmentalist	mayor	psychologist	tutor

_____   **1.** a decrease in trash along a highway

_____   **2.** a patient's mental health improves

_____   **3.** social patterns change

_____   **4.** a student's study habits change

_____   **5.** a ship's course suddenly changes

_____   **6.** a controversial human rights issue erupts

_____   **7.** citizens demand better public services

_____   **8.** wholesale food prices soar

_____   **9.** climate changes affect polar bears

_____   **10.** interest rates drop

5 An Inventor's Advice. One person who thrived on change was Benjamin Franklin. One of his famous sayings can be found by solving this puzzle. Rearrange the letters in each box to form another word. Put the number that matches the clue for the new word in the circle. The circled numbers in each row and column add up to 65.

After you figure out a word, write its first letter in the numbered blank at the bottom of the page. The first and last words have been filled in to get you started.

KAYOS ○ ___	**LATER** ○ ___	**MONAD** ㉕ **NOMAD**	**SMALL** ○ ___	**EXIST** ○ ___	= 65
TUTOR ○ ___	**FIRED** ○ ___	**SLIDE** ○ ___	**YEMEN** ○ ___	**PAGES** ○ ___	= 65
CHASE ○ ___	**NOBLE** ○ ___	**SEVER** ○ ___	**MANOR** ○ ___	**STRUT** ○ ___	= 65
ZONED ○ ___	**LEASE** ○ ___	**DOORS** ○ ___	**REINS** ○ ___	**MITES** ○ ___	= 65
SETUP ○ ___	**CURBS** ○ ___	**ALLOY** ① **LOYAL**	**RUNES** ○ ___	**TRINE** ○ ___	= 65
= 65	= 65	= 65	= 65	= 65	

✓**1.** Faithful; trustworthy
2. Agrees to; endorses
3. To clean vigorously
4. A freshwater fish
5. Confidence; faith; reliance
6. Details; bits of information
7. Shopping centers
8. Departs; takes off
9. Runs an engine in neutral

10. A fire engine's alarm
11. The inventor of dynamite
12. An artist's stand
13. Poetry
14. A synonym for foe
15. A citizen of Italy's capital city
16. Cooked in hot oil or fat
17. Smells; scents

18. Disturbed; distressed; bothered
19. A hospital employee
20. Twelve items
21. Pains; hurts
22. Stares
23. Watchful; attentive
24. Lifeless; inactive
✓**25.** A wanderer

Benjamin Franklin's words of advice:

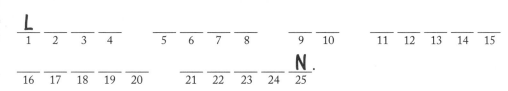

L̲ ̲ ̲ ̲   ̲ ̲ ̲ ̲   ̲ ̲   ̲ ̲ ̲ ̲ ̲
1 2 3 4   5 6 7 8   9 10   11 12 13 14 15

̲ ̲ ̲ ̲ ̲   ̲ ̲ ̲ ̲ N̲.
16 17 18 19 20   21 22 23 24 25

Words for Study

keynote	ballots	endowed	democracy
Convention	milestone	inalienable	self-reliance
multiracial	barrier	pedigree	tyranny
commentators	heritage	naysayers	fundamental

LESSON 19
The Face of Change

On July 27, 2004, Illinois Senator Barack Obama gave the keynote speech at the Democratic National Convention in Boston, Massachusetts. A first-term senator, Obama was not well known on the national stage, but his speech inspired the audience and instantly raised his political profile, casting him as a rising star within the Democratic Party.

In 2007, Obama announced a run for the U.S. presidency, launching a successful campaign and winning his party's nomination in August 2008 at the Democratic National Convention in Denver, Colorado.

Obama ran on a platform of "hope" and "change," promising to restore a sense of unity and common purpose to the nation. The son of a white American mother and a black African father, Obama reflected the increasingly multiracial identity of many Americans. Race became a major issue during the campaign, with some politicians and commentators claiming that Americans were not ready to elect a black president. Despite Obama's strong poll numbers, many political experts questioned whether white voters would in fact cast their ballots for the white candidate once they entered the privacy of the voting booth.

After a lengthy campaign, Obama won an election-night victory on November 4, 2008, against Republican candidate John McCain. On January 20, 2009, Barack Obama was sworn into office as the 44th president of the United States, becoming the nation's first black president. His appointment marked a major milestone in the struggle for equality and civil rights begun decades earlier.

The following excerpts are adapted from Obama's speeches at both Democratic conventions and from his victory speech on Election Day, 2008.

July 27, 2004

Keynote Speech, Democratic National Convention, Boston, Massachusetts

Tonight is a particular honor for me because—let's face it—my presence on this stage is pretty unlikely. My father was a foreign student, born and raised in a small village in Kenya. He grew up herding goats, went to school in a tin-roof shack. His father—my grandfather—was a cook, a domestic servant to the British.

But my grandfather had larger dreams for his son. Through hard work and persistence my father got a scholarship to study in a magical place, America, that shone as a beacon of freedom and opportunity to so many who had come before.

While studying here, my father met my mother. She was born in a town on the other side of the world, in Kansas. Her father worked on oil rigs and farms through most of the Depression. The day after Pearl Harbor my grandfather signed up for duty, joined the army, marched across Europe.

Back home, my grandmother raised their baby and went to work on a bomber assembly line. After the war, they studied on the G.I. Bill, bought a house, and later moved west all the way to Hawaii in search of opportunity.

And they, too, had big dreams for their daughter. A common dream, born of two continents.

My parents shared not only an improbable love; they shared an abiding faith in the possibilities of this nation. They would give me an African name, Barack, or "blessed," believing that in an open-minded America your name is no barrier to success.

They imagined me going to the best schools in the land, even though they weren't rich, because in a generous America you don't have to be rich to achieve your potential.

They are both passed away now. And yet, I know that, on this night, they look down on me with great pride.

I stand here today, grateful for the diversity of my heritage, aware that my parents' dreams live on in my two precious daughters. I stand here knowing that my story is part of the larger American story, that I owe a debt to all of those who came before me, and that, in no other country on earth, is my story even possible.

Tonight, we gather to affirm the greatness of our nation—not because of the height of our skyscrapers, or the power of our military, or the size of our economy. Our pride is based on a very simple assertion, summed up in a declaration made over two hundred years ago: "We hold these truths to be self-evident, that all men are created equal. That they are endowed by their Creator with certain inalienable rights. That among these are life, liberty and the pursuit of happiness."

Aug 28, 2008

Nomination acceptance speech, Democratic National Convention, Denver, Colorado

Four years ago, I stood before you and told you my story—of the brief union between a young man from Kenya and a young woman from Kansas who weren't well-off or well-known, but shared a belief that in America, their son could achieve whatever he put his mind to.

It is that promise that has always set this country apart—that through hard work and sacrifice, each of us can pursue our individual dreams but still come together as one American family, to ensure that the next generation can pursue their dreams as well.

That's why I stand here tonight. Because for two hundred and thirty-two years, at each moment when that promise was in danger, ordinary men and women—students and soldiers, farmers and teachers, nurses and janitors—found the courage to keep it alive.

I don't fit the typical pedigree, and I haven't spent my career in the halls of Washington.

But I stand before you tonight because all across America something is stirring. What the naysayers don't understand is that this election has never been about me. It's been about you.

For eighteen long months, you have stood up, one by one, and said enough to the politics of the past. You understand that in this election, the greatest risk we can take is to try the same old politics with the same old players and expect a different result. You have shown what history teaches us—that at defining moments like this one, the change we need doesn't come from Washington. Change comes to Washington. Change happens because the American people demand it—because they rise up and insist on new ideas and new leadership, a new politics for a new time.

America, this is one of those moments.

I believe that as hard as it will be, the change we need is coming. Because I've seen it. Because I've lived it.

November 4, 2008

Election-night victory speech, Chicago, Illinois
Hello, Chicago.

If there is anyone out there who still doubts that America is a place where all things are possible, who still wonders if the dream of our founders is alive in our time, who still questions the power of our democracy, tonight is your answer.

It's the answer told by lines that stretched around schools and churches in numbers this nation has never seen, by people who waited three

hours and four hours, many for the first time in their lives, because they believed that this time must be different, that their voices could be that difference.

It's the answer spoken by young and old, rich and poor, Democrat and Republican, black, white, Hispanic, Asian, Native American, gay, straight, disabled and not disabled. Americans who sent a message to the world that we have never been just a collection of individuals or a collection of red states and blue states.

We are, and always will be, the United States of America.

It's the answer that led those who've been told for so long by so many to be cynical and fearful and doubtful about what we can achieve to put their hands on the arc of history and bend it once more toward the hope of a better day.

It's been a long time coming, but tonight, because of what we did on this date, in this election, at this defining moment, change has come to America.

Our campaign was not hatched in the halls of Washington. It began in the backyards of Iowa and the living rooms of Vermont and the front porches of South Carolina. It was built by working men and women who dug into what little savings they had to give $5 and $10 and $20 to the cause.

It grew strength from the young people who rejected the myth of their generation's indifference, who left their homes and their families for jobs that offered little pay and less sleep.

It drew strength from the not-so-young people who braved the bitter cold and scorching heat to knock on doors of perfect strangers, and from the millions of Americans who volunteered and organized.

This is your victory.

Let's remember that it was a man from this state who first carried the banner of the Republican Party to the White House, a party founded on the values of self-reliance and individual liberty and national unity.

Those are values that we all share. And while the Democratic Party has won a great victory tonight, we do so with a measure of humility and determination to heal the divides that have held back our progress.

As Lincoln said to a nation far more divided than ours, we are not enemies but friends. Though passion may have strained, it must not break our bonds of affection.

Tonight we proved once more that the true strength of our nation comes not from the might of our arms or the scale of our wealth, but from the enduring power of our ideals: democracy, liberty, opportunity, and unyielding hope.

That's the true genius of America: that America can change. Our union can be perfected. What we've already achieved gives us hope for what we can and must achieve tomorrow.

This election had many firsts and many stories that will be told for generations. But one that's on my mind tonight is about a woman who cast her ballot in Atlanta. She's a lot like the millions of others who stood in line to make their voice heard in this election except for one thing: Ann Nixon Cooper is 106 years old.

She was born just a generation past slavery; a time when there were no cars on the road or planes in the sky; when someone like her couldn't vote for two reasons—because she was a woman and because of the color of her skin.

And tonight, I think about all that she's seen throughout her century in America—the heartache and the hope; the struggle and the progress; the times we were told that we can't, and the people who pressed on with that American creed: Yes we can.

At a time when women's voices were silenced and their hopes dismissed, she lived to see them stand up and speak out and reach for the ballot. Yes we can.

When there was despair in the dust bowl and depression across the land, she saw a nation conquer fear itself with a New Deal, new jobs, a new sense of common purpose. Yes we can.

When the bombs fell on our harbor and tyranny threatened the world, she was there to witness a generation rise to greatness and a democracy was saved. Yes we can.

She was there for the buses in Montgomery, the hoses in Birmingham, a bridge in Selma, and a preacher from Atlanta who told a people that "We Shall Overcome." Yes we can.

A man touched down on the moon, a wall came down in Berlin, a world was connected by our own science and imagination.

And this year, in this election, she touched her finger to a screen, and cast her vote, because after 106 years in America, through the best of times and the darkest of hours, she knows how America can change.

Yes we can.

America, we have come so far. We have seen so much. But there is so much more to do. So tonight, let us ask ourselves—if our children should live to see the next century; if my daughters should be so lucky to live as long as Ann Nixon Cooper, what change will they see? What progress will we have made?

This is our chance to answer that call. This is our moment.

This is our time, to put our people back to work and open doors of opportunity for our kids; to restore prosperity and promote the cause of peace; to reclaim the American dream and reaffirm that fundamental truth, that, out of many, we are one; that while we breathe, we hope. And where we are met with cynicism and doubts and those who tell us that we can't, we will respond with that timeless creed that sums up the spirit of a people: Yes, we can.

Thank you. God bless you. And may God bless the United States of America.

1 Understanding the Reading. Answer the following questions in good sentence form.

1. List three facts about Barack Obama that made him an appropriate symbol of change.

   _____

   _____

   _____

2. How did white voters prove the political commentators and experts wrong on November 4, 2008?

   _____

   _____

   _____

3. Why did Obama's election mark a major milestone in the struggle for equality and civil rights?

   _____

4. Why did Obama describe himself as an unlikely candidate for office?

   _____

   _____

   _____

5. According to Obama, how do things change in Washington?

   _____

   _____

   _____

6. How did young people "reject the myth of their generation's indifference"?

   _____

   _____

7. Why do you think Obama compares the political campaign to the Civil War? What connections might he see?

   _____

   _____

   _____

8. In your opinion, how is Obama's story part of the "American story"?

   _____

   _____

   _____

9. Why does Obama use a 106-year-old woman as a symbol of change?

_____

_____

_____

10. Name five things that have changed during Ann Nixon Cooper's lifetime, according to the speech.

_____

_____

_____

_____

_____

2 What Do You Think? Answer the following questions in brief but detailed paragraphs.

1. Obama asks the audience, "if our children should live to see the next century . . . what change will they see? What progress will we have made?" What do you think will have changed 100 years from now? Include reasons for your thinking.

_____

_____

_____

_____

_____

_____

_____

2. How does the phrase "Yes we can" relate to what Obama calls the "true genius of America"?

_____

_____

_____

_____

_____

_____

_____

3 History in the Making. In his speeches, Barack Obama refers to many major historical moments. Use a dictionary, encyclopedia, or the Internet to help you complete the sentences below. Each sentence deals with historical figures, places, or events mentioned in Obama's speeches.

1930s	the Civil War	John McCain	Rosa Parks
African Americans	Ann Nixon Cooper	Montgomery	Pearl Harbor
Neil Armstrong	the Dust Bowl	the New Deal	Franklin D. Roosevelt
Berlin	G.I. Bill	Richard Nixon	women
Birmingham	Martin Luther King, Jr.	November 4	World War II
George H. Bush	Abraham Lincoln	Barack Obama	

1. _____, a black woman, refused to give up her seat at the front of a bus to make room for a white passenger. Her actions set off the bus boycotts in _____, Alabama.

2. The _____ wall separated two parts of Germany from one another. The wall "fell" in 1989, when _____ was president.

3. In 1941, the Japanese bombed _____, prompting the United States to enter into _____. After the war, the _____ helped many veterans attend college.

4. _____ was a preacher and civil rights leader who delivered a famous "I Have a Dream" speech.

5. _____ and _____ were two groups that were not initially allowed to vote. _____ saw both of those groups win the right to cast a ballot.

6. _____ passed a major financial rescue plan, known as _____, during the _____.

7. _____ was one of the men who landed on the moon in 1969, during _____'s presidency.

8. Police released attack dogs on civil rights marchers in _____, Alabama.

9. The _____ was caused by a major drought that swept across American farmlands during the 1930s.

10. _____ lost the presidential race to _____ on _____, 2008.

11. _____ was the first Republican president. During his presidency, the nation fought _____ and abolished slavery.

4 Comprehension Check. Write the letter of the correct answer on the line to the left.

_____ 1. The idea that white voters would claim to support Obama and then vote for the white candidate in the privacy of the voting booth is an example of what kind of thinking?

   a. optimistic   **c.** multiracial

   b. cynical   **d.** idealistic

_____ 2. Obama mentions a "sense of common purpose." This could also be called:

   a. individualism   **c.** civility

   b. equality   **d.** responsibility

_____ 3. "Inalienable" rights are rights that cannot:

   a. be taken away   **c.** be defined

   b. be given to others **d.** belong to immigrants

_____ 4. The opposite of "prosperity" is:

   a. richness   **c.** poverty

   b. rejection   **d.** duty

_____ 5. A person who is prejudiced might have a problem with:

   a. diversity   **c.** elections

   b. democracy   **d.** liberty

_____ 6. Barack Obama describes his heritage as diverse. "Heritage" can refer to all of the following, except:

   a. lineage   **c.** background

   b. legacy   **d.** ambitions

_____ 7. When Obama mentions "red states and blue states," he is referring to what two types of states?

   a. Northern and Southern   **c.** diverse and segregated

   b. Republican and Democrat **d.** Eastern and Western

_____ 8. The opposite of "cynical and doubtful" would be:

   a. pessimistic and fearful   **c.** optimistic and hopeful

   b. idealistic and democratic **d.** diverse and hopeful

_____ 9. Another way to describe "self-reliance" would be:

   a. indifference   **c.** determination

   b. humility   **d.** independence

_____ 10. Obama says Ann Nixon Cooper was born "just a generation past slavery." That means slavery existed in the time of her:

   a. parents   **c.** great-grandparents

   b. grandparents   **d.** children

5 Biographies and Family Trees. In his speeches, Barack Obama discusses the heritage, legacy, and experiences of different generations. He describes the lives of his grandparents, parents, and himself. He tells his own life story, or biography, in order to explain why he is an unlikely candidate for the presidency. Fill out your own family tree below, including brief descriptions of each family member (their country of origin, profession, etc). Imagine you are running for a political office in the U.S. Using your family tree as reference, write a brief biography of your life and family background that explains how you are a likely or unlikely candidate for the office.

Grandfather   +   Grandmother   Grandfather   +   Grandmother

Father   +   Mother

Me

My Biography

_____

_____

_____

_____

_____

_____

_____

_____

_____

_____

_____

Words for Study

heir	subconsciously	overshadowed	seers
plight	sentimental	shoddy	kinship
competitive	amateur	librarian	Euphrates
underestimated	layman	spontaneous	bosom

LESSON 20

Heir to Tradition

Does the emphasis that so many writers place upon the present mean that we should forget about the past and concentrate on adjusting to the changes taking place around us now? In this excerpt from her book *How to Think About Ourselves,* Bonaro Overstreet presents a thoughtful response to this question.

* * *

"Sometimes I feel like a motherless child . . ." Thus go the words of the old spiritual, and in them is the haunt of earth's loneliest estate.

If anywhere in our experience there is proof that man does not live by bread alone, it is in the condition of the child left to find its own way in a precarious and confusing world. Relatives, or society at large, may see to it that the orphan does not go cold or hungry, but such elementary care leaves untouched some inner core of loneliness. The lack remains—a lack of a deep sense of belonging.

We recognize the plight of the orphan. Yet many, perhaps most, of us in a deep spiritual sense are voluntary orphans. We have cut ourselves off from the human tradition that is parent to the human present. As a result, there is an uneasiness that cannot be quieted by adding new possessions, by competitive triumphs in our activities, or by joining more organizations. It is the uneasiness of trying to build a new sense of values out of materials that are too flimsy to rely on, of never quite knowing what is important and what does not matter, of trying to go it too much alone, or desperate in aloneness, of running with whatever gang is handy to run with.

Biologists never tire of stressing the fact that man, and only man, is a tradition builder. Birds and beavers can repeat what birds and beavers have done before. But only the human being can begin where others before him have left off. He can do *what they have not done* because he can learn from *what they have done.*

Modern man, confused about his relationship to the past, has built a confused present. Only as a scientist and technologist has he confidently honored the past as it can best be honored by a tradition-building species: *he has learned from it.* He has learned not to repeat its blunders but to carry its triumphs on from stage to stage. In economics, politics, and religion, however, he has consistently dishonored the past. Either he has underestimated his debt to it by pretending to be self-made, or he has refused to budge beyond the stopping point of the past.

Psychiatrists have made it clear that an individual who is consciously or subconsciously at odds with his own past is likely to be an unhappy and sick individual. If he knows nothing at all about his past, he lacks something vital to his sense of completeness. If, on the other hand, he knows his past and resents it, he is again in a bad way. For the expectations and desires that he will bring to present situations and future plans will be so distorted by bitterness that they will cause further distortion. If by contrast he is tied to his past by a sentimental memory of it, he will remain mentally, emotionally, and socially immature. He will be dependent, inclined to cling to the familiar, possessive in friendship and marriage, prone to seek a leader.

Properly speaking, an individual's past is simply the *so-far element* in his life. It contains what he has learned so far, the people he has known so far, the problems he has solved or fumbled so far, the types of behaviors that he has, so far, found reason to condemn or admire. Thus the past is what is supposed to keep an individual from having to be, all his life, a rank amateur in his role as human being. Properly speaking, the past is what a person learns from—and goes on from. The tragedy, as psychiatrists are making us aware, is that the past too often becomes for an individual not something to go from, but something that prevents a healthy going on.

But neither the trained psychiatrist nor the observant layman, it seems to me, has yet paid enough attention to what it does to an individual to have a right or wrong relationship to that shared past we call the human tradition. The pasts that laymen and psychiatrists alike have talked about, in sizing up the behavior of people, have almost always been personal pasts. This man, we say, was once a boy who hated his father and loved his mother. This woman was once a girl who was overshadowed in all that she tried to do by a brilliant and beautiful younger sister.

But what was the relationship of this man or this woman to the longer past, the human past? How were they introduced to it? What were they encouraged to find in it? Has it given them any practical and dependable clues to what is worth wanting and admiring on the human level of life? What habits and attitudes of their own trace back to admiration of what has, throughout history, been proved to have worth?

It seems odd that no psychiatrist has yet—so far as I know—explored the biographical evidence which suggests that many individuals have triumphed over painful and dreary personal pasts because some fortunate accident encouraged them to make the human past their own. In one life story after another we find the theme repeated: that of the lost and lonely child who, through some circumstance, was brought into contact with tradition, was introduced to books through which he learned the difference between what is shoddy in human behavior and what is excellent.

To take one example, we may recall the story that the American writer Langston Hughes tells in his autobiography, *The Big Sea*. A small and lonely son of a despised race, he had the enormous good fortune to discover a public library and in it a librarian who, with a sure sense of the boy's need, introduced him to book after book—gave him the great past as his own; helped him to make it his personal background, so that the standards it set became the standards on which he was ready to stake his life.

Such contact with the past, obviously, is necessary not only to those who are having to compensate for a difficult personal past. For even the most fortunate among us, it is the background that contains more of understanding and compassion, more of courage and dedication, than even the best family background can hold. It both illumines the world in which the individual does his daily living and introduces him to an older and wider world than any he has known.

To say precisely what happens to us when we establish a warm, creative link with the long history of man on earth is as difficult as to say what happens when we experience a great love. We are still the selves we were. Yet we are no longer the selves we were, for we see the world around us so differently that our spontaneous reactions to it are different.

As individuals, we are more than the powers and limitations we were born with. We are, in fact, marked less by these than by *our habits of attention,* the *expectations* we bring to our meetings with life, and the *judgments* we pass upon people and events. Let any new insight change the focus of our attention—so that we notice what we did not notice before—or change our expectations and our habits of judgment, and we may in an instant move mentally and emotionally into a new environment,

even though we have not moved from our tracks. Something of this sort is what happens when we fall in love—either with one individual, or with the human race as it speaks for itself through the great tradition.

All through the ages the seers, prophets, saints, artists, and genuine lovers have tried mightily to make the experiences that have transformed them seem real to persons who cannot quite believe them because they have not had matching experiences of their own. When, by word or example, they are able to make it convincing that there is a non-ordinary approach to life which yields a tremendous sense of happiness and freedom, they are able to persuade others—some yearning few—to take a chance on a way of life the worth of which they have not yet tested for themselves.

Among these converts, many will still see so darkly that they will miss the road pointed out to them and stumble, instead, into a path that leads nowhere. Some few, however, will catch on to the fact that what is called for in their lives is a whole new focus of attention, a whole new set of habits and attitudes—ones that will break down the barriers by which they have been held apart from their world and the people in it. They are the few who actually discover the excitement of being human, and strangely enough, at the heart of that excitement, discover the peace that passes understanding.

In a profound sense, the individual who has come to feel his kinship to the human race and his responsible heirship to the human past has gone through such a transforming experience. He probably makes keener distinctions than ever before—for he knows, as never before, what he considers important. But he is no longer alone. He knows himself as a member of the human race.

1 Understanding the Reading. Put the letter of the best answer on the line.

1. Overstreet uses the example of the orphan to illustrate that _____.
   a. nobody chooses to be an orphan
   b. parents often neglect their children
   c. people need more than food, clothing, and shelter
   d. the care received by orphans is better than we often realize

2. The past, or tradition, in this reading is referred to as a(n) _____.
   a. burden
   b. heir
   c. orphan
   d. parent

3. *Odds,* as it is used by Overstreet in "Psychiatrists have made it clear that an individual who is at odds with his own past is likely to be an unhappy and sick individual" means _____.
   a. a number of points given to a weaker side in a contest
   b. a ratio expressing the probable outcome of an event
   c. in conflict or disagreement
   d. likelihood

4. According to the psychiatrists, which word *least* describes a person who is at odds with his past?
   a. dependent
   b. incomplete
   c. resentful
   d. vital

5. Overstreet's *main* disagreement with the typical view toward the past is that most of us _____.
   a. blame the past for all our present difficulties
   b. have a sentimental view of the past
   c. emphasize only our personal pasts
   d. spend too much time reliving past events

6. To explain her disagreement with the typical view of the past, Overstreet uses the example of _____.
   a. Langston Hughes's autobiography
   b. the orphan
   c. the girl who is overshadowed by her younger sister
   d. the "so-far element"

7. Overstreet contends that _____.
   a. an appreciation of tradition helps everyone who has had a difficult personal past
   b. people can be enriched by an understanding of tradition
   c. tradition is the strongest influence on our present lives
   d. tradition reminds us of how limited we are in our ability to bring about change

2 Reacting to the Reading. Answer the following questions in good sentence form.

1. According to Overstreet, many people concentrate on their personal pasts and pay little or no attention to the human past or tradition. What does she feel people can gain from establishing a "warm, creative link with the long history of man on earth"?

_____

_____

_____

_____

_____

_____

_____

2. Do you think that Overstreet is correct in her beliefs? Why or why not?

_____

_____

_____

_____

_____

_____

3. Suppose you decide that Overstreet is right—that "establishing a warm, creative link" with the past is important. How might you go about establishing this link?

_____

_____

_____

_____

_____

_____

3 A Poem by Langston Hughes. In the reading selection, Overstreet discusses how the American writer and poet Langston Hughes (1902–1967) made the human past his personal background. Read this poem of his, and then answer the questions.

The Negro Speaks of Rivers
by Langston Hughes

I've known rivers:
I've known rivers ancient as the world and older than the flow of human blood in human veins.

My soul has grown deep like the rivers.

I bathed in the Euphrates when dawns were young.
I built my hut near the Congo and it lulled me to sleep.
I looked upon the Nile and raised the pyramids above it.
I heard the singing of the Mississippi when Abe Lincoln went down to New Orleans,
    and I've seen its muddy bosom turn all golden in the sunset.

I've known rivers:
Ancient, dusky rivers.

My soul has grown deep like the rivers.

1. What is it? Where is it? Locate each of the following using a dictionary or other reference.

   a. the Euphrates _____

   b. the Congo _____

   c. the Nile _____

   d. New Orleans _____

2. Cite evidence from the poem that shows that Langston Hughes did, as Overstreet stated in the reading, make the human past his personal background.

   _____

   _____

   _____

   _____

3. Why do you think Hughes chose rivers rather than forests or mountains to express his link with the past?

   _____

   _____

   _____

4. Why do you think Hughes says that his "*soul* has grown deep" rather than his mind or his heart?

_____

_____

_____

_____

_____

4 Synonyms and Antonyms. Choose a synonym to fill in the first blank in each sentence. Choose an antonym to fill in the second blank.

Synonyms

ample

corrupt

despise

elevate

ignite

leaning

obstacle

rehabilitate

sentimental

shielded

Antonyms

admire

advantage

damage

extinguish

honorable

lower

stingy

unemotional

unprotected

unwillingness

1. Barrier and _____ are antonyms for _____.

2. Generous and _____ are antonyms for

    _____.

3. Kindle and _____ are antonyms for _____.

4. Restore and _____ are antonyms for _____.

5. Romantic and _____ are antonyms for

    _____.

6. Safe and _____ are antonyms for _____.

7. Scorn and _____ are antonyms for _____.

8. Tendency and _____ are antonyms for

    _____.

9. Unprincipled and _____ are antonyms for

    _____.

10. Uplift and _____ are antonyms for _____.

5 Spelling Check. One tradition with which we are familiar is Thanksgiving. In each of these items about the celebration of Thanksgiving, one of the underlined words may be misspelled. Write that word, spelled correctly, on the line. If none of the words is misspelled, write *all right* on the line.

_____

1. Although a day reserved for general thanksgiving—especially at harvest time—has been observed by almost every nation in almost every historacal period, Thanksgiving Day as observed in the United States has evolved as a unique American feast.

_____

2. Probably the first thanksgiving service in America, which was held on May 27, 1578, by the members of an expidition that had landed on the shores of Newfoundland, was conducted by an English minister who preached a thanksgiving sermon.

_____

3. Those, however, were merely thanksgiving services, and the origin of a *day* of thanksgiving such as we now celabrate must be granted to Governor Bradford of Plymouth.

_____

4. After landing on the desolate coast of New England in November 1620, the Pilgrums passed the winter with great suffering and watched the growth of the seed they planted in spring with great anxiety. For the lives of the colonists depended on the result.

_____

5. When the grain was cut and the harvest was found to be abundant, there was great rejoicing and the governor proclaimed a day of thanksgiving. He sent out four men in search of game, and they soon returned with a large number of wild foul, most of which were turkeys.

_____

6. Incidentally, one etymologist tells the doubtful but amusing story of how the turkey is said to have gotten its name from the doctor on Columbus's first voyage who exclaimed "Tukki!" (the Hebrew word for "big bird") on seeing this unusual specimen for the first time.

_____

7. The first Thanksgiving feast probably consisted of turkeys, ducks, geese, native squash and pumpkin. The provisions must have been abundant, for about one hundred fourty persons, including ninety Indians, were entertained for three days.

_____

8. The specific date of this festival is not known, but acording to records it must have occurred between September 23rd and November 11th in 1621.

9. On October 3, 1789, <u>George</u> Washington issued a <u>proclamation</u> appointing Thursday, November 26, 1789, as a day of <u>general</u> thanksgiving, and this day may be <u>considered</u> the first <u>national</u> Thanksgiving Day.

10. Thanksgiving days were <u>irregularly</u> celebrated after this and almost never in the South; but in 1864, President Lincoln issued a <u>proclamation</u> <u>appointing</u> the <u>forth</u> Thursday in November as Thanksgiving Day, with a view of having the day observed every year <u>thereafter</u>.

11. The <u>adoption</u> of the last Thursday in November as a <u>uniform</u> date for <u>observence</u> of Thanksgiving was largely due to the efforts of Mrs. Sarah J. Hale, a well-known author and <u>editor</u> of the late nineteenth <u>century</u>.

12. Although Thanksgiving Day is still observed by feasting and general <u>festivity</u>, the electronic era of television has resulted in millions of Americans being <u>thankfull</u> for the <u>broadcast</u> of football games rather than for the <u>abundance</u> of nature that brought about Thanksgiving Day in the first place.

1 Definitions. Match the words listed below with the correct definitions.

canopy	interval	palpitation	savvy
decade	maneuver	plight	shoddy
famine	milestone	precarious	technology
flux	obstacle	prominent	unabridged

_____ **1.** a covering hung over a throne, bed, or entrance

_____ **2.** a difficult condition or situation

_____ **3.** a continued flow or flood

_____ **4.** a drastic and wide-reaching shortage of food; severe hunger

_____ **5.** a period of ten years

_____ **6.** inferior; of poor quality

_____ **7.** a trembling or shaking; irregular or rapid beating of the heart

_____ **8.** not condensed; complete

_____ **9.** a planned military movement; a skillful plan or movement

_____ **10.** something that stands in the way or interferes

_____ **11.** risky and uncertain; dangerous, hazardous

_____ **12.** practical understanding or knowledge; common sense (slang)

_____ **13.** widely known; important

_____ **14.** the application of scientific and industrial skills to practical uses

_____ **15.** a distance or space between two objects or points; the time between two events

_____ **16.** an important event

2 Vocabulary Review. Write the letter of the best answer on the line.

1. A seer would most likely make _____.
   - **a.** conclusions
   - **b.** predictions
   - **c.** determinations
   - **d.** proclamations

2. An ecologist would be most concerned about _____.
   - **a.** tyranny
   - **b.** segregation
   - **c.** deforestation
   - **d.** monotony

3. A navigator often uses a _____.
   - **a.** winch
   - **b.** device
   - **c.** probe
   - **d.** compass

4. A person watching a sentimental movie might request a(n) _____.
   - **a.** handkerchief
   - **b.** intermission
   - **c.** snack
   - **d.** usher

5. A sociologist would probably not spend a lot of time studying _____.
   - **a.** battleships
   - **b.** courtships
   - **c.** friendships
   - **d.** kinships

6. Amateurs are generally _____.
   - **a.** unfriendly
   - **b.** unhealthy
   - **c.** unmarried
   - **d.** unpaid

7. A person prone to spontaneous actions is rarely _____.
   - **a.** conscious
   - **b.** self-conscious
   - **c.** subconscious
   - **d.** unconscious

8. The *hearth* is frequently used to symbolize _____ life.
   - **a.** domestic
   - **b.** international
   - **c.** patriotic
   - **d.** tropical

3 Vocabulary Review. Match the words listed below with what they best describe.

abridged	desolate	offensive	reliable
competitive	economical	portable	sentimental

_____ **1.** a 20,000 word dictionary

_____ **2.** a small television set

_____ **3.** a professional tennis player

_____ **4.** a scrapbook lover

_____ **5.** a thrifty householder

_____ **6.** a trustworthy employee

_____ **7.** an empty landscape

_____ **8.** a vulgar insult

4 Population Growth and Change. The chart below records the population in five different periods of American history beginning with the Jamestown settlement in 1607. Refer to both the chart and a dictionary, if necessary, to answer the questions.

Population Growth & Change

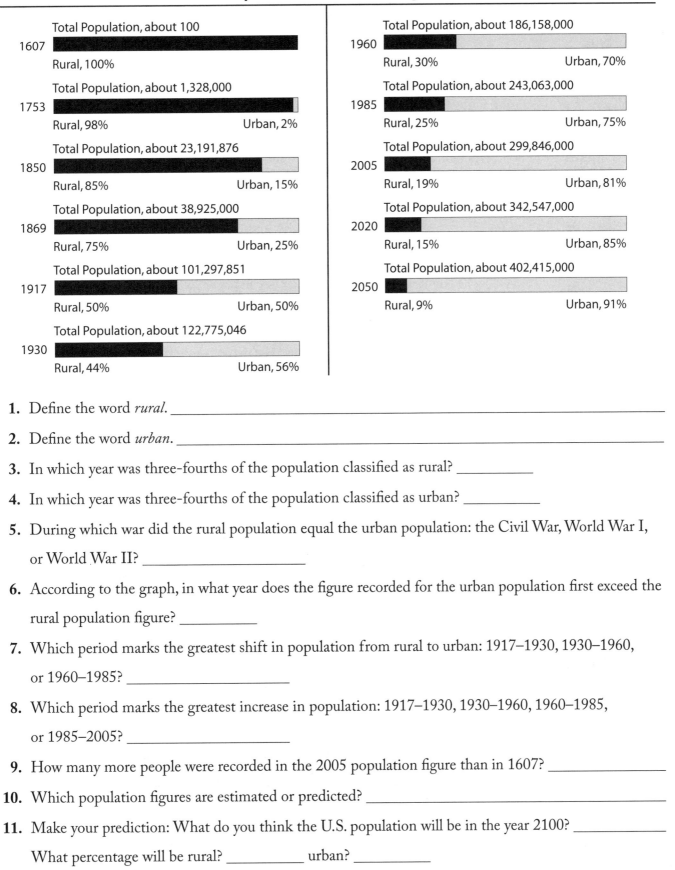

1. Define the word *rural*. _____

2. Define the word *urban*. _____

3. In which year was three-fourths of the population classified as rural? _____

4. In which year was three-fourths of the population classified as urban? _____

5. During which war did the rural population equal the urban population: the Civil War, World War I, or World War II? _____

6. According to the graph, in what year does the figure recorded for the urban population first exceed the rural population figure? _____

7. Which period marks the greatest shift in population from rural to urban: 1917–1930, 1930–1960, or 1960–1985? _____

8. Which period marks the greatest increase in population: 1917–1930, 1930–1960, 1960–1985, or 1985–2005? _____

9. How many more people were recorded in the 2005 population figure than in 1607? _____

10. Which population figures are estimated or predicted? _____

11. Make your prediction: What do you think the U.S. population will be in the year 2100? _____
    What percentage will be rural? _____ urban? _____

5 What Difference Does a Century Make? As you can see from the population statistics in the last exercise, a lot can change in one hundred years. Read the table which contains information about what the U.S. was like in 1900 and then a century later in 2000. Think about the kinds of changes that have occurred in the last one hundred years, and then answer the questions in **Parts A, B,** and **C.**

U.S. Population: 1900 vs. 2000

	1900	2000
1	The average person is a male in his early 20s who rents a home in the country.	The average person is a female in her mid-30s who owns a home in the city.
2	There are more males than females.	There are more females than males.
3	The largest five-year age group includes children from 0–5 years old.	The largest five-year age groups include adults 35–39 and 40–44.
4	The infant death rate is more than 10%.	The infant death rate is less than 1%.
5	1 out of every 3 people is under 15 years old.	1 out of every 5 people is under 15 years old.
6	4.1% of people are over age 65.	12.4% of people are over age 65.
7	122,000 people are over age 85.	4.2 million people are over age 85.
8	Average life expectancy is about 47 years.	Average life expectancy is about 77 years.
9	1 of every 8 residents is of a race other than white.	1 of every 4 residents is of a race other than white.
10	American Indian and Alaska Native have the highest percentage of people under age 15.	Multiracial (two or more races) have the highest percentage of people under age 15.
11	11.6% of people are black and 87.9% are white.	12.3% of people are black and 75.1% are white.
12	The census does not report data on the Hispanic population.	The Hispanic population represents 12.5% of the total U.S. population.
13	Asians and Pacific Islanders are almost all male.	There are slightly more female Asians and Pacific Islanders than males.
14	Black females outnumber black males.	Black females outnumber black males.
15	The census does not report data on multiracial populations.	Hawaii reports the largest (21.4%) multiracial population.
16	The most common household contains seven or more people.	The most common household contains two people.
17	Male family households with no wife are unlikely to include children.	Male family households with no wife are more likely to include children.
18	Over half of all occupied housing units are rented.	66% of all occupied housing units are owned.
19	The most populous state is New York with 7.3 million people.	The most populous state is California with almost 34 million people.

Source: U.S. Census Bureau

Part A The media headlines below relate to some of the statistics in the table. Read each headline, and then write the number or numbers of the statistics that relate to that headline. The first one is done for you.

_____12_____   **1.** U.S. Hispanic Population to Triple by 2050

_____   **2.** Infant Mortality Rates Drop

_____   **3.** Island Life in Multiracial Hawaii Shaped Obama

_____   **4.** U.S. Sees Major Growth in Elderly Population

_____   **5.** Why More and More Women Are Losing Custody Battles Over Their Children

_____   **6.** Family Size in America: Are Large Families Back?

_____   **7.** California Still Leads the Nation in Immigrant Population

_____   **8.** December 1906: Thousands of Filipino Men Rush to Hawaii in Search of Jobs

_____   **9.** White People of European Descent Will No Longer Be Majority by 2042

_____   **10.** Brooklyn Closes 14 Elementary Schools

Part B Read these predicted statistics for the year 2100, and think about what effect they might have on life in the U.S. Write your own headline for each statistic.

1. Females of every race outnumber males.

_____

2. 1 billion people are over age 85.

_____

3. The average person is a 50-year-old multiracial female.

_____

Part C What do you think life in the U.S. will be like in the 22nd century? Write a description of life in 2100, and include some predictions of your own.

_____

_____

_____

_____

_____

_____

_____

_____

_____

_____

_____

_____

_____

_____

_____

_____

_____

_____

_____

_____

_____

_____

_____

Answer Key

Lesson 1

1 Understanding the Reading

1. b	4. b	7. a	9. d
2. c	5. a	8. d	10. a
3. b	6. b		

2 What Do You Think?

1. Answers will vary. Accept any reasonable response.
2. Answers will vary. Accept any reasonable response.

3 Synonyms

1. display	6. amazing	11. overpower
2. confine	7. universal	12. hidden
3. burst	8. myth	13. dive
4. advertise	9. achievement	14. support
5. spellbound	10. disentangle	

4 Names That Have Made the Dictionary

1. Braille, (braille)
2. Poinsett, (poinsettia)
3. Jacuzzi, (Jacuzzi)
4. Fahrenheit, (Fahrenheit)
5. Lynch, (lynch)
6. Sandwich, (sandwich)
7. Derick (or Derrick), (derrick)
8. Nicot, (nicotine)

5 Challenges

1. 4, 3, 5, 2, 1
2. 5, 3, 4, 2, 1 or 5, 2, 3, 4, 1
3. 2, 5, 1, 3, 4 or 2, 5, 1, 4, 3

Lesson 2

1 Understanding the Reading

1. b	3. c	5. d	7. b
2. d	4. a	6. a	8. c

2 More about We and They

Answers will vary. Accept reasonable responses.

3 Antonyms

1. suddenly	6. dwindle	11. certainly
2. disfigure	7. frail	12. inflict
3. advanced	8. wastefulness	13. indifferent
4. fixed	9. jittery	14. dullness
5. careless	10. plain	

4 The Suffix -logy

1. zoology	5. ecology	9. sociology
2. meteorology	6. archaeology	10. theology
3. biology	7. pathology	11. etymology
4. psychology	8. geology	12. astrology

5 More about Melanesia

1. a	3. b	5. c
2. d	4. c	

Lesson 3

1 Understanding the Reading

Answers will vary. Reasonable responses include:

1. Ordinary people who saw movie stars dressed in fancy clothes dreamt about what it would be like to be Hollywood royalty.
2. The *Enquirer* made it easy for everyone to get news and photos of popular celebrities.
3. When TVs became affordable, TV shows—and their stars—became part of people's everyday lives.
4. *ET* brought celebrity news, photos, and information about celebrities' personal lives into America's living room.
5. The Internet makes it easy for fans to find photos of and information about their favorite TV and movie stars.
6. Reality shows make regular people into TV stars.

2 Reality Check

Answers will vary.

3 Synonyms and Antonyms

1. antonym	7. synonym	12. synonym
2. antonym	8. antonym	13. antonym
3. synonym	9. synonym	14. antonym
4. antonym	10. synonym	15. synonym
5. antonym	11. antonym	16. synonym
6. antonym		

4 The Suffix -ist

1. hypnotist	5. activist	9. alarmist
2. novelist	6. anthropologist	10. conformist
3. dramatist	7. etymologist	11. nonconformist
4. journalist	8. archaeologist	12. meteorologist

5 Working with Headings

1. Cooking Show	5. Crime Drama
2. Sitcom	6. Sporting Event
3. Newsmagazine	7. Nature Show
4. News Broadcast	8. Game Show

Extra Credit: Answers will vary.

Lesson 4

1 Understanding the Reading

1. a	4. c	7. b	9. a
2. d	5. d	8. d	10. b
3. b	6. c		

2 What Do You Think?

1. Answers will vary. Accept reasonable responses.
2. Answers will vary.
3. Answers will vary. Accept reasonable responses.

3 Word Relationships

1. b	4. d	7. a	9. c
2. c	5. d	8. d	10. b
3. c	6. c		

4 The Suffix -ism

1. escapism	5. terrorism	9. hypnotism
2. cynicism	6. materialism	10. skepticism
3. individualism	7. favoritism	11. idealism
4. heroism	8. capitalism	12. patriotism

5 Spelling Check

1. origin	5. humorous	8. *Bulletin*
2. following	6. correct	9. cartoon
3. correct	7. forty-two	10. portraits
4. etc.		

Lesson 5

1 Understanding the Story

1. b	4. d	7. b	9. c
2. a	5. d	8. a	10. c
3. c	6. c		

2 What Do You Think?

1. Mr. Parkenstacker pretends to be a cashier in a restaurant. Answers will vary on why he does this. Accept reasonable responses.
2. Answers will vary.
3. Answers will vary.

3 Which Word Does Not Fit?

1. question	7. fascination	12. unsuspecting
2. glaring	8. self-seeking	13. tragedy
3. printing	9. valuable	14. suggest
4. restaurant	10. stately	15. stillness
5. idealistic	11. soar	16. Wilhelmina
6. Montreal		

4 More about O. Henry

1. cleverly, scholarly, continually
2. originally, eventually, determinedly
3. necessity, majority, prosperity
4. objective, offensive, subjective
5. unbearable, valuable, unmistakable
6. confirmation, assumption, abbreviation
7. indication, limitation, quotation
8. cheerless, boundless, countless
9. bewilderment, fulfillment, bombardment
10. observation, relations, separation

5 Pretenses in the Park

1. wallflower	4. skeptic	7. manipulator
2. escapist	5. alarmist	8. braggart
3. immigrant	6. Scrooge	9. quibbler

Review: Lessons 1–5

1 Definitions

1. organism	7. technique	12. modesty
2. luxury	8. neutrality	13. economy
3. leisure	9. excerpt	14. illusion
4. trivia	10. assumption	15. fiction
5. status	11. feat	16. penalty
6. prosperity		

2 Word Review

1. ecologist, glaring
2. executive, remarkably
3. immune, favoritism
4. Pierre, South Dakota
5. nonconformist, unbearable
6. minister, theology
7. accurately, entry
8. opposition, Nonetheless
9. Biology, organisms
10. ideal, instinct

3 Synonyms and Antonyms

1. plentiful, scarce
2. skepticism, conviction
3. imaginary, actual
4. cheerless, lighthearted
5. meekly, boastfully
6. elimination, addition
7. confined, boundless
8. frill, necessity
9. modest, pretentious
10. upright, dishonorable
11. significant, uneventful
12. unbiased, subjective

4 A Poem about Appearances

1. Each of the blind men thinks that the part of the elephant that he touches is representative of the whole.
2. There are differences of opinion among them about what an elephant is like. Each of them believes his opinion is right.
3. Answers will vary. Accept reasonable responses.
4. Answers will vary. Reasonable responses include: Appearances can be deceiving, especially if we are not open-minded. Knowing only partial facts can distort our perceptions of reality. We all tend to believe our opinions are correct and anyone who disagrees with us is wrong.

5 Faraway Places

1. Guam	5. Fiji	8. Tahiti
2. Vietnam	6. Hollywood	9. New Guinea
3. Budapest	7. Australia	10. Tasmania
4. Hawaii		

Lesson 6

1 Understanding the Reading

1. a	4. c	7. d	9. a
2. b	5. a	8. b	10. c
3. d	6. c		

2 What Do You Think?

Reasonable responses include:

1. No. He probably only heard stories from other people and repeated them himself.
2. Yes, because travel by foot through the sand would have been difficult and would have taken a long time.

212   Answer Key

3. Polo was impressed with the Khan's communication system because messages could be sent very quickly over long distances. He was justified in having this opinion because travel by foot and even horseback was slow in those days. The Khan's ability to send messages 300 miles in a day was an extraordinary achievement so long ago.

4. Yes. Although some of his stories may have been exaggerated, he tells of many things he could not have known unless he visited the country.

3 Ancient China

1. legend
2. evidence
3. bamboo
4. type
5. society
6. language
7. press
8. technology
9. books
10. revolution
11. wealthy
12. knowledge
13. invention
14. magnets
15. explorer
16. explosive
17. rockets
18. warfare
19. currency
20. commerce

4 Early Explorers

1. explorers, discovered, document, vague, extraordinary
2. traders, colonized, ancient, continent, scholars
3. navigated, treacherous, flimsy, Similar, sailed
4. traditional, fantastic, validity, legends, underlie
5. mariner, ancestors, voyages, exhibit, extended
6. scale, fleets, treasure, vessels, Compare
7. travels, exception, commenced, following, medieval
8. recount, narrative, resulting, complete, insight

5 Animals of Myth

Reasonable responses include:

1. A sailor might fear the Kraken the most. It is huge and lives in the ocean.
2. They might be afraid they would hear its voice and be lured to their deaths.
3. I would rather meet a unicorn because it would not be dangerous.
4. I would most expect to meet a gryphon in the mountains, where it lives.

Lesson 7

1 Understanding the Reading

Answers will vary. Reasonable responses may include:

1. Charbonneau and Sacagawea speak the Shoshone language. Without them, Lewis has to rely on a language of signs to communicate with the Shoshone. That makes the encounter more difficult and leads to some distrust.

2. Answers may include any three of the following:
   He gives the women gifts and paints their cheeks with red paint, a symbol of peace.
   He lays down his gun and advances carrying a flag.
   He smokes several pipes with the warriors, and then tells them his purpose is friendly.
   He presents the flag as a symbol of peace and union.

3. Lewis writes that so far all the tribes have understood the language of signs. He says the language is imperfect and prone to error, but that the major ideas are seldom mistaken.

4. The chief tells him that the river below runs westward a long way before losing itself in "a great lake of ill-tasting water." Since the Pacific Ocean is to the west and its water is salty, he is likely describing the ocean.

5. Cameahwait believes the Shoshone would no longer have to hide in the mountains and live on roots and berries. They would be able to live in the country of the buffalo and eat as their enemies do. They would be able to stand up to the Minnetarees who murder the Shoshone and steal their horses.

6. Lewis describes the Shoshone as "ignorant" and "fickle" and calls them "savages." He seems to suggest that the Shoshone are cowardly for distrusting him.

7. a. He threatens the Shoshone by saying that if they continue to think meanly of his party no white men will ever come trade with them. He is trying to pressure them to come with him, since he knows how badly they want guns.

   b. He tries to shame them by suggesting that they should be brave enough to come with him and witness the truth of what he has said. He is trying to insult the warriors so that they will want to prove him wrong and come with him.

   c. He gives Cameahwait his gun and tells the chief that he can use it as he wishes. He is trying to restore the warriors' confidence in him by showing he has nothing to fear and has not betrayed them.

   d. He lies and tells the Shoshone that Clark left a letter saying he's been slightly delayed. Lewis is trying to buy time so Clark's party will reach them before the Indians leave him and spread the alarm.

8. The trip would be much more difficult and much slower without horses, and Lewis fears his men would become so discouraged that they would give up.

9. It turns out that Sacagawea is a sister of Chief Cameahwait. She also meets up with an Indian woman who had been taken prisoner at the same time with her, and who had afterwards escaped from the Minnetarees and returned to her tribe. Sacagawea's story proves that the Minnetarees have attacked the Shoshone tribe and taken some females captive.

2 What Do You Think?

1. The Shoshone chief and warriors embrace Lewis warmly and take him to their camp. Sacagawea, a Shoshone woman, agrees to help Lewis and Clark on the expedition. The tribe welcomes the chance to trade with the white strangers, etc.

2. The Shoshone have good reason to fear strangers. They are under attack by the Minnetarees of Fort de Prairie, who murder them, steal their horses, and take some of the women prisoner. The Shoshone may have also had some negative encounters with whites in the past.

3. The Shoshone could have decided that Lewis was a liar and was out to harm them. The chief could have used Lewis's gun to shoot him. The warriors could have fled into the woods and spread the alarm to other tribes.

4. Answers will vary.

5. Answers will vary.

3 Words in Context

1. b	4. c	7. d	9. a
2. a	5. c	8. b	10. d
3. d	6. a		

4 Spelling Check

1. selected, buffalo
2. gazing, animal, forgotten, rather
3. recollected, operation
4. until, turned
5. struck, depth, hastily
6. defense, suddenly
7. novel, endeavored
8. ground, torn, talons
9. alarm, mysterious
10. felt, gratified
11. animal, color, crouched
12. destroy, expense, proceeded, tiger, buffalo
13. route, enchanted

5 Powers of Observation

Answers will vary.

Lesson 8

1 Understanding the Reading

Answers will vary. Reasonable responses may include:

1. a. The open water freezes so that a ship can no longer sail or break through the ice. The summer ice can form early, trapping a ship in the ice pack all winter.

   b. As the ice breaks up, it forms great pressure that can crush a ship. Giant pieces of ice are tossed around and are very dangerous.

   c. During the melt, cracks form in the ice pack. People can fall through the ice.

2. The dogs must be kept healthy and fit so they can help the explorers cross the ice. Sports and games keep the men's spirits up and also help them get important mental and physical exercise. Such activities help cut down on boredom.

3. Shackleton worries that the ship will drift past all land and into a dangerous area of the open sea. The party must reach land in order to survive. He needs the ice pack to open so the ship can be released.

4. The smoke shows that the ice is beginning to break up near the ship. If a wide enough area were to open, the ship could try to sail. But if ice floes were to break up and create a lot of pressure close to the ship, the ship could be crushed.

5. Shackleton says the ship is more than just a floating home; it is the center of his ambitions, hopes, and desires.

6. Shackleton must immediately change his focus and adjust to a new goal. His "old mark" was his goal to cross the Antarctic by foot. It "went to ground" when the ship was trapped in the ice and destroyed. His "new mark" is to ensure the safety and survival of his entire party.

7. Shackleton envies the seals because they are "at home" and relaxed amidst the chaos of the ice. They do not have worries or responsibilities. On the other hand, he and the men must now fight to survive in a dangerous environment, and Shackleton must bear the responsibility of leading his entire party to safety.

8. Ship: Pros—shelter, protection, feeling of home and safety, ability to move through the ocean

   Ship: Cons—men and dogs cannot get exercise, ship can be trapped in ice and crushed with men aboard, ship crowded, routine can cause boredom, ship can sink

   Floe: Pros—men and dogs can exercise, don't feel as trapped, men can train the dog teams, fresh air, less boredom

   Floe: Cons—less shelter from the cold and the weather, cracks can open and swallow a person up, ice pressure can smash floe and send giant pieces of ice flying, floe can break up and become too small to live on

2 Comprehension Check

1. hedgerows	6. ice pressure	11. young ice
2. drift	7. lead	12. loose pack
3. grinding	8. floe	13. rafting
4. frost-smoke	9. corrugating	14. Antarctic
5. iceberg	10. close pack	15. ice pack

3 Shades of Meaning

1. c	4. a	7. a	10. a
2. a	5. c	8. d	11. c
3. d	6. b	9. d	12. b

4 Looking Closely at Language

Part A

1. The pack ice, like a jigsaw puzzle, is made up of many pieces of ice that only fit together in a certain way.

2. The ocean is the "mighty giant" lying beneath the ice. The description shows how small and powerless the men feel when faced with the power of nature, which seems mysterious and frightening.

3. Shackleton compares the frost-smoke to the smoke of a great prairie fire and to the steam of warships. All three forms of smoke warn of an unstoppable and life-threatening force approaching from afar.

4. The image suggests that Shackleton views the ship as home, a source of safety and comfort. Once the light dies out, Shackleton feels he has lost all connection to those things.

5. Shackleton describes the ship as having gaping wounds and says it is "almost like a living being." He describes the ship as "dying" and as having a "sentient life," two things that are only possible for living creatures.

6. Describing the *Endurance* as a person who is wounded and dying makes the physical description of the ship's destruction more painful and creates a sense of loss and sadness similar to the death of a person.

7. Shackleton compares the floe to a boat by calling it "our drifting home" and noting that it has "no rudder to guide it, no sail to give it speed." The floe is like a boat since it drifts on the surface of the water, moved by wind and current. The crew's last home was a boat, so it makes sense that all three things are connected in Shackleton's mind.

8. Shackleton describes the Antarctic winter as "a siege;" he compares the frost-smoke to "warships steaming in line ahead;" he describes the ship's struggle as "a one-sided battle;" he describes the ship as wounded; and he compares the noise of the ship's beams breaking to "heavy gunfire."

Part B
Answers will vary.

5 Labeling a Storyboard
Answers will vary.

Lesson 9

1 Understanding the Reading

1. c	4. c	7. d	9. d
2. a	5. b	8. a	10. b
3. d	6. b		

2 What Do You Think?
Answers will vary. Accept reasonable responses.

3 Word Relationships

1. b	4. b	7. a	9. d
2. c	5. d	8. b	10. c
3. a	6. c		

4 Still More Prefixes

1. concurred	5. emitted	8. semifinal
2. provoked	6. permissible	9. submit
3. adhere	7. super-duper	10. circumvent
4. contrary		

5 A Look Back

1. It has been blown far off course. The wind has blown it into the Antarctic Ocean where it is surrounded by icebergs, snow, and ice.

2. Any two of the following: tyrannous and strong; o'ertaking wings; pursued with yell and blow; loud roar'd the blast.

3. Any two of the following: wondrous cold; ice, mast-high, came floating by; as green as emerald; the snowy cliffs; cracked and growl'd; roar'd and howl'd like noises in a swound.

4. Answers will vary.

Lesson 10

1 Understanding the Reading.

1. Aristotle lived long before Galileo was born.

2. The German scientists might have begun a space program in Germany.

3. Pluto is very small, and it is not like the other planets.

4. The U.S may have refused to take Tito because it was afraid something would happen to him.

5. The U.N. was probably recognizing major discoveries that were being made and that were on the horizon for the field of astronomy.

6. One kind of space junk is abandoned space probes. Another kind is bits and pieces of wrecked satellites.

7. Anything that an astronaut might have dropped while in space, like a tool, could be space junk.

8. Reusable shuttles made it less expensive to travel in space because a new spaceship did not have to be built each time. Also, it took less time to get the shuttle ready than to start from scratch.

2 What Do You Think?
Answers will vary.

3 Synonym Review

1. rocket	8. characteristic	14. explore
2. consider	9. rise	15. position
3. adhere	10. watch	16. foreign
4. lost	11. flawed	17. habit
5. icy	12. competent	18. fantastic
6. delicate	13. crash	19. investigation
7. remains		

4 Put Events in Order
3, 1, 4, 2, 8, 6, 5, 7

5 Make Your Own Time Line
Answers will vary. Accept reasonable responses.

Review: Lessons 1–10

1 Definitions

1. endurance	7. disposition	12. administration
2. circumstance	8. mariner	13. illumination
3. navigator	9. intruder	14. sepulcher
4. generation	10. observatory	15. pros and cons
5. exposition	11. rudder	16. expedition
6. porthole		

2 Vocabulary Review

1. b	5. c	9. b	13. c
2. c	6. a	10. c	14. c
3. a	7. c	11. b	15. a
4. b	8. a	12. b	16. d

3 Antonym Review

1. construct	6. enemy	11. rudderless
2. tiny	7. despise	12. effortless
3. minimize	8. incompetent	13. undecided
4. unconscious	9. predator	14. eager
5. trivial	10. orderly	15. inadequately

4 Today's Explorers

1. ex, dis, un, sub, under
2. extra, con, dis, per, re
3. ex, re, re, com, ad
4. dis, de, re, de, dis
5. en, de, self, inter, en

5 Discovery Time Line

500 BC	Hanno sails down the northwestern coast of Africa.
AD 530	St. Brendan sails the Atlantic Ocean.
982–986	Eric the Red discovers Greenland.
1001–2	Leif Erikson is the first European to reach North America.
1271	Marco Polo begins his exploration of Asia, Mongolia, China, and Persia.
1325–54	Ibn Battutah explores North Africa, the Middle East, India, and Asia.
1405–33	Zheng He travels throughout Southeast Asia, East Africa, and Arabia.
1492	Christopher Columbus lands in San Salvador.
1497–98	Amerigo Vespucci discovers North and South America.
1497–1504	Vasco da Gama sails around the Cape of Good Hope and reaches India.
1519–21	Ferdinand Magellan circumnavigates the world.
1609–11	Henry Hudson explores eastern coast of North America and Canada.
1768–1779	James Cook explores the Pacific, South Pacific, and Arctic Ocean.
1804	Lewis and Clark set out to explore the western territories of the U.S.
1805	Sacagawea gives birth to a son, Jean Baptiste.
1806	Lewis and Clark return home to St. Louis.
1909	Robert Peary and Matthew Henson reach the North Pole.
1911	Roald Amundsen reaches the South Pole.
1914	Sir Ernest Shackleton sets out across Antarctica toward the South Pole.
1934	Beebe and Barton reach a record-breaking depth of 3,028 feet below sea level.
1960	Auguste Piccard takes the *Trieste* submersible to a depth of 32,500 feet.
1961	Yuri Gagarin is the first person to orbit Earth.
1969	Neil Armstrong is the first person to walk on the moon.
2004	The Cassini probe reaches Saturn.
2008	The Messenger spacecraft maps the surface of Mercury.
2014	Humans land on Mars?
2050	Answers will vary.
3000	Answers will vary.

Lesson 11

1 Understanding the Reading

1. b
2. a
3. a
4. b
5. c
6. b
7. c
8. c
9. c

2 What Do You Think?

1. Chief Seattle's statement supports "A Fable for Tomorrow" because he says that when we harm the environment we harm ourselves. He says that all things are connected and related, and that whatever happens to the earth, happens to man as well.
2. Answers will vary. Reasonable responses include: Many Americans use biodegradable products. They recycle. They do not litter. They fight against pollution. They tend gardens.
3. Answers will vary. Reasonable responses include: Many Americans use products that pollute the atmosphere or environment. They cut down trees without replanting. They pollute waters by dumping garbage or sewage into them. They litter public places. They don't bother to recycle or to buy recycled products.
4. Answers will vary. Accept reasonable responses.

3 What Is the Nobel Prize?

1. anniversary, distinction, economics, substantial, enrichment
2. distinguished, accumulated, massive, portion, estate
3. abundance, tragedy, fateful, capable, incident
4. indignant, rebuild, determinedly, reliable, minimize
5. dedicated, ambitions, ample, exertion, inevitable
6. precisely, patents, discredited, reclusive, sociable

4 Global Warming

Part A

1. T
2. T
3. F
4. T
5. ?
6. F
7. F
8. T

Part B

Answers will vary.

5 Names in Nature

1. b
2. b
3. b
4. a
5. c
6. c
7. b
8. a
9. b
10. c

Lesson 12

1 Understanding the Reading: Part 1

1. d
2. c
3. a
4. c
5. a
6. b
7. b
8. d
9. c
10. a

2 Understanding the Reading: Part 2

1. If the preserves contribute to their financial well-being, people will be more interested and active in protecting the rainforest.

2. If the land is better used, people will not abandon it and move on to clear land in other parts of the forest.

3. a. Plants of the rainforest may become a source of important medicines.
   b. A healthy rainforest will absorb greenhouse gases and help reduce global warming.
   c. The native peoples of the rainforest are disappearing as the rainforest disappears. Their knowledge of the forest and their cultures are valuable and should be preserved.

What do you think?

Answers will vary.

3 Synonyms and Antonyms

1. abundant, skimpy
2. observe, ignore
3. decompose, develop
4. dismiss, employ
5. inducement, deterrent
6. harmony, strife
7. contaminate, purify
8. affirm, deny
9. noteworthy, insignificant
10. withered, thriving
11. practical, impossible
12. prosperous, needy

4 Two Environmentalists

1. ecologists, century, career, submit, conservation
2. environment, regulate, inconvenient, advocate, well-being
3. latter, enabled, devoted, controversial, culmination
4. condemned, pesticides, forbidding, comprehend, consciousness
5. intriguing, personality, stark, rebel, characterization
6. obvious, flunked, journalism, gravitate, graduate
7. inclined, activism, hitchhiked, inseparable, passion
8. uncompromising, evoke, canyons, commitment, inspired

Lesson 13

1 Understanding the Reading

1. a. a deep narrow gully; a gorge
   b. a road or trail that follows a winding, zigzag course up a steep grade
   c. loose fragments formed by breaking up or wearing away rock
   d. a mixture of water and other material such as soil, rock, or sand

2. The setting is the Cascade Range of mountains in the western U.S.

3. A mining company is about to start mining copper there.

4. He is the leader of Friends of the Earth.

5. He is a mineral engineer.

6. Park used that example to show how mining could improve the economic standard of living of people in the area of the mine.

7. Both Brower and Park agree that the ruins and debris left from the mining operation are ugly and spoil the beauty of the area. They both feel it was wrong to leave such a mess.

8. Brower believes in the conservation of natural resources, in recycling resources, and even going without some things in order to conserve some resources for future generations. Park believes that it is essential to use minerals to maintain and improve people's standard of living.

What do you think?

Answers will vary. Accept reasonable responses.

2 The Earth: A Cartoonist's Point of View

Reasonable responses include:

1. He would probably agree with the cartoonist's point that man pollutes his environment and destroys the beauty of nature.

2. He would probably also agree that man's littering of his environment with trash is objectionable.

3. Answers will vary.

3 Word Families

1. vigorous, vigor
2. prosperity, prosper, prosperous
3. Consistency, consistently, consistent, inconsistent
4. emphasize, emphatic, emphasis
5. probability, improbable, probable
6. complicated, complicate, complication

4 America's Resources

1. Florida
2. Horseshoe
3. Ontario, Erie, Huron, Michigan, Superior
4. Hernando
5. Minnesota
6. South Dakota
7. 1872
8. Utah
9. Colorado
10. Arizona
11. Hawaii
12. William

5 Can You Crack the Code?

1. copper
2. gold
3. tin
4. iron
5. lead
6. mercury
7. silver
8. chromium
9. manganese
10. cobalt

Lesson 14

1 Understanding the Story

1. a
2. d
3. d
4. c
5. c
6. b
7. c
8. d
9. a
10. b

2 What Do You Think?

Answers will vary. Reasonable responses include:

1. T.J. is persistent in trying to achieve his dream. He works hard and sets a good example for the others. He has a strong sense of purpose. He has knowledge and experience in growing things. He has a strong desire to have land on which to grow something.

2. The boys like the idea of a secret project. It gives them something to work together on. The uniqueness of the idea appeals to them. The project captures the imagination.

3 Word Relationships

1. b
2. c
3. a
4. d
5. c
6. b
7. d
8. a
9. b
10. c

4 From the Earth

1. hemlock
2. buckwheat
3. spearmint
4. sunflower
5. foxglove
6. goldenrod
7. arrowroot
8. horseradish
9. pennyroyal
10. heartsease

5 Arbor Day

1. Territory, agriculture, pioneers, necessity
2. encouraged, proposed, observe, participating
3. National, beautify, research, region
4. activist or ecologist, ecologist or activist, essential, pollutants, diversity
5. deforestation, worldwide, recovering, serious, habitats

Lesson 15

1 Understanding the Story

1. The gang wants to plant grass and trees. T.J. tells them it will take a while to grow trees, but he goes along with their idea of planting grass when he sees how much it means to them. He gets them to agree to a row of watermelons, though.
2. Blackie steps on the young grass. The others don't do anything, because they can see he feels bad about what he did.
3. They are picking out the kind of watermelon seeds to buy from a catalog.
4. The owner is angry at the boys for being on his roof and for hauling up the dirt and planting grass there. He believes the weight on the roof could cause it to sag.
5. At first T.J. fights back because he believes his rights are being violated. The other boys have had more experience with adult authority and know they can't win. They are willing to leave the grass for the owner's men to remove, but T.J. looks at the earth as his, and doesn't want the men to touch it.
6. T.J. and the boys clear the grass and earth from the roof themselves.

2 What Do You Think?

1. Answers will vary. Accept reasonable responses.
2. Reasonable responses to why T.J. ran away include: He was homesick. He wanted to go back to where he could plant and raise a crop. He had suffered a great disappointment. He had seen his work destroyed. Opinions on the second part of the question will vary.

3 Which Word Does Not Fit?

1. Atlas
2. traverse
3. Polynesian
4. despair
5. abstain
6. switchback
7. humble
8. laurel
9. wriggle
10. waddle
11. bale
12. Arcadia
13. confer
14. wither
15. junction

4 Homonym Review

1. doe—dough
2. Rome—roam
3. prey—pray
4. burrow—burro
5. council—counsel
6. aisle—isle
7. load—lode
8. sew—sow
9. principle—principal
10. bale—bail

5 A Logic Problem

	Jones	Kelly	Lane	Nyuyen	artichokes	asparagus	broccoli	cauliflower
Alan	N	N	Y	N	N	Y	N	N
Juanita	N	Y	N	N	N	N	Y	N
Dennis	N	N	N	Y	Y	N	N	N
Lucy	Y	N	N	N	N	N	N	Y
artichokes	N	N	N	Y				
asparagus	N	N	Y	N				
broccoli	N	Y	N	N				
cauliflower	Y	N	N	N				

Lucy Jones planted cauliflower.

Juanita Kelly planted broccoli.

Alan Lane planted asparagus.

Dennis Nguyen planted artichokes.

Review: Lessons 1–15

1 Definitions

1. diverse
2. swath
3. terrain
4. vigor
5. bravado
6. anonymous
7. substantial
8. emphatic
9. vegetation
10. levy
11. sediment
12. resolve
13. capability
14. estimate
15. diagnosis
16. cache

2 Using Context Clues: Part 1

1. angler—alder
2. consistently—desecration
3. spirited—skyrocketed
4. parapet—pondered
5. dabble—economics
6. recalled—insulting
7. contribution—infinitely
8. Characterized—transmitted
9. principles—council

3 Using Context Clues: Part 2

1. c
2. a
3. a
4. b
5. c
6. a
7. c

4 Save the Earth: Go Green!

1. 2, 5, 4, 3, 1
2. 4, 6, 1 or 2, 3, 5, 2 or 1
3. 2 or 3 or 4, 2 or 3 or 4, 5, 1, 2 or 3 or 4
4. 2, 4, 3, 7, 6, 1, 5

5 A Poet's Point of View

Reasonable responses include:

1. We have shut ourselves off from the natural world. We shield ourselves from direct contact with the outside world and know it only through what we are told and shown by the media.
2. Humankind will continue to grow more distant and separated from nature. We will continue to lose touch with the natural world by refusing to be concerned.
3. Answers will vary.

Lesson 16

1 Understanding the Reading

I. A. Open fireplace
   B. Fuel supply
   C. Tinderbox
   D. Coal furnace
II. A. Outhouse
   B. Baths
      1. Water
      2. Kitchen
III. A. Night log
   B. Curfew
   C. Water pitcher
   D. Bed warmer

2 What Do You Think?

1. Answers will vary. Accept reasonable responses.
2. Answers will vary.

3 Using Context Clues

1. All, nothing, endures
2. nature, trial, silly
3. constantly, consist, actually, believe
4. fact, pace, human
5. Wars, caused, institutions, organized
6. years, reverse, Refrain, matters
7. change, inevitable, dominant, sensible
8. change, remain, same

4 Writing about Change

Answers will vary.

5 Inventors and Their Inventions

1. Robert Fulton
2. Eli Whitney
3. Samuel F. B. Morse
4. Charles Goodyear
5. Cyrus McCormick
6. Samuel Colt
7. Elias Howe
8. George Westinghouse
9. Alexander Graham Bell
10. Thomas Edison
11. George Eastman
12. William Burroughs
13. George W. Carver
14. Ransom E. Olds
15. Lee DeForest

Lesson 17

1 Understanding the Play

1. Stepan thinks that Ivan has come to borrow money.
2. Ivan intends to ask Natalia to marry him.
3. They begin to quarrel over the ownership of some meadowland.
4. Answers will vary. Students who believe that the argument pertains to trivial matters may cite Natalia's statement that "the meadows are worth very little" and Ivan's willingness to give them to her. Other students may feel that five acres worth "a few hundred roubles" would be a serious matter. Students may also cite Natalia's statement that it is "the injustice of the thing" and Ivan's being "concerned with the principle" as indicating that the argument pertains to serious matters.
5. First, he offers to give the meadows to Natalia. Later, he threatens to take the matter to court.
6. She finds out he had come to propose marriage to her.
7. Answers will vary. Reasonable responses include: His daughter is very changeable; first she is angry with Ivan, then she wants him back. It is difficult to get a grown daughter married and on her own.
8. The play is intended to be humorous. Supporting evidence will vary. Students may cite the exaggerated reactions of the characters, the foolishness of the argument, the fact that both Ivan and Natalia claim to be dying at the end, and similar examples as evidence.

2 You Be the Playwright

Answers will vary. The following is what actually happens. When Ivan returns, Natalia apologizes and tells him the meadows are really his. Then she tries to lead the conversation to a point where he will propose to her. Instead, another argument breaks out, this time about the relative worth of their hunting dogs. Stepan is again drawn into the fray. Finally Ivan faints. Natalia and Stepan think he is dead. But Ivan recovers and Stepan tells him that Natalia consents to his proposal (although Ivan hasn't actually proposed to her yet). Ivan and Natalia hesitantly express their mutual happiness, but they resume their argument as Stepan calls for champagne and the curtain falls.

3 More about Anton Chekhov

1. monotonously, monotony, monotonous
2. Uninspired, inspiration, inspired
3. severity, severely, severe
4. reliably, unreliable, reliability
5. wretchedly, wretchedness, wretched
6. irritate, irritable, irritation
7. censorship, censor, uncensored
8. immodest, modesty, modest
9. mortally, mortal, immortality, immortal

4 Foreign Currency

1. dollar		7. dinar		12. ringgit
2. yuan		8. shekel		13. peso
3. krone		9. yen		14. rouble
4. pound		10. won		15. rand
5. euro		11. kwacha		16. dong
6. rupee				

5 Synonym Review

1. danger	7. adaptable	12. household
2. foundation	8. climb	13. difficult
3. ponder	9. leaning	14. flutter
4. harvest	10. influence	15. obvious
5. scheme	11. splendid	16. flow
6. pause		

Lesson 18

1 Understanding the Reading

1. d	3. c	5. d	7. b
2. d	4. a	6. c	8. c

2 Optimists and Pessimists

Answers will vary. Reasonable responses include:

2. a. I can be friends with anyone, I just may have to try harder with some people.
   b. No one wants to hear from me—I don't have friends.
3. a. It is our ability to adapt to change that helps us grow stronger.
   b. If you don't adapt to change, you die.
4. a. We can all do our small part to make this world better—right now, in our own way.
   b. It's too late to make the world better. We're doomed.
5. a. We can make our own changes and design our own future.
   b. Nothing has changed to make the world better, and it never will.

3 Antonym Review

1. opponent		6. pleasant		11. antisocial
2. willful		7. negative		12. optimistic
3. general		8. employee		13. safe
4. few		9. groups		14. local
5. unusual		10. passive		

4 Signs of Change

1. environmentalist		5. navigator		8. grocer
2. psychologist		6. activist		9. ecologist
3. sociologist		7. mayor		10. economist
4. tutor				

5 An Inventor's Advice

KAYOS	LATER	MONAD	SMALL	EXIST
2	23	25	7	8
OKAYS	ALERT	NOMAD	MALLS	EXITS
TUTOR	FIRED	SLIDE	YEMEN	PAGES
4	16	9	14	22
TROUT	FRIED	IDLES	ENEMY	GAPES
CHASE	NOBLE	SEVER	MANOR	STRUT
21	11	13	15	5
ACHES	NOBEL	VERSE	ROMAN	TRUST
ZONED	LEASE	DOORS	REINS	MITES
20	12	17	10	6
DOZEN	EASEL	ODORS	SIREN	ITEMS
SETUP	CURBS	ALLOY	RUNES	TRINE
18	3	1	19	24
UPSET	SCRUB	LOYAL	NURSE	INERT

Quote: Lost time is never found again.

Lesson 19

1 Understanding the Reading

1. Reasonable responses include:
   He was a new senator. He was a young politician. He came from a multiracial background. He didn't have the "typical pedigree" of most presidential candidates. He didn't spend his career "in the halls of Washington."
2. White voters cast their ballots for Obama, rather than voting for the white candidate in the privacy of the voting booth.
3. Obama was elected as the first African-American president.
4. Obama didn't have a traditional background—his father started out as a goat herder in Kenya; he came into politics as an outsider with a multiracial heritage and a strange name; he rose to the top on his own merits.

5. The American people bring change to Washington by demanding it. They rise up and insist on new ideas and new leadership.

6. Young people worked hard for the campaign, working long hours and late nights, and showed up in big numbers on Election Day.

7. Answers will vary. Reasonable responses include:
   There were racial tensions between blacks and whites during the campaign. The country seemed to be divided into red states and blue states. The campaign seemed like a hard fought battle.

8. Answers will vary.

9. Answers will vary. Reasonable responses include:
   She offers proof of how much things can change in one person's lifetime. She lived through many historical events, and her life story helps people see how far the nation has come.

10. Reasonable responses include:
    Cars were invented. Planes were invented. Women and African Americans won the vote. The civil rights movement occurred. A man landed on the moon. Computers and the Internet were invented. The Dust Bowl, The New Deal, and WWII occurred. The Berlin wall fell. Touch-screen voting was invented. An African American president was elected.

2 What Do You Think?

1. Answers will vary.

2. Answers will vary.

3 History in the Making

1. Rosa Parks, Montgomery
2. Berlin, George H. Bush
3. Pearl Harbor, World War II, G.I. Bill
4. Martin Luther King, Jr.
5. African Americans, women, Ann Nixon Cooper
6. Franklin Roosevelt, The New Deal, 1930s
7. Neil Armstrong, Richard Nixon
8. Birmingham
9. The Dust Bowl
10. John McCain, Barack Obama, November 4
11. Abraham Lincoln, The Civil War

4 Comprehension Check

1. b	4. c	7. b	9. d
2. d	5. a	8. c	10. a
3. a	6. d		

5 Biographies and Family Trees

Answers will vary. Accept reasonable responses.

Lesson 20

1 Understanding the Reading

1. c	3. c	5. c	7. b
2. d	4. d	6. a	

2 Reacting to the Reading

Reasonable responses include:

1. People can gain new insights and understand the world better. They see the world around them differently and an older, wider world opens to them. People are able to develop a value system based on the experiences and wisdom of many people in the past. People can develop new habits and attitudes. They discover a background that is richer than any single family can provide.

2. Answers will vary. Accept reasonable responses.

3. To establish a link with the past one might: read the great classics of the past; study history, philosophy, anthropology; become acquainted with great works of art; visit museums; talk with older people and with those who have studied the past.

3 A Poem by Langston Hughes

1. a. A river in southwest Asia flowing from Turkey to the Persian Gulf
   b. A river of central Africa rising in Zaire and emptying into the Atlantic
   c. The world's longest river, rising in Burundi and emptying into the Mediterranean Sea at Egypt
   d. A city in southeast Louisiana near the mouth of the Mississippi River

Reasonable responses include:

2. Hughes says he has "known rivers ancient as the world," "bathed in the Euphrates when dawns were young," "raised the pyramids above" the Nile, and "heard the singing of the Mississippi when Abe Lincoln went down to New Orleans." His "soul has grown deep" by making these experiences of the human past his own.

3. Hughes compares rivers with the flow of blood in human veins, life lines that keep lands and people alive through the ages. Forests die and mountains wear away; both are stationary. But rivers flow on forever; always remaining, always changing.

4. If Hughes had said his mind had "grown deep" he would imply that only his thinking had been affected. Likewise saying his heart had "grown deep" would imply that only his feelings were involved. The concept of soul encompasses both the mind and the heart and implies that his whole spirit has been enriched by his learning.

4 Synonyms and Antonyms

1. obstacle, advantage	6. shielded, unprotected
2. ample, stingy	7. despise, admire
3. ignite, extinguish	8. leaning, unwillingness
4. rehabilitate, damage	9. corrupt, honorable
5. sentimental, unemotional	10. elevate, lower

5 Spelling Check

1. historical	5. fowl	9. all right
2. expedition	6. all right	10. fourth
3. celebrate	7. forty	11. observance
4. Pilgrims	8. according	12. thankful

Review: Lessons 1–20

1 Definitions

1. canopy	7. palpitation	12. savvy
2. plight	8. unabridged	13. controversy
3. flux	9. maneuver	14. technology
4. famine	10. obstacle	15. interval
5. decade	11. precarious	16. milestone
6. shoddy		

2 Vocabulary Review

1. b	3. d	5. a	7. b
2. c	4. a	6. d	8. a

3 Vocabulary Review

1. abridged	4. sentimental	7. desolate
2. portable	5. economical	8. offensive
3. competitive	6. reliable	

4 Population Growth and Change

1. Pertaining to country, farming, or agricultural areas
2. Pertaining to city areas or highly populated areas
3. 1869
4. 1985
5. World War I
6. 1930
7. 1930–1960
8. 1960–1985
9. 299,845,900
10. 1607, 2020, 2050
11. Answers will vary.

5 What Difference Does a Century Make?

Part A

1. 12	5. 17	8. 13, 15
2. 4	6. 16	9. 9, 11, 12
3. 15	7. 19	10. 5
4. 6, 7, 8		

Part B

Sample responses:

1. Women Who Can't Find Mates Give Birth to Clones
2. Shortage in Housing for Elderly Forces Millions into Shelters
3. White Men Are No Longer a Majority in America

Part C

Answers will vary.